Preference Pollution

Economics, Cognition, and Society

This series provides a forum for theoretical and empirical investigations of social phenomena. It promotes works that focus on the interactions among cognitive processes, individual behavior, and social outcomes. It is especially open to interdisciplinary books that are genuinely integrative.

Titles in the Series

Preference Pollution

How Markets Create the Desires We Dislike

David George

Ann Arbor

THE UNIVERSITY OF MICHIGAN PRESS

Copyright © by the University of Michigan 2001
All rights reserved
Published in the United States of America by
The University of Michigan Press
Manufactured in the United States of America
⊗ Printed on acid-free paper

2004   2003   2002   2001   4   3   2   1

A CIP catalog record for this book is available from the British Library.

Library of Congress Cataloging-in-Publication Data applied for
ISBN 0-472-11220-1 (cloth: alk. paper)

To my father and to the memory of my mother

Contents

Acknowledgments

My interest in the market's influence on tastes has a considerable history, fast approaching thirty years. To step back and give deserved recognition to those who have helped along the way is thus all the more daunting.

I am extraordinarily grateful to series editor Timur Kuran for the care and frank criticism he has provided, and to social science editor Ellen McCarthy for her support above and beyond the call of duty. And the editors were not alone in such support. The task of reading works-in-progress, like dieting and exercising, can be something that one intends to do but fails to carry out. Those who came through and offered important comments include Robert Goldfarb, Doug Porpora, Tim Brennan, Tyler Cowen, and Steven Worland, and I wish to thank them all.

In the incubation stage of developing ideas the loneliness can at times be excruciating. There are several scholars who during the 1980s expressed enough interest or offered enough advice to keep the project moving and by so doing indirectly helped to make this book a reality. I wish to thank, in particular, Lynn Holmes, Tucker Taylor, Amartya Sen, Mark Lutz, Albert Hirschman, Claus Offe, Martha Nussbaum, and Michael S. McPherson. I also wish to recognize the encouraging comments of the late Kenneth Boulding. Over the last decade, the comments, criticisms, and support offered by Roger McCain, David Colander, Vivian Walsh, Herbert Gintis, and the late Richard Herrnstein have been of enormous help as well.

Within the workplace and the home are those whom we naturally are with more often and whose contributions are more apt to get lost in the noise of everyday events. At La Salle University, several people stand out. Professor Emeritus Joseph Flubacher created an atmosphere in our department appreciative of moral inquiry that mainstream departments have been slower to embrace. While all colleagues in my department have offered words of encouragement, I owe special thanks to Richard Mshomba for advice on clearing the publication hurdles and to David Robison, John Grady, and Joe Cairo for their helpful advice. Thanks are also due to other colleagues at La Salle. Michael Kerlin and Mark Moreau of philosophy, David Falcone of psychology, and Walt Schubert of finance provided other disciplinary perspectives. Rita Mall offered plenty of emotional support and along with Richard DiDio and Elaine Mshomba assisted in the crafting of a title. Student support was provided by Marc Santugini, Robert Scheible, and Danica Andrews. Thanks as well to La Salle University for offering a semester's leave that provided the critical time needed in the project's early stages.

As one greatly concerned about contemporary trends toward overwork, I like to view myself as a relatively slow writer by design and one who has managed to avoid the dreaded disease of workaholism. Family members of most any writer can probably attest to the naïveté of any such characterization of one engaged in the writing of a book, and my family is no exception. My deepest thanks to my wife, Patty, for her indulgence and support when indulgence and support were what I so desperately needed. Thanks to Rebecca and Alexander for adjusting gracefully to a writer's deadlines as well.

Let me end with some thanks to those whose contributions predate the first time I committed to paper a thought about preferences. Extended conversations with my late uncle, L. J. George, a conservative defender of the marketplace, taught me at a fairly early age the art of good argumentation. That we each heard the other and modified our positions in consequence I am certain. That I learned to take more time to develop my arguments with care I am equally certain.

A number of my chapters draw on articles published elsewhere. Parts of chapters 2 and 3 appeared in "Does the Market Create Preferred Preferences?" *Review of Social Economy* 51 (1993): 323–46. Parts of chapter 2 and 4 were originally published in "Coping Rationally with Unpreferred Preferences," *Eastern Economic Journal* 24, no. 2 (1998): 181–94. Portions of the material in chapters 5 and 6 appear in "Unpreferred Preferences: Unavoidable or a Failure of the Market?" *Eastern Economic Journal* 27, no. 4 (fall 2001). The latter part of chapter 8 appeared in "Working Longer Hours: Pressure from the Boss or Pressure from the Marketers?" *Review of Social Economy* 55 (1997): 33–65, and in a revised version, "Driven to Spend: Longer Work Hours a Byproduct of Market Forces," in *Working Time: International Trends, Theory, and Policy Perspectives,* edited by Lonnie Golden and Deborah M. Figart (New York: Routledge, 2001): 127–42. I thank the publishers of these articles for permission to use them here.

There are two other individuals whose help preceded my first work on preferences. Well after my first paper had been written I turned to the philosophy literature and repeatedly came across the names of two scholars whose classes I had had the privilege of taking while an undergraduate at the University of Michigan. Richard Brandt taught the introductory philosophy class that I took in 1967. Richard Hare (a visiting professor at Michigan) taught the moral philosophy course I enrolled in a year later. I have little doubt that their utilitarian leanings planted the seeds of my later ideas, for as the years have passed I have ever more often come across references to their work in the philosophical writings on rational choice.

Finally, I am grateful to "an unknown economist." While working on a paper on visual perception with a faculty member at UCLA in 1972 I first started thinking about "preferences for preferences." As a means of determining whether my ideas were indeed fresh and worth pursuing, I went to the economics department and started knocking on doors to see if the criticisms of the market that I was formulating had already been made. I must thank a professor whose name I cannot recall (I never introduced myself to him nor did he to me). He let me know in no uncertain terms that the very notion of a "preference for a preference" was unheard of within economics. For the frankness of this response I must thank him. Its strength was enough to convince me to pursue a graduate degree and career in economics.

CHAPTER 1

Introduction

The Widening Scope of the Market

When historians look back upon the final quarter of the twentieth century, the spread of market capitalism will likely stand out as the period's truly defining event. And while it is the private ownership of the means of production that a century ago stood as the central symbol of market capitalism, it is the free market that has come to best represent such systems in more recent years and the free market that has gained the most followers.

As recently as the 1970s, to be "competitive" was to "try hard." To speak of a sports team in such a way said little about success and was often a polite way of describing those teams that suffered through particularly bad years. Coincident with the rise in markets, *competitive* has been liberated from any connection with failure, and has even begun to be used as a synonym for *successful*. While it remains impossible to be too rich or too thin, it has become nearly as impossible to be too "competitive" or too "market oriented."

The United States has been in the vanguard of the move toward markets but by no means alone. Nor have "for-profit" businesses been the only ones defining their success through their ability to compete. Enterprises that remain firmly nonprofit have not been reluctant to define themselves anew as sellers in the market. Hospitals and universities that only a few years ago would have resisted any suggestions that they advertise or market their services today follow procedures indistinguishable from the profit sector. Just as surely, professionals who traditionally saw themselves as only tangentially related to the market—doctors, nurses, lawyers, teachers, professors—are throwing off their inhibitions and looking at themselves as market participants with "customers" standing where once there were students, patients, and clients.[1]

Market forces have not always enjoyed such popularity. Though the critiques have been many, two in particular stand out, one usually associated with the political Left, the other with the political Right. Consider first the often-heard complaint coming from the liberal side. While the market may be remarkably adept at fulfilling the wants of the financially secure, goes this argument, it is far less able to adequately fulfill the basic needs of a sizable portion of the population. The market thus comes under attack for devoting large segments of land to the production of food for the pets of the well-off while the children of the poor go hungry and for channeling the energies and equipment of medical providers to cosmetic surgery for the affluent while the basic treatable illnesses of many are ignored.[2]

While the liberal argument views market forces as insufficiently sensitive to those in the bottom half, conservatives tend to see precisely the reverse. A fear of a steadily sinking "lowest common denominator" forms the organizing point for their dissatisfaction. The relatively lower-paid and less educated segment of society is perceived to be gaining influence in the marketplace as a result of their rising incomes, and standards are seen to be endangered as a consequence.[3]

There are problems with each of these criticisms of markets. The first—that they ignore the desires of the poor—is not really a complaint about markets in general. Rather, as mainstream economists have rightly pointed out, it amounts to dissatisfaction with the outcome of *labor* markets, and it thus follows that there is in principle a solution that does not interfere with the market's dominant role in determining output. Redistributing purchasing power from the haves to the have-nots is all that would seem to be required to ensure that discretionary spending could not occur unless the basic needs of all had been satisfied.

The conservative argument similarly does not hold up well if closely examined. For the "dumbing down" complaint would really only pertain to a very limited set of mass-produced items, a set that appears to be shrinking in an age of targeted markets that the information revolution has made possible. In short, though a highbrow sensibility may lament what lowbrows consume, their choices are not themselves as directly influenced by the lowbrow decisions as might once have been true.

In addition to these shortcomings, the liberal critique and conservative critique share a feature that makes them contingent in nature. Though differing in their interpretation of what segment of society suffers from the market's workings, each presupposes income inequality. For the conservatives, the choices made by those at the lower end have negative effects upon those at the top. For the liberals, the choices of those at the top wastefully exhaust resources and by so doing unfairly curtail the range of choices that are possible for those at the bottom. And thus for each, actions to increase income equality, whether seen as justified or not in their own right, would be actions yielding as a fortunate by-product the lessening of the perceived problems with market forces.

Though recent years have brought rising income inequality, this has not been the main focus of liberal "equalization" efforts. Since efforts to achieve greater economic opportunities for previously excluded segments of the population have brought results, liberals have been directing more of their attention to economic innovation and growth and less to distribution, and the attractiveness of the market has been correspondingly growing. Among conservatives, the libertarian strain that values freedom to choose and rejects elitism has similarly been more "classically liberal" and inclined to accord ever greater respect to market outcomes. To be sure, there have been regrets expressed on both sides over these developments. Writing in the conservative periodical *Commentary,* Adam Wolfson describes approvingly nineteenth-century America, when "choice itself was tightly constrained by moral and civic considerations, by custom and by local legislation," with "[p]rofane and blasphemous speech . . . proscribed, pornographic materials . . . censored, [and] gambling . . . prohibited" (1997, 49). Wolfson goes on to observe, with regret, that the "'right to choose' is something which not only upper-middle-class liberals but all Americans take for granted" (49).

Todd Gitlin, writing in the liberal journal *Dissent,* puts an entirely different interpretation on the hegemony of "free choice." For him, it is not conservatives parroting capitalism's critics that has resulted in a shared embrace of choice. Rather, it is an emerging left-wing culture, well represented in academia by "cultural studies," that has altered the Left's outlook in a way that makes it more compatible with conservative libertarian perspectives. A cultural critic following a cultural studies perspective, by treating the choice made by the average consumer as more indicative of worth than the opinion of the critic, "purports to stand four-square for the people against capitalism. The consumer sovereignty touted by a capitalist society as the grandest possible means for judging merit finds a reverberation among its ostensible adversaries" (Gitlin 1997, 80).

To sum up, "freedom to choose" is the zeitgeist of the era, a first principle on which groups having otherwise little in common can agree. Abortion advocates have long been most comfortable with phrasing their position as a "woman's right to choose," and more recently cigarette companies have responded to the mounting opposition to their product by seeking to focus attention on a person's right to choose to smoke. But to invoke "freedom to choose" is not to trump one's opponents, as the continuation of the abortion wars and the cigarette wars attests. For the public recognizes that one person's choice can on occasion unjustly restrict another's opportunities. Thus the foes of abortion view the fetus as indeed a person and see a woman's choice of abortion as precluding the fetus's future potential choices that becoming a full human would allow. And thus those contesting the right to smoke speak on behalf of those who will be unable to exercise their right to breathe clean air.

As these examples should suggest, opposition to the exercise of choice in modern society is often based on the infringement of someone else's "right to choose." It is thus not surprising that when no third parties suffer spillover costs (or when the existence of such effects is contestable), the case for restricting the "freedom to choose" is greatly weakened. And thus it is that the opposition to the "classic vices" has lost such support in just those years when the market model has been so ascendant. To the extent that prostitution, gambling, and the use of drugs cannot be shown to impose costs on bystanders, what possible basis can there be for restricting the freedom of others to choose these activities?

The Widening Grasp of Addictions

Whether or not "addictions" in the sense that the experts use the term are on the rise is one question. Whether or not the word itself is on the rise is another. And as any survey of popular magazines and newspapers will reveal, there can be little doubt about the popularity of this word. For it is now being used in contexts where it would not have appeared only a few years ago.

The mental health professionals are more circumspect than the public in describing an activity as addictive. In the *Journal of Addictive Behavior* over a five-year period, fifty-six of the articles dealt with smoking, fifty-three with alcohol, fifty-three with substance abuse, and twenty-nine with eating disorders. Together these four themes accounted for all of the articles dealing with specific addictions. When used by the lay public, the uses of the word *addiction* are much richer indeed, and it continues to appear in ever more novel contexts.[4] Besides the classic addictions, one finds claims of addiction to gambling, addiction to sexual activity (of all different sorts), addiction to the Internet, and addiction to one's work.[5]

There appear to be two features that set the experts' examples of addictive activities apart from the public's broader class of examples. First, in every case of a professionally recognized addiction there is a "smoking gun," usually in the form of an object that is in some form or other ingested into the body, and as a result there are physically observable changes that can be linked to the use of the substance. Second, in most every case of such addictions, it is an accepted fact that use of the substance causes physical harm and shortens life expectancy.[6] Here we have a feature that to professional psychologists and the lay public alike appears to render use of the substance "irrational." As economists rightly note, however, shortened life expectancy is not a convincing criterion for questioning the rationality of an agent's choice. For there are plenty of things that people voluntarily do that lessen life expectancy but that would be very odd to describe as irrational. To drive in excess of what is absolutely necessary for the acquisition of life's basics is to increase the risk of serious injury or even death, but few have any problem with preferences for such travel. To be close to other human beings raises one's chance of untimely violent death. Clearly, while the fact of physical harm or risk of harm may tempt us to declare a voluntary action as irrational, the reasoning is thus highly problematic.

Operating as closet "subjectivists" or "mentalists," the general public is more willing to allow a person's word speak for him, and to treat a person's declaration that he is addicted to something as sufficient evidence that he in fact is. This is not the place to resolve the long-standing debate between empiricists and mentalists, nor is it the place to resolve more recent disagreements over whether or not a verbal report shall be classified as a "behavior." It is, however, the place to note a problem with both the professional and popular description of the state of being an addict. As described in an editorial appearing on the very first page of the very first issue of *Addictive Behavior,* "[A]lcoholism constitutes a disease process whereby the individual exhibits *total loss of control* over his drinking" (Miller and Hersen 1975, 1; emphasis added). And just as the alcoholic is described as one simply unable to stop himself from drinking, whether speaking colloquially or professionally, the addictive personality is described as simply "unable" to resist indulging in the addictive activity.

Again, it is possible to turn to mainstream economics to see the problem with such characterizations. To be "out of control" would seem to carry with it the implication that one's actions would not be influenced by a change of incentives. One who is swept up by a tornado cannot exert any influence upon where she will land. Offering a million-dollar reward if she will land in one spot rather than another cannot alter the outcome, an outcome that is fully "out of her control." With any imaginable addiction, this is not the case. A credible offer of one million dollars conditional on remaining heroin-free for one month would succeed in getting many, many addicts to freely give up their habits for this length of time. For the less gripping sorts of "addiction," this is more obvious still. Shopping addicts and Internet addicts would likely find the offer of such a sum of money too good to resist. It may not be true that each and every addict "has his price," but there can be little doubt that the great majority does.[7]

This is not a new point and has figured prominently in the recent attempts of economists to provide insights about addictions.[8] But economists have steered away from the question that this book will largely be concerned with. What do markets and addictions have to do with one another? Is their simultaneous historical rise a spurious correlation or might a causal connection be at work? As a first step in getting to such questions, a brief consideration of how economists have responded to the question of changing tastes is in order.

The Galbraithian Challenge

Extending back to at least the 1930s, mainstream economists have generally resisted directing their analytical efforts toward the study of preference change. Two different rationales have been offered for such resistance. First is the claim that preference creation and preference change are topics simply lying outside the scope of economics. We have here not any claim about the possibility, in principle, of studying what determines preferences and what changes them. What we do have is a denial that this is a project that should occupy economists. Following Lionel Robbins's often cited claim, economics would be defined as the study of the efficient means of responding to *given* ends (Robbins 1952, chap. 1). This position may be understood as something of a reverse "turf war." Rather than staking new ground for their analytical talents, economists taking this position are on the contrary claiming no responsibility for the study of some issues that might, on the surface, appear to be within their domain. Rather than questioning the importance of what determines tastes, they are, like the proverbial bureaucrat, choosing to refer the curious party elsewhere.

This first reason for ignoring preference change applies mainly to the positive side of economics. The study of how and why preferences change is judged to fall outside the subject's boundaries. A second reason for ignoring preference change pertains to the normative side of the discipline. The widely accepted claim for some time has been that there is simply no basis for making any normative judgments when a preference change occurs. Someone whose tastes change from reading the *National Enquirer* to reading the *New York Times* (or from playing pushpin to reading Pushkin) is not someone, by the official line, for whom a welfare change in well-being can be traced. This conclusion follows from the convention of treating a single agent with different preference rankings over time as analytically equivalent to two agents with different preferences at a single moment in time. To be able to rank the well-being of the "different agents" would be nice, most economists would likely agree, but happens to be impossible.[9]

This official position of the neoclassical economists did not deter John Kenneth Galbraith from arguing in his 1958 book, *The Affluent Society,* that it was troubling for the American economy, ever more reliant on advertising and marketing, to be measuring its success by the satisfaction of the very wants that it had created. Galbraith's argument, while never embraced by mainstream economists, did resonate with cultural critics of the period.

Concerns about the harmful effects of the market's persuasive processes have never disappeared, but these concerns have taken a backseat to other issues for critics of contemporary capitalism. Beginning with Michael Harrington's 1962 classic, *The Other America,* attention has been more often centered on America's underclass. This worked against the Galbraithian critique in two distinct ways. First, it drew attention to the fact that concern with "preference manipulation" was primarily a preoccupation of the economically secure. Those liberated from the fear of poverty might indeed care very much about their fitness and personal growth, and might indeed resent the efforts of sellers to persuade them to spend in ways that do not further these ends. But such concerns came to seem somewhat narcissistic and of secondary status from a broader social perspective. Second, and at least as significantly, the Galbraithian exercise of pointing to particular examples of objectionable taste manipulation (tail fins on cars being the most memorable example) likely began to seem too elitist to be easily digested by the spreading populist mood of the 1960s. How could one feel solidarity with the underclass of the nation while simultaneously poking fun at the objects that might attract their increased purchasing power were the agenda of reform to succeed?

Albert Hirschman (1982a) notes that critics of the historical unfolding of capitalism can be usefully divided into two camps. Those in one group claim that capitalism "goes too far," displaying great success in the transformation of inefficient economic practices that predate it, but eventually eroding parts of the social infrastructure that are critical for its success. Those in the other group instead see the major problem as "not going far enough," as existing comfortably with social inefficiencies and injustices inherited from earlier social arrangements.

The Galbraithian critique seems to best fit the first of these. The market was praised for its ability to furnish the basics of life but strongly criticized for its proclivity to replace sensible tastes with superfluous created tastes. In contrast to this, liberal critics of social inequalities were not usually inclined to attribute maldistribution of income, power, and wealth to capitalism's natural unfolding. Capitalism was faulted for peacefully coexisting with social injustices, not for creating them. Since gender, race, and ethnic prejudices were common long before the rise of the modern market economy, capitalism was found guilty not of creating the pathologies but of not going far enough to alleviate them. (This distinction may help to explain why the movement of women, African Americans, and other previously underrepresented groups into the mainstream, a liberal goal, has historically coincided with the strengthening of capitalism. To help members of these groups has not required reversing capitalism's trajectory, but merely helping to undo wrongs that it was not equipped to undo on its own.)

The Hirschman distinction between those critiques that judge the market as too powerful and those that judge it as too weak not only separates Galbraith's concerns from those that replaced it, but also draws attention to a particular weakness in Galbraith's argument. For it is not hard to come up with examples where the complaint directed at the market is not that it shapes tastes but that it *fails* to do so. In other words, the market is sometimes faulted for catering to preexisting tastes rather than ignoring these tastes and inculcating superior ones. This kind of criticism is directed with particular force at the entertainment industry. Television producers must often face the complaint that television panders rather than leads, that it indulges relatively immature tastes rather than aiding in the shaping of more sophisticated tastes.

There is particular irony to be found in the battle for survival being waged by public television in the United States. One time known as "educational television," PBS still sees one of its missions to be the development of new and improved tastes in the American public. Thus in this realm, at least, it is a *public* rather than a private provider that seeks to change tastes. And it is, of course, the commercial networks that are criticized precisely for their unwillingness to do so! The Galbraithian argument appears to have been stood on its head.[10]

There is an initial temptation to rescue Galbraith by simply conceding that his argument was too specific. By this rescue attempt, one would acknowledge that the market's tendency to pander to our tastes is indeed also at times a problem but would also insist that Galbraith only wished to focus his attention on a particular type of market pathology, namely, *objectionable* preference change. But any such defense is doomed to fail. For it must not be overlooked that the basis for his objection to preference manipulation had much more to do with the manipulative act itself than with what changes in taste this manipulation caused. In other words, he directed his criticism at what he chose to call the "dependence effect," suggesting that it was problematic to praise an economic system for satisfying tastes that the system itself had created. To concede that there are instances when the market's shortcoming is its proclivity to pander rather than to create tastes for its products clearly makes it impossible to accept the Galbraithian critique in its present form.

Thickening the Plot

To reject Galbraith's argument as it was presented is not to reject the intuition that likely prompted the argument. And as my personal experiences convinced me some time ago, the forces of the market were not operating to my advantage as a consumer in quite the way the textbooks taught. The standard line regarding rational choice as communicated in Paul Samuelson's *Economics* (already in its seventh edition when I read it) was compelling but at the same time something that troubled me. In reflecting on my eating habits, the claims of rationality seemed not to apply. I would regularly and voluntarily direct myself to McDonald's, order two cheeseburgers, french fries, and Coke, and yet be troubled by the thought that the market was responding to my desires. For there was clearly some sense in which I wanted to be acting differently than I was. Either I had to resolve the paradox or accept the label of hypocrite par excellence. I was a regular critic of so much of the commercial sphere, yet here I was through my actions giving an unequivocal "vote" for the spread of a true symbol of that sphere, McDonald's restaurants.

None of my early attempts to resolve the conflict seemed to in any way put at risk the essentials of rational choice theory. For I realized that feelings of conflict or even of "regret" were not sufficient to undo the essential arguments. I might, after all, regret that my decision to purchase the McDonald's meal was simultaneously the decision to *not* purchase some almost equally desirable meal from some other restaurant. Regret, in other words, might often stem from the brute fact that to make a selection from one's choice set is very often to simultaneously reject another desirable option. And even if the two cheeseburgers, fries, and Coke were far more desired by me than anything else in my choice set, there would still be another possible explanation for my feelings of regret. For regret might just be the consequence of not being able to have something that was unavailable. Perhaps my dissatisfaction was tied to the fact that I yearned to have *more* purchasing power and the more attractive bundle that would have thus been available.

While in some circumstances internal conflict might indeed follow from either of these—having to forgo the next best option in one's choice set or recognizing that a favored something was not in the choice set—neither of these could capture properly the internal dissatisfaction that my eating habits created. This became apparent when I thought about what my decision would have been had I been able to make it well in advance of the actual meal. Were I to have decided what I would eat twenty-four hours prior to consumption, I realized I would not have chosen the cheeseburger, fries, and Coke nearly so often. I would have likely opted, at least part of the time, for healthier choices. This is not to say that a spartan existence would have prevailed if there had always been time between choice and actual consumption. It *is* to say that health would have more often entered into my thinking. What is more, it became clear that the regret I experienced was very different from the two sorts mentioned above. I did not regret not being able to have my McDonald's bundle *and* some other bundle that I was forgoing (the "wanting to have my cake and eat it too" sort of regret). Nor did my consumption of this bundle cause me to regret not having been able to have some unattainable bundle. Rather, I clearly seemed to regret consuming what I was *rather than something else that was available.* But this served to open up new questions. If, as seemed reasonable, the standard economic line that an agent chooses the preferred item from the choice set was correct, how could it be that I both preferred the McDonald's bundle and preferred some other, healthier bundle?

The solution to this paradox will provide the uniting theme of this book. My proposed addition to the standard theory of rational choice will permit the resolution of a number of puzzles, one of which is worth giving attention to here. Consider the following three statements: (1) I am a rational person who selects what is optimal from the choices available; (2) although other choices are available, I have currently selected the McDonald's meal; (3) I report that in the best of all possible worlds, given currently prevailing prices and given my income, I would have chosen something else.

The strongest defenders and the harshest critics of the economist's rational choice model might have difficulty finding common ground, but they would be in agreement that only two of these three statements could be true. The defender would most likely focus critical attention on the third statement. For me to make such a claim would signal either confusion or dishonesty on my part, according to this view.[11] My considered, deliberate selection would be taken to reveal that the McDonald's meal is optimal, even if it does carry with it an increased risk, however slight, of ill health as well as unwanted calories. Critics of the rational choice model, on the other hand, would turn a critical eye on the first statement. From the observation that people report dissatisfaction with their free choices, they would ask us to reject the assumption of rationality. By their analysis, my reported dissatisfaction with my choice would be a clear signal that I lack fully rational faculties (see, e.g., Thaler 1991; Schwartz 1998).

Neither the "anti–rational choice" rejection of statement 1 nor the "pro–rational choice" rejection of statement 3 is, I would argue, acceptable. It is true that certain subjective claims of doing other than what one prefers to do are based on definitions of *prefer* that are not what the economist has in mind. However, it will be demonstrated at a later point that even after all the definitional differences are taken into account, agents do sometimes express dissatisfaction with their choices in a way that is incompatible with orthodox choice theory.

But to toss out the rationality assumption is at least as troubling. Models that ask us to treat the rational agent as in fact something else have become common.[12] Recasting a person as not one agent, but two (or even more), or characterizing people as comprised of two or more simultaneous preference orderings may result in the substitution of the standard model with a richer model having greater explanatory power, but it seriously compromises a most vital component of the rational choice model, namely, the normative dimension. To evaluate the efficiency characteristics of competing economic arrangements requires a basis for saying unequivocally when an agent is becoming better or worse off. The postmodern agent that emerges from the rejection of the rationality assumption brings with her a severe loss of the ability to make evaluative judgments. Clearly, a better way must be found.

Resolving a Paradox

But how is it possible to accept all three of the above claims? The analytical tool that will make this possible is a "second-order preference."[13] Let M represent the McDonald's meal that has already been described. Let H represent a similarly priced, more healthy alternative. The personal conflict described above is the simultaneous occurrence of a regular, or "first order," preference for M (that is, "M preferred H") and a second-order preference for H (that is, "H preferred M" is a preference that is preferred to "M preferred H"). Quite simply, my preference was something that I very definitely "had," or "felt" or "experienced" but was just as surely something that I would have preferred to have not "had" or "felt" or "experienced."

　　If such a higher-order preference, a preference for a particular preference, is introduced, the above paradox is resolved. Just as (1) says, I can be treated as a rational agent who selects what is best from the alternatives available. And as (2) says, I selected the McDonald's meal. But it is also possible now to accept statement (3), namely, that, holding my income and prices steady, in the best of all possible worlds I would have found myself choosing a different bundle. For in the best of all possible worlds I would have found myself experiencing a different preference ranking. Rather than suffering from a preference for M, I would have been experiencing a different preference, and as a result would have also found it in my interest to choose H.

　　From a strictly descriptive standpoint, the admission of second-order preferences into the discussion can undoubtedly be of value. Following the advice of Albert Hirschman, this richer rendering of the rational agent can aid in the resolution of otherwise paradoxical behavior (1985, 8–11). But such positive pursuits will remain very much secondary in the chapters that follow. The question to be ultimately addressed is this: How should we rate the market in its sensitivity to second-order preferences? Is there any inclination to produce unpreferred preferences? Does a sufficient market for preference shaping exist to protect, from a normative standpoint, the current-day prestige of the market as an economic organizing principle? Or might a serious shortcoming emerge?

In the twentieth century economists were nearly silent on the question of second-order preferences. But this was not always true. John Stuart Mill, who straddled the line between economics and philosophy (to the disadvantage of his contribution to each, some would undoubtedly claim), had the following to say:

> A person whose desires and impulses are his own—are the expression of his own nature, as it has been developed and modified by his own culture—is said to have a character. One whose desires and impulses are not his own, has no character. (1962, chap. 3, qtd. in Heap et al. 1992, 80)

Even while stressing the importance of taste formation, Mill minimized the significance of economic institutions in the taste-shaping enterprise. It was the other social institutions—school, church, family, neighborhood—that occupied center stage in the engineering of preferences.[14] At the time that Mill wrote, this might have been a reasonable conclusion to have reached. Sellers of that period were surely more prone to shape the tastes of customers than would have been true had perfect competition prevailed. But it is equally apparent that preference formation on their part was far less common than it has become in the century and a half since.

By Mill's account, to not have desires that are one's own (similar to having unpreferred preferences) was to be without character. Similar claims have been made in more recent years. According to the philosopher Terence Penelhum, "Someone achieves self-identity, or finds himself, if the desires that move him to act are, for the most part, desires that he recognizes and wishes to be the ones to move him" (1979, 304–5). For Harry Frankfurt, to have a free will is to be moved by desires that one wishes to be moved by (1971, 14–15). My unhappiness at consuming cheeseburgers, fries, and Cokes would classify me, following Frankfurt's way of characterizing matters, as one who acted freely upon the will that he had, but not as one who had a free will. For this will ("disposition to action") was not the will I wished to have.

In the chapter to follow, I will more thoroughly explore second-order preferences and the controversies that have surrounded them. In chapter 3, some welfare conclusions will be spelled out, conclusions that will not paint a very flattering picture of the market. Economists are in general agreement that spillover effects, whether positive or negative, have inefficiencies associated with them. The market delivers too much of that which creates spillover costs (whether in the act of producing or consuming) and too little of that which creates spillover benefits. The rejuvenated conservatives of the last twenty years have mounted counteroffensives against liberal critiques of the free market. The spillover problem provides one example, the recurrent conservative theme being that government is not the only source of solutions to the problem. People's sense of right and wrong and their desire for social approval provide mechanisms by which the damaging effect of spillovers may be avoided without government participation in the matter.

But to the extent that ideology matters and shapes us in ways that are not necessarily efficient, it will be my argument that the market-embracing nations of the world are heading in precisely the wrong direction when it comes to the shaping of our tastes. Imagine if overnight laws against noxious externalities were overturned. Imagine as well that people were unable to sense the damage that their actions were causing to others. We might expect a sudden rise in pollution, not out of thoughtlessness but because polluting was in the interest of the polluter and of no apparent harm to others. By the book's conclusion, I hope to have shown that something not unlike this has been occurring within market economies over the last century. Unrestricted persuasion has attained a legitimacy it did not have in earlier historical epochs. The consequence has been a slide away from what has been called, among other things, "character development," the achievement of "self-identity," and the attainment of "free will." To put it mildly, this amounts to a substantial welfare loss.

CHAPTER 2

Freedom to Choose

Free Choice and Free Will

The strong case for a free-market economy rests on the assumption that people can intelligently choose, but precisely what it means to exercise "free choice" has rarely been of much concern to economists. If *free* is taken to signify "costless" and *choice* to signify the item chosen ("vanilla ice cream is my choice"), economists would necessarily have some difficulties with the expression. Indeed, with these the accepted definitions, Milton Friedman's dictum that there is "no such thing as a free lunch" might be brought to bear on free choice itself. To choose one thing is always to forgo something else, and in that sense, there is "no such thing as a free choice."

If, on the other hand, the intended meaning of "free choice" is nothing more than "able to select for oneself," then it would be possible to agree that among the items in an agent's choice set a free choice is indeed possible. But even if this definition is the intended one, economists would not be hesitant to issue another warning. Anyone exercising "free choice" in this second sense ("free to select") still has constraints that make this a limited freedom. If items A and B are each possibilities, but C and D are not, the agent has "free choice" over the first two but not over the latter two.

What is meant by a free choice is, it thus appears, less than obvious. What is meant by a "free will" is more problematic still. By one account, an agent is exercising a free will when he makes a free choice in the second sense just considered, that is, when he chooses the preferred item from his choice set. While free will, by this interpretation, is necessary for the expression of a free choice, it would be absent only in rather exceptional situations. So, for example, consider an agent responding to a posthypnotic suggestion. If free to choose either a one-dollar bill or a twenty-dollar bill, the choice of the one-dollar bill would lead most to describe the agent as neither having exercised a "free will" nor as having made a free choice.

According to the philosopher Harry Frankfurt, it is incorrect to link the exercise of a free choice so closely with the condition of having a free will.[1] By his account, one may freely choose among the available options without having exercised a free will. At the same time, it is the potential for having a free will that sets humans apart from all other sentient beings. While animals do, according to him, exercise a free choice among the available options, they cannot, by their very nature, have a free will. Frankfurt's argument is worth considering since my eventual claim will be that market forces are deficient in the creation of Frankfurt's sort of free will. Now according to him,

> [O]ne essential difference between persons and other creatures is to be found in the structure of a person's will. Human beings are not alone in having desires and motives, or in making choices. . . . It seems to be peculiarly characteristic of humans, however, that they are able to form what I shall call "second-order desires" or "desires of the second order."
>
> Besides wanting and choosing and being moved *to do* this or that, men may also want to have (or not to have) certain desires and motives. They are capable of wanting to be different, in their preferences and purposes, from what they are. Many animals appear to have the capacity for what I shall call "first-order desires" or "desires of the first order," which are simply desires to do or not to do one thing or another. No animal other than man, however, appears to have the capacity for reflective self-evaluation that is manifested in the formation of second-order desires. (1971, 6–7)

Frankfurt makes it clear at other points that a first-order desire does not necessarily move an agent to act (1971, 8). In essence, for *every* valued object in the agent's choice set (and not just the preferred object) the agent has a first-order desire. Let "a Milky Way," "a Nestle's Crunch," and "nothing" comprise the elements in an agent's choice set. If "nothing" is ranked the lowest, then it can be concluded that the agent has a "desire" for both the Milky Way and the Nestle's Crunch. This is only to say that he would prefer having either of them to having nothing at all. If "nothing" is assigned a utility level of zero, this agent can be described as having a desire for an item if the utility value assigned to it is positive. Second-order desires, in contrast, are positive evaluations of *desires* for things rather than positive evaluations of the things themselves. If this agent would prefer having "a desire for a Milky Way" to "a desire for nothing" (and similarly ranks a desire for a Nestle's Crunch), and gets no utility from "a desire for nothing" (assigns a zero value to it), then it is possible to say that he has a second-order desire for each desire.

By Frankfurt's account, the desire that moves one to act is one's "will." This is roughly analogous to what an economist would call a preference. As Frankfurt puts it, "To identify an agent's will is either to identify the desire (or desires) by which he is motivated in some action he performs or to identify the desire (or desires) by which he will or would be motivated when or if he acts. An agent's will, then, is identical with one or more of his first-order desires" (1971, 8). This returns us to the question of what it might mean to have a free will. Let A and B be the only two choices available to Mary and assume that she prefers A to B. Mary's desire for A would be described by Frankfurt as her will, since it is this desire that moves her to act. It might seem to follow from this that she is in possession of a "free will." True, her choices are limited, but as the introductory student is often reminded, such limits are an essential feature of the human condition. The market economy, if functioning reasonably, provides Mary with a wide selection of bundles from which to select. It thus seems sensible to say that with respect to the bundles that are available to her, she exercises free will.

Frankfurt, however, would find this unacceptable and would treat Mary's choice of A as insufficient evidence that she has a free will. The choice would be taken to reveal only that she has been free to act upon the will that she has. In other words, if a desire for A happens to be Mary's will, her ability to choose A does not serve as evidence that her will is free. The evidence that her will is free would be an indication from her that she was content having a desire for A be her will and that if she were able to select the desire that would move her to act she would choose just this desire.

To speak of "desires" rather than "preference orderings" can complicate matters, particularly when discussion focuses on the second order. Now at the second order, the things that Mary does or does not desire are first-order desires. Just as it was possible for her to have a desire for A and a desire for B as well, so too is it possible for her to have a desire for a "desire for A" while at the same time also desiring a "desire for B." Recall again that Mary's will was equated with the strongest of the first-order desires—the one that drives her to act. The second-order desire that the agent would select, if possible, to be the desire that would move her to act is referred to by Frankfurt as her second-order volition. Furthermore, Mary would be said to be experiencing a free will only if the desire that is her will (i.e., the desire that moves her to act) is the desire that is her volition (i.e., the desire that she desires to have move her to act.)

Before reexpressing this in the language of preference orderings, consider another example. I am pressed for time as I walk toward my car and notice that a friend I have not seen in a while just happens to be walking in my direction. I see myself as having two options: stop and chat for a few minutes (call this A) or hurriedly nod hello and move on (call this B). Suppose that each of these are desires since I would prefer each option to doing absolutely nothing. Suppose also that the desire for B happens to be my will in that it is the stronger of the desires, and therefore is the one that will move me to act.

At the second order the objects of valuation are, of course, desires. Suppose that each of the possible desires is in itself pleasant and that I thus have a second-order desire for each; that is, a "desire to desire to stop and chat for a few minutes" and a "desire to desire to nod hello and move on." Suppose also that the first of these second-order desires is the stronger of the two, and is thus my volition. Following Frankfurt's terminology, this would mean that if I were enjoying a free will, I would select A as the desire that moved me to act. Inasmuch as I am instead moved by the desire for B (i.e., B is my "will") I am, unfortunately, not currently experiencing a free will. I certainly have the freedom to act upon an unwanted will that is now mine, but I do not have a *free* will, in the sense of a desire that I chose to be the one moving me to act.

Preferences to the Rescue: A Simplification

When it comes to a command of mathematics, there is no doubt that economists outshine philosophers, but when it comes to command of language, the nod usually goes to the philosophers. Despite this, the economist's explanatory structure of a "preference ordering" is far more effective (and economical) in communicating Frankfurt's thesis than is his explanatory structure of "desires."[2]

The column labeled "Conflict" that appears in table 2.1 summarizes via preference rankings the state of being moved to act by a preference that is not itself preferred. While preferring to have a preference for A (that is, preferring that "A pref B" be one's first-order preference rather than "B pref A"), the agent is stuck with (B pref A) as his preference. As a consequence, he freely chooses B, since, given the first-order preference that prevails, this choice leaves him better off than would A.[3] The column labeled "Harmony" portrays the better situation of an agent who experiences the first-order ranking that he prefers, and who thus finds it optimal to choose that which he prefers and prefers to prefer as well. Each of these agents is

TABLE 2.1.

	Conflict	Harmony
Second-order preference	(A pref B) pref (B pref A)	(A pref B) pref (B pref A)
First-order preference	B pref A	A pref B
Choice	B	A

exercising a "freedom to act on the will that he has," which is to say that each is able to select the highest item in the first-order preference ranking. But it is not true that each has a free will in the Frankfurtian sense. For the conflicted agent, the will that he has is not the one he wishes to have. While he wishes to be experiencing a preference for A, he is experiencing a preference for B. For the contented agent, on the other hand, the first-order preference (the will that moves him to act) is precisely that which he wishes to have. Free will prevails in the Frankfurtian sense, since he has the preference he prefers having.

Expressing Frankfurt's claims in this way holds at least three expositional advantages. First, where there were previously two first-order desires—one for B and one for A—there is now a single first-order preference ranking. Similarly, rather than having to confront two second-order desires, one for a "desire for A" and the other for a "desire for B," we can now speak of a single second-order preference ranking.

Second, there is no need to restrict the discussion to those activities and those preferences for activities that are "desirable." As I already suggested, something might be usefully described as "desired" if having it is better than having nothing. This limitation is no longer necessary. In the above example, B and A might each be undesirable since the ranking of things does not require that these things be "better than doing or having nothing." All it requires is that the agent prefer any particular element to whatever lies to its right. It is entirely possible that some or all of the available elements could be undesirable. Such would be the case if the agent would prefer doing nothing (not an option) to the possibilities that she must select from. This sort of situation is brought home with particular force in the novel *Sophie's Choice*. The protagonist was given three choices. Hand her young son over to the Nazis, hand her young daughter over to the Nazis, or do nothing and have them both taken from her. Clearly, none of these options was desired, but, macabre as it might sound, we could speak of one being preferred relative to the other options.

As a third advantage, not only does a recasting of the argument in terms of preference orderings render more manageable Frankfurt's argument, it also brings to light the problematic nature of his word choice. An agent's freedom to act upon his will would appear to be an impossible condition to achieve if it were ever true that there was even one element *not* in his choice set that was preferable to anything *within* his choice set. Thus an agent who prefers flying like a bird to walking and prefers walking to crawling might be said to never exercise freedom to act in accord with his will when he merely walks. For the preferred element is chronically outside the choice set. Just as surely, there is likely always some preference ranking that an agent would regard as preferable to what is available to a mere mortal (e.g., preferring to prefer no hostile emotions), and by Frankfurt's definition we would appear forced to say that such an agent could not have a free will. Clearly, the economic insight that scarcity is our existential condition becomes relevant. Rather than speak of an agent who is "free to act upon his will" and one who has "free will," it would be more accurate to speak of "more or less freedom to act upon his will" and to speak of a "freer or less free will."

Frequent Sightings: Disregarded Preferences and Regretted Preferences

A second-order preference will be defined throughout this book in a way that fits well with the economist's definition of a first-order preference. The choice of A over B when both are available reveals a preference for the former relative to the latter. This is true regardless of the nature of A and B. And what forms the recurrent thread of this book is how important questions arise about the market's functioning when A and B are allowed to be "preference rankings of things" rather than themselves "things." Remaining within the economic tradition, I will not be undertaking any analysis of what distinguishes that which is preferred from that which is not. To do so would introduce complexity that could only detract from the main ideas.[4] There are, however, two definitional problems that can cause great confusion and that are worth some consideration. The first has to do with just what it means to say that a choice reveals a preference, while the second has to do with a danger of overdiagnosing the state of being moved to act by unpreferred preferences.

The economist's assumption that preference is revealed by choice meets with resistance largely because there is a rival definition of preference that is confused with the economist's definition. By this rival meaning, it is not at all unusual for someone to claim that she sometimes acts contrary to her preference. This is most strikingly apparent in the case of someone who has just managed to quit smoking. Let N represent "not smoke" and S represent "smoke." To the economist, the fact that N is the choice when both N and S are options stands as sufficient evidence that N is preferred to S. It would not be unusual, however, to hear an agent announce that beating the smoking habit consisted of learning to act contrary to her preference; that while S is preferred to N, it is the unpreferred N that she has chosen. Are such claims simply inconsistent with the assumption of revealed preference? How is it possible for (S pref N) to be the agent's preference ranking, for both S and N to be available, and yet for N to be her choice?

It is tempting to turn to second-order preferences to resolve this paradox. For it might be reasoned that although (S pref N) is her first-order preference and [(N pref S) pref (S pref N)] her second-order preference, rather than give in to her unpreferred preference, she elects to act "as if" she has the preferred preference. Martin Hollis reasons in just this manner, but builds his argument on a flawed definition of the second-order preference as a better ranking of the *same elements* as appear in the first-order ranking (1983, 254). By definition, the agent is better off if she smokes if (S pref N) is her first-order ranking. Overcoming the habit is the act of changing her preference, of having it become true that (N pref S), from which the choice of N follows.

The difference between the economist's assumed link between preference and choice and the more general usage that suggests otherwise is traceable to the economist's treatment of preferences as "overall" in scope while popular usage, in contrast, is inclined to treat them as "intrinsic" (see Baier 1977, 218). An intrinsic preference is a preference for the "thing in itself" or "activity in itself" independently of what is distantly contingent on the preference's fulfillment. Thus, even the agent who is successful at giving up cigarettes may be one who continues to have an intrinsic preference to smoke. That is, the act of having a single cigarette thought of in isolation from whatever effects this might eventually have (slightly increased risk of death, increased likelihood of preferring to smoke next time) might be preferred to not smoking. But this agent's abstention would reveal that he has an "all things considered" or overall preference to not smoke.[5]

Failure to make this distinction likely accounts for much of the resistance to the claim that "agents do what they prefer," for too frequently the critic of this claim has in mind an intrinsic preference when the claimant has in mind an overall preference. Though not made explicit, rational choice theory defines preferences as overall in nature. To prefer A to B is to prefer the future that is contingent on selecting A. Consider the recovering alcoholic. Informal language is such that the following might be stated and well understood: "Although I would prefer to have a drink, I will abstain. For I realize that fulfilling this preference will not be in my long-term interest. Having the one drink will lead me to have more, and I will likely become intoxicated, wake up with a hangover, and lessen the long-term likelihood of beating the drinking habit."

Making such a claim indicates an *intrinsic* preference for a drink. The thought of the immediate future, isolated from any effect that the actions chosen will have on the more distant future, leads the agent to rate a drink as better than any of the alternatives. His decision to not indulge is indeed a decision to *not* do what he prefers in the intrinsic sense. However, his voluntary abstinence indicates an *overall* preference to so act, an overall preference made clear in the specifics mentioned in the above hypothetical quotation, but not usually so obvious.[6]

While the habit of defining preference in a narrow intrinsic sense may obscure the frequency of unpreferred preferences, there is a related fuzziness in definitions that results in too frequent spottings. This related problem stems from a failure to distinguish not doing a particular something because it is not the *preferred* option from not doing something because it is not *an option at all.*

To illustrate, suppose that someone is asked to identify the city that is the country music capital of the world and is promised an all-expense paid trip to the city in question if a correct answer is given. Suppose that the agent knows the city to be Nashville and thus prefers to give Nashville (N) as his answer. But further suppose that this agent has a stronger desire to visit Paris (P) than to visit Nashville. Would it be correct to say that he has a first-order preference to utter "N" but a second-order preference to utter "P"? That is, would it be correct to say that although (N pref P) is this agent's first-order preference ranking, he has at the same time [(P pref N) pref (N pref P)] as his second-order preference? Certainly the casual rhetoric used in situations having a formal resemblance to what has been described suggests so. For a full understanding would be communicated by this agent were he to announce, "Although I will freely offer 'Nashville' as my answer, I truly wish that it was 'Paris' that I found to be my preferred response."[7]

In a certain respect this agent does wish that his preference were different, but this sort of case must be distinguished from the sorts of conflict that have already been discussed. For if his preference had been (P pref N) he would have given P as his answer, but he would have then gone away empty-handed. It appears that the discontent afflicting the agent is traceable to the items in his *choice set* rather than to the preference he is experiencing. To better see this, it will be helpful to give a fuller definition to three hypothetical choices, only two of which are actually available. Let these choices be not just the uttering of a city's name, but uttering the name and then doing whatever is contingent on the utterance. Suppose that

P = give Paris as answer and go to Paris as a result
p = give Paris as answer but go nowhere as a result
N = give Nashville as answer and go to Nashville as a result.

Further suppose that this agent has a first-order preference ranking (P pref N pref p) and that this ranking happens to be the highest element in his second-order preference ranking. If this is so, he is clearly not in the grip of a preference that he would prefer not to be experiencing. Rather, P is not in his choice set, and he is thus forced to choose between N and p, the former of which ranks above the latter. If the elements in the first-order preference ranking are specified only over the *available* elements, then P would not be included, and it would follow that the agent has first-order preference (N pref p) and second-order preference [(N pref p) pref (p pref N)]. He prefers to give Nashville as his answer, and is content with this preference, given the true available options.

It would be a mistake to conclude from the above that second-order preferences are a preoccupation of our age, constantly being brought into discussions where they do not belong. Recognition of the idea that agents can evaluate their tastes remains uncommon. And it remains an idea that the "rational agent" who is the chief actor in economic discussions has never even considered.

Homo Economicus: More Animal Than Human?

The economist's analytical tools emerge from the above discussion as powerful devices for refining Frankfurt's major argument. But the economist's favorite biological fiction, *homo economicus,* emerges in a considerably less dignified light. For the most well known economic version of humanity neglects entirely the line of second-order preferences in table 2.1. By this interpretation, people make choices and are treated as being motivated in their choices by preferences for this over that, but are never assumed to reflect upon and evaluate these preferences.[8] More sophisticated versions of the human agent have been cropping up in the professional journals and scholarly books that question this and will receive attention later in this writing. But the version that continues to thoroughly dominate the textbooks—the general population's window to the economist's world—remains steadfastly tied to a sort of agent that Frankfurt chooses to call a "wanton." And according to Frankfurt:

> What distinguishes the rational wanton from other rational agents is that he is not concerned with the desirability of his desires themselves. He ignores the question of what his will is to be. Not only does he pursue whatever course of action he is most strongly inclined to pursue, but he does not care which of his inclinations is the strongest. (1971, 11)

According to *Webster's New Collegiate,* a wanton is, among other things, "a pampered person or child," or a "frolicsome child or animal," or "a person given to luxurious self-enjoyment." Whether any of these capture well Frankfurt's intended meaning is debatable, but it seems clear he was seeking a label for one who did not at all correspond with most visions of what a fully developed human being would be.

It might be argued that economic activity of humans is radically distinguishable from the economic activity of other living creatures. "Trucking and bartering" remains, by all accounts, something that only humans choose to do, and as a consequence markets only have relevance in human cultures. In addition, the division of labor, the phenomenon that, according to Adam Smith, most facilitated dynamic economic growth, barely can be observed in the animal kingdom, and when it is observed typically consists of "wired-in" specialization on the basis of a creature's gender. It is thus undeniable that the creatures that hold center stage in the economics textbooks and economics journals are not to be confused with other species.

Despite this obvious difference, the implied posture of *homo economicus* toward her desires is the same as an animal's posture. Neither creature embraces, rejects, or has the ability to evaluate its preferences. Some of the introductory texts have sought to convey the full generality of demand theory by reporting empirical findings that animals have downward sloping demand curves as surely as do humans.[9] So, for example, if the number of pecks of a bar that are required to issue forth a fixed quantity of food is increased, then the representative pigeon will, just as positive theory predicts, opt for less. The rise in the "price" will have lowered the "quantity demanded." That there is an implicit wantonness characterizing both humans and pigeons goes unmentioned, undoubtedly in large measure because it is not a feature that economists even imagine could be different. But if Frankfurt's argument is accepted, then there is a critical difference between the pigeon electing to lessen its intake of seed when the price rises, and a human agent reacting similarly when the price of something that he purchases increases. The pigeon is fully uncritical of its tastes. It cannot, according to Frankfurt, embrace them or view them with displeasure. They are just an unexamined canvas on which the pigeon lives its life, unlike what is true for the human agent with second-order preferences.

Early Economic Stirrings

For John Locke, discontent over one's choice provided the basis for his judgment that we ought to take an agent at his word rather than his action. As he put it, "[T]he question still remains, *how men come often to prefer the worse to the better,* and to choose that, which, by their own confession, has made them miserable" (qtd. in Levy 1982, 9). For Bernard Mandeville, in contrast, it was one's actual choice that revealed one's preference:

> I don't call things Pleasures which Men say are best, but such as they seem to be most pleased with; how can I believe that a Man's chief Delight is in the Embellishments of the Mind, when I see him ever employ'd about and daily pursue the Pleasures that are contrary to them? (Qtd. in Levy 1982, 21)

Earlier I presented the following paradox; I (1) am rational and select what is optimal, (2) select a McDonald's meal from among the options available, and (3) report that holding prices and income constant, in the best of all possible worlds I would have chosen something else. I characterized critics of the rational choice model as using reports such as this one as evidence that the rationality assumption is inaccurate. Locke might be placed in this group. He takes the agent at his word and assumes that the agent does not like his choice. For Mandeville, in contrast, statements that one prefers x while choosing y are simply not to be taken seriously.

If my interpretation is accepted, we appear to have a defender and a critic of the rationality assumption of neoclassicism, each writing well before Adam Smith. But it was with the writings of the nineteenth-century utilitarians that deeper considerations of rational choice appeared. Jeremy Bentham's allegation that "quantity of pleasure being equal, push-pin is as good as poetry" (qtd. in Bronfenbrenner 1977, 95) is probably his most cited claim. As quaint and time-bound as it is, this message remains at the very core of rational choice theory.

This is not to suggest that there has not been opposition. And it was probably John Stuart Mill who came closest to overturning the Bentham dictum. Mill asks us to distinguish between two types of pleasure:

> It is quite compatible with the principles of utility to recognize the fact that some kinds of pleasure are more desirable and more valuable than others . . . there is no known Epicurean theory of life which does not assign to the pleasures of the intellect, of the feelings and imagination, and of the moral sentiments, a much higher value as pleasures than to those of mere sensation. (Qtd. in Hahnel and Albert 1990, 27)

It was perhaps this passage, and others like it, that most contributed to the less than flattering evaluations of Mill's later writings. He symbolizes the end of the classical period because the neoclassical revolution took off soon after his final works were first appearing. In addition, even within the classical tradition, it was not possible to reconcile his argument with the utilitarianism he appeared to embrace. Simply put, how could a utilitarian claim that a given amount of utility from one source was better or worse than the *same amount* of utility from some other source?

Mill appears to have come close to suggesting the existence of second-order preferences, with the claim that the act of reflecting on the goods that provided a person with utility might itself raise or lower the utility associated with the good itself. If this interpretation is correct, it would appear that Mill's thinking was closer to Aristotle's (to be considered in a later chapter) than to what I am putting forth. For he appears to have assumed that there was a social consensus on which preferences were desirable and which were not. Were it otherwise, he would have had to allow for the possibility that some agents might value the pleasures of "mere sensation" more than they valued an equivalent amount of pleasure derived from intellectual pursuits. In short, the assumption that second-order preferences are subjective is not to be found in the writings of Mill.

Marginalized by the Marginalists

With the introduction of marginal analysis to economic theory in the latter half of the nineteenth century, attention strayed far from the philosophical. In retrospect, the early neoclassical project might be understood as a powerful answer to the critique of capitalism laid down by Karl Marx. The efficiency features of competitive markets could be formally demonstrated, as could the "fairness" of labor markets in paying workers amounts equal to their marginal products. The entire normative project rested precariously on a number of assumptions, and academic economics became known, to friend and foe alike, as an exercise in deductive logic more than an empirical science. Among the assumptions that were central to the enterprise was that agents chose what they found to be optimal, subject to the constraints they faced. Firms maximized profits, and consumers maximized utility. While profit was measurable and utility was not, it was no more an issue whether consumers were content with their "utility functions" than it was an issue whether firms were content with their "profit functions." Each was a brute fact.

This is not to say that all believed that the source of preferences should not concern the economist. John Maurice Clark had the following observation:

> We thought of the self as a sovereign will, in some sense independent of the universe. Men had their wants, and the universe granted or denied their gratification. Production consisted in turning out goods and services to suit these pre-existing wants. Now, however, we find a self which is but a series of attitudes toward the universe; a set of tendencies to react and to seek, which are themselves the joint product of

certain underlying tendencies, developed and given their shape and direction by the universe outside. Our wants . . . are molded by our environment just as surely as are the means of satisfaction. (Clark 1936, 100)

Clark was well aware that mainstream economists would be unswayed by his proposal for expanding the subject's scope and would stress that they "begin by taking wants as we find them," that "one want is as good as another in our eyes," and that it is the ethicist who could concentrate attention on the relative goodness of wants (1936, 100). Writing nearly a half century later, Milton Friedman indeed offered such an argument.

> The economist has little to say about the formation of wants; this is the province of the psychologist. The economist's task is to trace the consequences of any given set of wants. The legitimacy of justification for this abstraction must rest ultimately, in this case as with any other abstraction, on the light that is shed and the power to predict that is yielded by the abstraction. (Qtd. in Hahnel and Albert 1990, 76)

Clark anticipated that the ethicist would be the one whom the economist would regard as best suited to pursue the topic of taste change, but for Friedman it was the psychologist. This difference may be partly the result of psychology's growth vis-à-vis moral philosophy in the years separating Clark and Friedman. But even if it were true that ethicists were fewer in number, it does not follow that the normative side of economics was on the wane. For in the years separating Clark and Friedman, welfare economics was growing in substance and rigor. What is more, Milton Friedman, more than any other economist of the last half century, has served as the example of economist as advocate, and not just scientist. He, as much as any, has made it his responsibility to spell out the efficiency features of the free market and the moral grounds for such markets. Yet, rather than turn to the *ethicist* for the study of the market's influence on tastes, he would have us turn to the *psychologist*. A positive analysis might result, but a normative inquiry would still be lacking. And as Robert Pollak indeed noted, in commenting on emerging research interests of the 1960s and 1970s, the "impetus to incorporate taste formation and change into economic analysis has come primarily from those interested in household behavior rather than welfare, and the principal focus . . . has been empirical demand analysis" (1978, 374). But other paths were also being followed, paths that turned attention again to the normative dimension of changing preferences.

Partial Reentry: The Second Order as Servant of the First Order

Standing apart from the strictly positive literature is an article by Burton Weisbrod and two by Amartya Sen, all written in the 1970s.[10] Weisbrod operated in a neoclassical format, with utility functions rather than preference rankings being his engine of analysis. Sen, in contrast, relied on preference rankings, and at least partly as a result of this has been extensively cited by philosophers and decision theorists, as well as by economists.

Included in the title of Weisbrod's article is the question, "What kind of utility functions do we want?" This creates an initial impression that he is receptive to second-order preference rankings. But his loyalty to orthodoxy leads him to greatly limit the extent to which the ranking of utility functions is possible. After agreeing that "[t]he customary proposition that one type of utility function cannot be compared to another within an economic efficiency framework is correct in general" (1977, 994), he goes on to conclude that some very stringent conditions must be met before a comparison of utility functions is even possible. More specifically, he asserts that "one type of utility function, and the expected consumption bundle it generates, may be said to be preferred to another, and the expected consumption bundle it generates, if and only if (a) the two expected consumption bundles are different and (b) the same consumption bundle is preferred no matter which utility function is used to evaluate the two bundles" (993).

These conditions can be reexpressed in terms of preference rankings. Doing so will make it apparent that one of Weisbrod's conditions is not fulfilled in the instances of preference change that have served as examples here. The claim that a smoker has a second-order preference to not smoke has been taken to indicate that the person is better off "preferring to not smoke while not smoking" [(N pref S) and N] than she is "preferring to smoke while smoking" [(S pref N) and S]. More generally, it has been taken to be axiomatically true that the agent is better off "having the preference she prefers and acting on it" than "having the preference she would rather not have and acting on it."

There is a temptation to resist this axiom, and an example raised by Frankfurt may have contributed to such resistance. Frankfurt offers the example of a psychotherapist treating narcotics addicts who believes that his ability to help his clients would be facilitated if he were to experience the desires for drugs that they experience. In Frankfurt's words,

> It is entirely possible . . . that although he wants to be moved by a desire to take the drug, he does not want this desire to be effective. He

may not want it to move him all the way to action. He need not be interested in finding out what it is like to take the drug. And insofar as he now wants only to *want* to take it, and not to *take* it, there is nothing in what he now wants that would be satisfied by the drug itself. (1971, 9)

Allowing T to represent "take the drug" and N to represent "not take the drug," it may appear that this provides an instance wherein [(T pref N) and N] is preferred to [(T pref N) and T]. But this translation of Frankfurt's example would be mistaken. For as was discussed earlier in this chapter, to "desire" something is not synonymous with "preferring" that something in an overall sense. My interpretation of Frankfurt's example is best presented if more than two courses of action are possible. Let A = have lunch, B = shoot heroin, and C = do nothing. Frankfurt appears to be describing a case in which a physician treating the addict hopes to get closer to his patients by merely having a desire but not an overall preference for heroin. That is, the physician described wishes to go from a state of [(A pref C pref B) and A] to a state of [(A pref B pref C) and A]. A desire for the heroin would be experienced (since heroin would be preferred to doing nothing) but would be insufficient to interfere with his strongest desire to have lunch. To have had an overall preference, in contrast, would have meant that consuming heroin was preferred to any alternative use of his time.

Returning to the smoking example, by Weisbrod's criteria, condition (a) is met but condition (b) is not.[11] S is preferred in one of the rankings and N in the other. Neither is preferred in *both*. Weisbrod's criterion (b), in short, appears to directly contradict a clear implication of the second-order preference model that has been presented here. Despite this, claims much like it appear elsewhere in the literature (see, e.g., Frank 1987, 593; Dixit and Norman 1978, 2; Cowen 1993, 256).

It is necessary to expand the two-element example in order to provide a clearer sense of what the fulfillment of condition (b) entails. Let there be three elements, A, B, and C. Suppose that when the agent's first-order preference is (A pref B pref C), elements A and B are not available and, as a consequence, C is her choice. Further suppose that when her first-order preference shifts to (B pref A pref C), B suddenly becomes available and becomes her choice. According to Weisbrod, the latter preference is preferable, since the choice that follows from it is preferred to the choice accompanying the other preference, and this preference holds whichever of the two first-order rankings one refers to. The agent's second-order preference for (B pref A pref C) over (A pref B pref C) is thus strictly instrumental in nature. It amounts to a strategy for being able to attain a more highly ranked element in the original preference ranking and is not in any sense an exercise in embracing or rejecting this original ranking qua ranking.

Operating within the structure of preference rankings rather than utility functions, Amartya Sen places no similar requirement on second-order preferences. He presents a guilt-ridden meat-eater saying, "'I wish I had a vegetarian's tastes, for I disapprove of the killing of animals, but I find vegetarian food so revolting that I can't bear to eat it, so I do eat meat.'"[12] Letting M stand for "eating meat" and V stand for "eating vegetables," this agent is reporting (1) that [(V pref M) pref (M pref V)] is his second-order preference, (2) that if (V pref M) were his first-order preference, V would be his choice, but (3) that since (M pref V) is his first-order preference, M is what he chooses. Within Sen's writings on second-order preferences, to simply assert that the agent has a second-order preference for one thing over another carries with it an implicit assumption that the elements within the first-order ranking are within the agent's choice set, both before and after any preference change. Quite clearly, he does not adhere to Weisbrod's criterion (b), for it is not required by him that "the same consumption bundle is preferred no matter which utility function is used to evaluate the two bundles."

In spite of this difference, the context in which Sen introduces the second-order preference creates the impression that he would agree with Weisbrod. Sen argues that behaving "as if" one has a preference (whether one has this preference or not) is a device for overcoming the prisoner's dilemma. To summarize his argument, table 2.2 presents the fabled dilemma. The number on the left in each of the cells represents agent 1's payoff, the number on the right agent 2's payoff. If agent 1 is rational and self-interested, his first-order preference ranking (stated in terms of his payoffs) would naturally be (4 pref 3 pref 2 pref 1), which would lead to the selection of clearly dominant strategy B. If agent 2 had an equivalent ranking of her potential payoffs, she too would select B, and the result would be a payoff of 2 for each agent. As Sen argues, if each agent were to behave "as if" he or she valued the other's well-being in addition to his or her own, the dilemma might be overcome. As one example considered by Sen, each

TABLE 2.2.

		Agent 2	
		Strategy A	Strategy B
	Strategy A	3, 3	1, 4
Agent 1			
	Strategy B	4, 1	2, 2

agent might prefer having "other-regarding preferences" that lead to the ranking of outcomes on the basis of the sum of payoffs enjoyed (1974, 60–62). This would result in first-order preference ranking (3 pref 4 pref 1 pref 2) for each agent (the agent's personal payoff alone is still being used to express each outcome), the selection of A by each (the now dominant choice), and the attainment of a payoff of 3 for each. For each agent, the first-order preference and outcome would have changed as shown in table 2.3. What is significant to note is that 3 ranks higher than 2 for both the "selfish" and the "other-regarding" agent. Since a different "bundle" (in this case, "payoff") is realized following the changed ordering, it follows that both of the Weisbrod criteria are fulfilled.

Sen's decision to introduce second-order preferences was motivated by a very particular concern, namely, the desire to give a richer rendering of the way in which prisoner's dilemmas could be overcome. None of his work since his seminal papers has taken the study of second-order preferences any further. Those who have chosen to develop models of conflicted agents have usually chosen to leave higher-order preferences out of the discussion. At least two suggestions have been made as to why this might be so. Albert Hirschman sees a major problem in their being revealed more readily through words than action. In his words:

> If second-order preferences are permanently discordant with the agent's choices, then they tend to lose their credibility as being really "there" and will in the longer run be downgraded to "meaningless, hypocritical mutterings and remonstrances." (1982b, 71)

And later:

> If . . . the two kinds of preferences are permanently at odds so that the agent always acts against his better judgment, then again, this [second-order preference] cannot only be dismissed as wholly ineffective, but doubts will arise whether it is really there at all. (1985, 9)

While Hirschman's concerns stem from the positivist grounding of economics, Martin Bronfenbrenner raises mathematical concerns that

TABLE 2.3.

Type Agent	First-Order Preference	Outcome
Selfish	4 pref 3 pref 2 pref 1	2
Other-regarding	3 pref 4 pref 1 pref 2	3

should not be ignored. After acknowledging that "some of us sometimes wish our utility functions were other than what they are," he goes on to caution that any formal development of this within the neoclassical framework "opens up whole new cans of worms, about utility *functionals* made up of utility functions, with *optima optimorum* located on 'notional' rather than actual utility functions, on the costs and benefits of shifting from one function to another within a given functional, and similar messy problems."[13]

A mark of good theorizing is economy of explanatory structure. Among economists there are healthy doubts about the introduction of complex modes of analysis that may add little to our understanding and that often isolate those familiar with the techniques from others who should be part of the conversation. To the extent that Bronfenbrenner believed that regret over choice could be captured in a simpler way than provided by second-order preferences, he deserves praise. But to the extent that he was motivated by an unexamined devotion to the standard modes of analysis, he does not. Like the proverbial drunk who insists on looking for his dropped keys under the streetlight despite knowing that they fell elsewhere, avoiding models that diverge from standard modes of analysis makes it nearly impossible to discover what second-order preferences permit to be discovered, namely, welfare assessments of preference change. Some within the mainstream camp have, nevertheless, insisted on searching beneath the streetlight. And some have failed to appreciate the strong normative implications provided by second-order preferences by failing to properly separate them from their more manageable rivals, the multiple-selves models.

Second-Order Preference as a Coexistent "Second Self"?

A second-order preference ranking differs from a first-order preference ranking in the elements that are being ranked. The latter ranks "bundles," or "activities" or "states of the world"; the former ranks "rankings of bundles" or "rankings of activities," or "rankings of states of the world." Basic as this distinction may be, it appears to have been forgotten in the "multiple utility" and "multiple selves" models of internal conflict.[14] Multiple-utility models are those that treat the agent as simultaneously having more than one ranking of the same elements. Multiple-selves models are those that retain the assumption of "one ranking per agent" at a single moment while also treating the agent as in fact two, three, or more agents, each having its own ranking.

The claim that an agent has more than just one preference ranking of a given set of elements has sometimes been conflated with the very differ-

ent claim that an agent has both a first-order and a second-order preference ranking. Timothy Brennan points out that "one of the fundamental
components of the concept of economic rationality is that preference
orderings are 'complete,' that all alternative actions an agent can take are
comparable. The idea that all actions can be ranked may be called the *single utility* assumption" (1989, 189). Brennan goes on to contrast the "single utility" assumption with those multiple-utility models that violate this
assumption, and he chooses to include in this latter category those models
that treat the agent as having "preferences over preferences" (190).

Grouping the second-order preference model with multiple-utility
models deprives this model of most of its power. For unlike the multiple-
utility models, the introduction of second-order preferences does not
require the relaxation of the single-utility assumption. This might, on the
surface, seem incorrect, and it is worth considering why.

When *preference* was earlier offered as a replacement for *desire,* I
praised the former for making more tractable the task of separating the
first order from the second order. For by Frankfurt's account an agent has
at any moment many first-order desires and many second-order desires as
well. By speaking instead of preference rankings, we were left with an
agent having a single first-order ranking and a single second-order ranking, a transition that was economical in the very best sense of the word.

In spite of this useful simplification, a semantic imprecision may help
to explain why second-order preferences have too often been wrongly
grouped with multiple-selves models of internal conflict. Now an agent
who behaves "as if" she were made up of two persons, one wanting to
smoke and the other wanting not to or one wanting to save while the other
wants to spend, is, by the two-selves account, quite simply the analytical
equivalent of two closely intertwined people. One feature of such models is
the violation of the most basic assumption of the rational choice model,
namely, that if A is preferred to B at a particular time, it is not also possible that B is preferred to A. By the two-selves account, however, the
"agent," if we still grant this name to the contiguous being that is usually
referred to as such, has more than a single ranking. Attempts to speak of
"the" flesh-and-blood individual becoming better or worse off by moving
up or down "her" preference ranking become problematic indeed.

There is a definitional confusion that may at least partly explain why
the second-order preference approach has been wrongly classified as a
variation of a multiple-selves approach. Suppose there to be a recovering
alcoholic with a first-order preference to have a drink (D) and a second-
order preference to abstain (A). That is, suppose there to be an agent with
first-order preference ranking (D pref A) and second-order preference
ranking [(A pref D) pref (D pref A)]. Now to speak of the latter of these as

a "second-order preference" is to speak somewhat informally. More formally, it is a "second-order preference ranking," and just as it is not uncommon to hear the first "thing" in a first-order preference ranking sometimes referred to as the preference ("Gloria's preference is a glass of merlot"), so too it is not unusual to hear the "thing" lying at the top of the second-order preference ranking referred to as a "second-order preference." One following such a convention would speak of the above agent having as his second-order preference "A pref D."

This verbal convention carries with it the risk of not properly distinguishing the second-order preference approach from the multiple-selves approach. For there is a temptation to speak of the second-order preference in the above case as "D pref A" and to speak of the first-order preference as "A pref D," in other words, a temptation to speak of the agent as having a second-order preference to abstain and a first-order preference to drink. In short, a certain laziness in the language leads to a sliding between the two meanings of a preference (a "ranking" and a "highest ranked thing"). And such a practice carries with it a great risk of conflating the second-order preference approach to summarizing internal conflict with the two-selves approach. For we are left, after all, with an agent who both prefers D to A and prefers A to D at a single moment in time. This is an unfortunate mistake. While it is true that for the multiple-selves model the agent might simultaneously experience (D pref A) and (A pref D), for the second-order preference model the assumption that both are not simultaneously possible—an assumption having great normative significance—is not in the least compromised. Rather, the agent has first-order ranking (D pref A) and second-order ranking [(A pref D) pref (D pref A)], preference rankings over entirely different elements.

Inconsistent Time Preferences

Separate from the literature that posits the simultaneous existence of two or more selves is a more formalized literature that attempts to explain what lies behind "inconsistent time preferences," the observed tendency for a person's preference for future consumption to change as the future draws closer. From a seminal article by Richard Strotz in the 1950s to the works of David Laibson in recent years, the favored explanation for such time-inconsistency has been the existence of "hyperbolic" as opposed to "exponential" time discounting.[15]

Suppose there to be an agent needing to decide in January how to allocate ten thousand dollars between the months of November and December. Let one option be to allot six thousand dollars to November and four thousand dollars to December (call this option A). Let the other option be to allot seven thousand dollars to November and three thousand dollars to December (option B). Suppose that she chooses alternative A. Were she to have an exponential discount function, this would remain her preferred allocation throughout the year. Given the opportunity to change her decision in February, March, or any succeeding month, she would elect not to do so because A would remain the preferred option. But were she to have instead a hyperbolic discount function, her preference might flip at some point over the course of the year, with B suddenly being preferred to A.

These models of time inconsistency draw attention to a particular sort of internal conflict but suffer from two shortcomings. First, they are not sufficiently broad in capturing internal regret over one's discounting proclivities. For the clear implication is that only in those instances when the first-order preference with respect to future activity *changes* as the future draws closer is internal turmoil possible. The just-considered agent who in January chose option A over B would be said to be in conflict if by July she were to find herself preferring B to A. Were she, however, to prefer A to B in January and throughout the rest of the year, no conflict would be said to exist. With the use of second-order preferences this clearly need not be the case. It is entirely possible that the agent continuously prefers A to B despite having a second-order preference to prefer a third option, C, that would allocate five thousand dollars to each month. What is more, some of the most nascent conflicts over orders of preference are precisely of this type. A severely addicted heroin addict having a preference on December 31 to shoot up might be one who had the same preference regarding December 31 a year before, a month before, and a day before. This would still be very much a conflict if at each of these moments he would simultaneously prefer not preferring to ingest heroin. Indeed, some of the most painful conflicts between the first- and second-order preference rankings are likely characterized by just such "consistency" through time. The conflicted overweight person who prefers a low-calorie 6:30 restaurant dinner from 8:00 in the morning until 6:25 in the evening and a high-calorie meal when the time comes to order at 6:26 has some conflict, to be sure. The conflicted overweight person who prefers a *high*-calorie dinner from morning clear through to mealtime (while preferring to prefer the low-calorie alternative throughout) may have no "inconsistent time preferences" but is at least as deserving of sympathy since the changing of her preferences seems to be a more formidable task.

The second shortcoming is the very circumscribed ability of "inconsistent time preferences" to allow welfare conclusions to be drawn. As with most variations of multiple-selves models in which these selves exist simultaneously, defining the agent as an unfolding set of selves through time suggests that Pareto improvements are not possible since one self's gain is another's loss. As Hausman and McPherson state:

> If Jones does not have a consistent preference ranking, then there is no way one can say whether anything is better for Jones than anything else. If Jones has two or more preference rankings which conflict with one another, then there is no way one can say whether x is better for Jones than y unless x happens to be above y in all of Jones' rankings. Without privileging one of the rankings, one cannot say which ranking would be best for Jones to keep and which would be best to drop. Indeed one cannot even make *sense* of the notion of how good it is for Jones to have one preference ranking rather than another without invoking some preference ranking.[16]

Not all would quite agree. David Laibson's model permits the present self's imposition of constraint on future selves to be an unambiguous welfare gain, but only if certain fairly restrictive conditions are met. By Laibson's account, constraining the ability of current self to liquidate assets will lower the welfare of current self by lowering current consumption, but might simultaneously benefit current self if she cares about her future selves by also constraining the myopic spending by future selves. As Laibson demonstrates, with appropriate parameterization of the model, the latter effect can dominate the former, and "all selves" may gain.[17] But while the second-order preference approach can draw welfare conclusions for two-period models, Laibson's approach cannot. The agent gains through restraints only if the "pain" of doing without is outweighed by the pleasure of seeing future selves restrained in their myopic behaviors. With a two-period model this latter gain is wholly absent. The present self that is being constrained has no pleasure to derive from anticipating the future restraints, for they are irrelevant to the future since only one period beyond the present remains.

In contrast to this, constraints on liquidity can be welfare enhancing within a two-period model via the second-order preference approach as long as constraints succeed in shaping preferences. To illustrate, let A = five hundred dollars now and five hundred dollars later, and B = one thousand dollars now and zero dollars later. If the agent has stable second-order preference (A pref B) pref (B pref A), and if ruling out B has the effect of changing the agent's first-order preference from (A pref B) to (B pref A), then a clear Pareto improvement has occurred.

Second-Order Preference or "Second Self"?
A Summary Evaluation

At a number of points in this chapter the special attributes of a second-order preference ranking have been noted, but it will be useful at this point to summarize in one place their advantages relative to the competition.

1. *At the level of general understanding, the second-order preference explanation of internal conflict sheds new light, while the multiple-selves and multiple-utility explanations do not.*

To explain internal conflict by postulating two (or more) selves is to take seriously a metaphor that people offer primarily as a portrayal of their limited grasp of their situation. Telling one who feels "as if" she has many selves that she *does* have many selves fails to in any way clear up the enigma. Similarly, to tell one who at some level feels that more than one alternative is "the best" that more than one is indeed "the best" is not very effective in shedding new light on the paradox. For proponents of Milton Friedman's methodological perspective this would not in any way be a shortcoming. If the only purpose of theory is to allow sound predictions to be made, the multiple-selves and multiple-utility models might indeed be judged successful. To proponents of almost any other perspective, however, models that shed light are, ceteris paribus, more valuable than those that do not. The second-order preference approach to understanding unhappiness over one's freely chosen action, when understood, creates a sense of solving a riddle. It is consistent with the assumption that one *does* do what one prefers. If one is unhappy with one's free choice, it is usually understandable as an instance of being "saddled" with a preference that one wishes not to be experiencing.

2. *The second-order preference approach retains the integrity of the "maximizing individual."*

As Lawrence Boland has argued, the assumption that an agent "maximizes" is metaphysical in nature, and "Metaphysical statements can be false but we may never know because they are the assumptions of a research program which are deliberately put beyond question."[18] Multiple-selves models clearly do reject the metaphysical statement that "an agent maximizes." Part of the agent may do so but not an agent defined in any conventional sense. Multiple-utility models are likewise forced to reject this most basic core assumption of conventional economics. By this approach, the agent may maximize with respect to one of his rankings but not with respect to another simultaneously experienced ranking.

Consider again an agent facing the decision of whether or not to smoke. If he chooses to smoke while claiming to be the victim of a bad habit, proponents of the multiple-selves model would say that one of the agent's selves prefers smoking while another one of the agent's selves prefers not smoking.[19] Similarly, proponents of a multiple-utility approach would require that the agent be understood as having conflicting rankings; for it would simultaneously be true that (S pref N) and that (N pref S). Whichever approach is followed, it is clear that the reflexivity assumption is violated.

In contrast, with the second-order preference approach, the agent's decision to smoke when N is within the choice set leads to the conclusion that the agent's preference ranking is (S pref N). The possibility that the ranking is the reverse is rejected, as the reflexivity assumption would require. The agent's dissatisfaction with his situation is taken to signify that he would prefer having a different preference ranking, namely, a preference to not smoke rather than a preference to smoke. The fact that the agent is not experiencing (N pref S) as his preference is not treated as an indication of irrationality but is rather taken to reveal that this particular preference ranking was not in the choice set.[20] Nothing about this state of affairs suggests irrationality. The agent is, as it were, "saddled" with (S pref N), a preference ranking that he would prefer not to have. Contrary to the other approaches, this manner of portraying the agent's situation is loyal to the core metaphysical assumption of standard economics.

It might on the surface seem peculiar to be offering adherence to a core assumption as a virtue. For my entire project builds on the relaxation of one particular core assumption, namely, the assumption that agents "end" at their first-order preferences. Is it hypocritical to base one's project on the *rejection* of a core assumption while at the same time making one's case by praising the *retention* of another such basic assumption? Not when the significance of the "maximizing individual" assumption is fully considered. Simply put, adherence to the assumption of a unitary maximizing agent is necessary if agents are to be held morally responsible for their choices and if market forces are to be assessed normatively. To further consideration of these issues I now turn.

3. *The coherence of moral responsibility of the individual agent is preserved by the second-order approach but difficult to defend by the other approaches.*

The examples of conflict between the first order and the second order thus far considered have been more prudential than moral in nature.[21] The agent preferring to eat excessively but preferring to prefer moderation is not guilty of a moral wrongdoing if that is understood to entail harm imposed on others. There is nothing preventing us, however, from applying the analytical structure in contexts with clear moral implications. To take an example where moral consensus prevails, let D = "do not harm" and M = "murder." By a two-selves approach, an agent experiencing conflict is an agent for whom it is simultaneously true that "D pref M" and "M pref D." Suppose that the "partial self" for whom the latter preference holds gains the upper hand and that this agent proceeds to commit a murder. Is he morally responsible? Isn't there a moral side to this person who was overwhelmed by an immoral side? Is it fair to hold the entire agent morally responsible and charge the entire agent with murder? Obviously the convenience of the two-selves approach falls short on these sorts of questions.

While it is true that second-order preferences enrich and complicate normative analysis, they do not similarly make incoherent the notion of individual moral responsibility. The agent who prefers to murder and thus murders is morally liable in his entirety regardless of what his second-order preference happens to be. The contrite murderer may wish to have had a different preference but this does lessen his responsibility for the act. And the fact that external circumstances may have created the preference to murder does not lessen the agent's moral responsibility, any more than the temptation of an unlocked car absolves the car thief from responsibility for his act.

4. *Normative assessment of a change in an agent's preferences is straightforward with the second-order preference approach but not with the competing approaches.*[22]

As noted earlier in this chapter, normative inferences could be drawn from David Laibson's model only if very special conditions held. For the earlier models of multiple selves, the normative implications were weaker still, with a gain for one self invariably being at the expense of another. This point was recognized by early proponents of the multiple-selves model, Richard Thaler and H. M. Shefrin (1980, 31) but was contested some years prior to Laibson's mathematically sophisticated effort. Thomas Schelling sought to expand the then wholly nonnormative multiple-selves models by casting the conflict within the agent as a conflict between a "farsighted self" and an "impulsive self," the latter being narrowly present-oriented, while the former had the greater good of the agent in mind (1984).

This vision of the farsighted self as an entity that acts to successfully control the less responsible spontaneous self presents a problem. It presupposes that control by the farsighted self is always preferable to control by the spontaneous self, an assumption that has been seriously questioned.[23] For multiple-utility models as well, a normative ambiguity follows when one of the preference rankings replaces another as a guide to action. In contrast to this, as emphasized in this chapter, there are strong welfare implications associated with preference change if the agent undergoing the change has a stable second-order preference ranking. Moreover, to accept second-order preferences does not commit one to placing the "restrained" self on a higher plane than the "spontaneous" self. There are agents with preferences that they be restrained who have second-order preferences that they be more spontaneous, other agents who are spontaneous who would prefer to prefer being more restrained, others who are content with their preferences for spontaneity, and still others who are content with their restrained dispositions. Somewhat paradoxically, while the second-order preference model places fewer restrictions on what agents wish to be like, it is more able to evaluate changes in the preferences that move an agent to act.

It is this third advantage of second-order preferences that provides a segue to the next chapter. The ability to evaluate preference change suggests a more general ability to evaluate one set of preferences in relation to another. The economists whose works on second-order preferences have been noted in this chapter have kept the evaluative project at a strictly "personal" level, so to speak. That is, the evaluation of preferences has been treated as an ability that humans possess and that economists would be well advised to recognize when they seek to construct models of rational agents that bear a reasonable resemblance to reality. Unconsidered has been a more global sort of normative question, namely, do market forces perform well in the way that they shape preferences? To this more compelling question we now turn.

CHAPTER 3

Market Failure in the Shaping of Tastes

It was noted in the opening chapter that economists have been inclined to treat the issue of changing preferences as a topic lying outside their subject's domain. As a normative issue, the neglect has been prompted less by beliefs about turf than by a general consensus that evaluations are not even possible.

Among the public, the question of how tastes are formed is not usually seen as something for economists to attempt to answer. While the production of goods and services is psychologically located wholly within this abstraction called the "economy," the production of *preferences* is rightly viewed as a project shared by a wide range of institutions.[1] Biological makeup as well as all sorts of social institutions are rightly noted to shape people's tastes, with market forces being just one more element in an already crowded field. To acknowledge this does not mean, however, that we should be any less inclined to assess the efficiency characteristics of economic actors in their taste-shaping role than we are to assess their efficiency in their more "monopolized" product-shaping role.

As the preceding chapter may have indicated, the questioning of received theory's view of the choice process has been prompted less by normative goals than by an attempt to construct a richer, more compelling picture of humans that might lead to more accurate predictions. The belief that the strong case for free markets would thus be weakened has been less common.

To be sure, Galbraith was not the last to criticize market-created tastes. But such criticisms have not been like what will be developed in this chapter. According to von Weiszacker (1971), it is the market's tendency to pander to existing myopic tastes rather than to agents' imminent tastes that represents a shortcoming. Bowles sees the problem as a traditional third-party sort of issue, when he urges "a broader concept of market failure" that recognizes that "because our preferences have non-contractual effects on others, how we acquire them is a matter of public concern."[2] For Sunstein, the harm of particular tastes is borne by the person exercising the taste, but the basis for concluding that there is indeed harm occurring is that unjust conditions preceded the taste's formation, not that the agent would prefer to be without such a taste.

> Severe deprivation—including poverty—can be an obstacle to the development of good preferences, choices, and beliefs. For example, a society in which people "prefer" to become drug addicts, or violent criminals, has a serious problem. Such preferences are likely to be an artifact of existing social norms, and those norms may disserve human freedom or well-being. (1997, 5)

For Robert Lane, neither inequality nor third-party effects are necessary preconditions to deficient preference formation. But the claim of deficiency is problematic since the two-selves model rather than first- and second-order preferences form the background for his charge. According to Lane,

> A person wants heroin, wants to gamble with meager savings, wants violent revenge. The enduring self is not to be sacrificed to the wants of the temporary self. All too often, however, the market is the ally of the temporary self against the enduring self. (1991, 460)

While perhaps compelling at an intuitive level to market critics, no basis is given for believing that overall social welfare is decreased by such bias in favor of the "temporary self." And as argued in the last chapter's concluding section, absent the introduction of second-order preferences to replace "two selves," no strong welfare conclusions are possible.

It might seem odd that while increasing mention of second-order preferences has historically coincided with increasing interest in market shortcomings in preference production, the two have not been linked.[3] A likely reason for this failure to make a connection has been the assumption, usually implicit, that having a second-order preference for x is a sufficient condition for having a first-order preference for x. The recurrent point has been that people have the ability to reflect upon and evaluate their experienced tastes, and that some behavior that might otherwise be anomalous can be usefully thought of as action designed to shape one's future preferences. Albert Hirschman, for example, writes, "Human beings are capable of evaluating and criticizing the entire set of their preferences as 'revealed' by their purchases and other actions in terms of alternative sets of preferences: in other words, they can behold several sets of preferences at the same time and then face the problem of deciding which set to live by."[4]

While there is nothing inherently wrong with this focus of attention, an unintended by-product might have been a downgrading of the existential significance of discord between the orders of preference. In other words, the concern with the long-run task of choosing one's preference ranking may have drawn attention away from the short-run reality of living with discord.

Bilateral Exploitation?

Consider first a primitive economy consisting of just two people, Ronald and Margaret, each self-supporting in the basics of life and each the recipient of a package that descends each day from the sky. Let Ronald's package consist of four small bottles of wine, and Margaret's consist of four desserts. In figure 3.1a this is represented by means of an Edgeworth Box. Ronald's origin is in the lower left, Margaret's in the upper right. Ronald's quantity of desserts is measured left to right, Margaret's right to left. Similarly, Ronald's quantity of wine is measured bottom to top, Margaret's top to bottom. Each point on or within the Edgeworth Box represents a particular allocation of the two goods.

Prior to trading, Ronald and Margaret would be located in the upper left corner, with Ronald having four wines but no desserts and Margaret having four desserts but no wines. Suppose that after each becomes aware of what the other has, each wishes to engage in some trade. Further suppose that if neither were to engage in any marketing efforts, each would be willing to engage in a one-for-one swap. This would leave Ronald with three wines and one dessert and Margaret with three desserts and one wine, and would place them at point A in figure 3.1a.

Suppose next that Ronald realizes he can get a better price for the drinks that he is selling by engaging in virtually costless "sales promotion." Specifically, suppose that by saying the right words he can significantly stimulate Margaret's appetite for wine, so much so that she would now be willing to sacrifice fully three of her desserts for just one wine. This outcome is represented by point B, and such an action would leave Ronald clearly better off; for at B he would have more desserts but no fewer drinks than at A.

Before considering points C and D in figure 3.1a, it will be useful to summarize where matters stand in terms of figure 3.1b. Each agent must decide to either not engage in marketing efforts or to do so. In each cell appears Ronald's rankings of the four points shown in figure 3.1a, and the point that would be attained, given the particular pair of actions shown. To this point Margaret has abstained from any marketing efforts, and it thus follows that only the two boxes on the left side would be possibilities. Each of these two shows the same ranking of the four points by Ronald. Point B is clearly ranked the highest since it has at least as much of one of

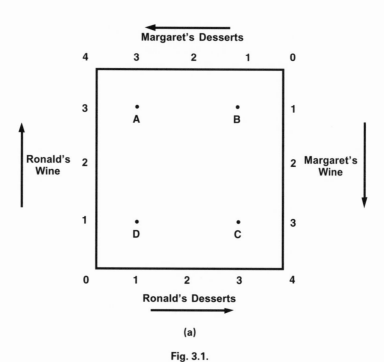

(a)

Fig. 3.1.

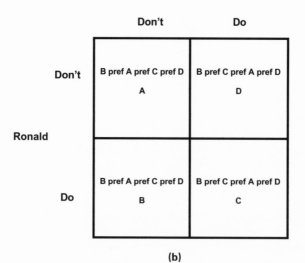

(b)

the two items for Ronald than do the other three points, and has more of at least one item. By similar reasoning, point D must be the lowest ranked. Since a starting assumption was that Ronald wished to sell just one drink if the terms of trade were one for one, point A must be ranked higher than point C. It follows from these considerations that Ronald would choose to market his drinks since by so doing he would end up at B rather than A. The lower left in 3.1b is, in other words, superior to the upper left.

But what if Margaret had followed an equivalent strategy? That is, what if she too had taken actions that caused the desserts that she owned to become more attractive to Ronald? Just as marketing improved the terms of trade for Ronald, such action would improve the terms of trade for Margaret. Assume that she finds that by marketing her product (when he does not market his) she is able to coax forth three wines from Ronald, instead of just the one that would be possible absent any marketing.

Returning to figure 3.1b, this is reflected in the changed preference ordering that Ronald experiences in response to Margaret's sales efforts. While B is still his most preferred outcome and D his least preferred, Margaret's efforts have resulted in points A and C switching positions in the ordering. The predicted outcomes follow straightforwardly. Just as Ronald's decision to market his product when Margaret did not market hers led to the attainment of B (lower left), so a reversal of roles would be expected to lead to the attainment of point D. And if both were to market their products, C would prevail. For, holding terms of trade constant at 1, each would like to trade for more of the other's product than was true prior to the adoption of marketing.

What follows from the above is that both Ronald and Margaret would find it worthwhile to market regardless of what each believes the other will do. This can be seen in figure 3.1b. Just as it was demonstrated that marketing was in Ronald's interest even if he believed that Margaret would abstain from similar efforts, it can be seen that marketing is also in his interest if he believes that she will do likewise. For given the preference ranking shown on the right, marketing results in the attainment of the second item in the ranking (point C), whereas abstaining results in attainment of the last item (point D).

Are any conclusions possible about marketing's effect on the well-being of Ronald and Margaret? A prisoner's dilemma is, it turns out, possible but not inevitable. To see this, it will be helpful to simplify the preference rankings that are shown in the upper left and lower right boxes. Since both of these rankings have B appearing highest in the ranking and D lowest, and since neither of these points is the attained one in either box, nothing will be sacrificed by their removal. Doing so better highlights the effect that marketing exerts in this primitive economy. Had neither agent sought to persuade the other, each would have had first-order preference (A pref C) and outcome A. As a result of each marketing, each instead experiences first-order preference (C pref A) and outcome C.

What welfare effects persuasive marketing has had depends on the agents' respective second-order rankings. Suppose that Ronald has a mild diabetic condition and is strongly advised by his doctor to limit his sugar intake, and that Margaret suffers from a condition that makes the consumption of more than a glass of wine each day risky. With these particular health limitations, it would not be surprising if each would prefer preferring point A relative to C. For at point A Ronald's intake of sugar is within the recommended bounds, and Margaret's intake of wine is likewise not excessive. Because each agent would have second-order ranking [(A pref C) pref (C pref A)], each would have been harmed by the other's marketing efforts.

Suppose instead that the health conditions were reversed, with Ronald the one whose health puts him at particular risk for excessive alcohol consumption, and Margaret the mild diabetic mindful of the need to curb her taste for sugar. Each would be expected to have second-order ranking [(C pref A) pref (A pref C)], and each would have thus benefited from the marketing efforts of the other. And, of course, as if normative results were not already tepid, the possibility that mutual marketing benefits one party and harms the other cannot be ruled out. This becomes clear if we allow the health status of both Ronald and Margaret to be such that sugar poses no threat while anything over one wine a day does. Marketing in this case would have left Ronald better off, with Margaret's efforts having moved him out of wine and into desserts. Just as clearly, Margaret herself would have suffered a loss, as Ronald's efforts would have left her with an unpreferred preference for more wine than she would have preferred absent any marketing. Clearly, this two-person model leaves us with ambiguous results. More must be done if stronger welfare conclusions are to emerge.

Too Much of a Good Thing: The Limits of Preference Improvement

It was argued in the previous chapter that Harry Frankfurt went too far by describing an agent's will as "free" only if the agent had precisely those preferences she preferred having. I noted that it is simply not often possible to attain such an extreme ideal, and that it made more sense to speak of the freedom of the will as a matter of degree. To this must now be added a related consideration. Even if it is technically possible for an agent to attain a preference that is, ceteris paribus, superior to the preference it replaces, it may possibly be just too costly to make such a move worthwhile. From the mere fact that the preference that prevails is lower in the second-order ranking than some other attainable preference, it does not follow that an inefficiency prevails.

I have sought simplicity to this point by keeping the number of items in the first-order ranking to a minimum. A limitation to two items (the usual practice) resulted in second-order rankings with just two items as well. In such examples, the agent either had her preferred preference ranking or had "the unpreferred ranking." In reality, of course, there are a limitless number of preference rankings that market forces might bring about. And, let it be emphasized again, even if there *were* maximal efficiency in the production of preferences, an agent's *most* preferred preference ranking would be unlikely to prevail.

In figure 3.2a appears an indifference curve over different combinations of "preference ranking" and "income." Each of the rankings is over many elements, with each element being a bundle of goods and services. The further along the vertical axis, the more preferred is the particular preference ranking. Just where within one's preference ranking one is able to locate depends in part on one's purchasing power. For this reason, an agent would be indifferent over different combinations of preference rankings and income. Consider points A and B in figure 3.2a. At point A the agent might be described as having relatively preferred preferences but little income with which to act, while at point B she has relatively unpreferred preferences but a relatively large income.

It is tempting to reason that the agent would be better off having little income when in the grip of unpreferred preferences. From this it would seem to follow that any point directly to the left of B would be preferable to B, since this would be a way of preventing the fulfillment of "bad preferences." But this would be incorrect. For when preferences are defined in an "overall" sense, one is necessarily better off having what one prefers than not having what one prefers, regardless of what one's second-order ranking happens to be. Matters are somewhat more complicated now since each preference ranking that appears along the vertical axis consists of a great many bundles rather than just over two, but the same principle still applies. Given that one is experiencing a particular preference ranking, one seeks to be as far to the left in this ranking as possible, and the greater one's purchasing power, the farther to the left one may indeed be.

Figure 3.2b shows a budget constraint along with two indifference curves. The constraint rests on the assumption that the more one is willing to pay (e.g., to weight reduction specialists or to clinics that promise to cut

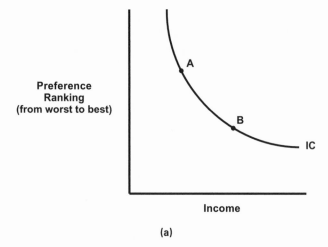

(a)

Fig. 3.2.

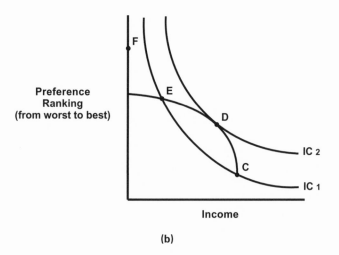

(b)

the urge to smoke), the greater will be the improvement in one's preference ranking. The nonlinear shape of the constraint is meant to emphasize that a well-defined market in which one pays a constant price for each preference improvement does not exist. If this agent allocated no resources to the improvement of her preferences, she would be at point C. The agent's tastes are such that the attainment of an improved ranking is deemed worth the sacrifice of some money and permits the attainment of a higher indifference curve at point D. Points E and F are included to emphasize that there are rather different explanations for why an agent may not have a ranking that is preferred to the prevailing ranking. Point F represents an unattainable preference ranking. Point E, in contrast, represents an attainable ranking but one judged not worth what it costs to achieve.

To summarize, it cannot be concluded from the fact that the preferences that prevail are less than "ideal" that a market inefficiency prevails. The agent may choose to have less than her most preferred preference ranking simply because the best is unattainable (as an existential fact) and might choose to not take the steps necessary to the attainment of the best preference ranking because of the expense of such a project.

To this point in the chapter no demonstration of market failure has emerged. It has been shown that preference change rated as beneficial by the agent is compatible with profit-maximizing strategies of sellers, and it has been further argued that unhappiness with extant preferences is not a sufficient reason for concluding that inefficiency prevails. A stronger argument clearly remains to be made.

Too Little of a Good Thing: Market Deficiency in Preference Shaping

The benefit or harm that the actions of one person do to an innocent bystander is not sufficient evidence that a market inefficiency exists. "Pecuniary" externalities affect the well-being of third parties but do not weaken the strong argument for relying upon the forces of the market. When cigars became trendy just a few years ago, demand rose dramatically. The incomes received by workers in the cigar industry grew as a result, as did returns to shareholders. Since some of those who took up cigars were at the same time swearing off cigarettes, workers and shareholders in that industry were likely harmed monetarily. Pecuniary externalities there surely were, but though such externalities arbitrarily redistributed well-being, they did not lead to anything that deserves to be called allocative inefficiencies. On the basis of the demand shift, it was thus not possible to say that the market was suddenly overproducing or underproducing cigars.

Market inefficiency in influencing preferences only becomes apparent when it is recognized that the changes in preferences emanating from advertising and other forces of the market are by their nature externalities, and when it is also recognized that these externalities are "nonpecuniary" in nature. An agent may speak of "having" a preference, but courts of law do not treat this as a property right. When a seller creates in an agent a preference that the agent rates as inferior to what it replaces, it is not possible for the agent to seek monetary compensation in a court of law.[5] Similarly, a seller has no means of extracting payment for the creation of a preference that an agent judges to be superior to the preference that is replaced.

Since the externalities are "nonpecuniary"—the benefit or harm does not come in the form of altered prices—welfare theory suggests that market forces will too rarely improve preferences and too often change them for the worse. It is admittedly somewhat odd to categorize these occurrences as externalities. The name, after all, derives from the fact that individuals "external" to the buyer and the seller bear costs or realize benefits. Thus, when a car is refueled with Exxon gasoline, not only are the owner of the car and those associated with the Exxon Corporation affected, but so too are those "third parties" whose air will be fouled ever so slightly by the additional driving that the filled tank will make possible. And thus, to take an example of a positive externality, when the exterior of a house is graced with a new coat of Sherwin-Williams paint, not only are the owner of the house and those with Sherwin-Williams affiliations affected, but those who have occasion to gaze upon the house.

In contrast to this, the "externality" associated with a preference change is an "externality" borne by the *buyer*. Consider that the seller's actions, if successful, cause people who would not otherwise be buyers to voluntarily become so. Since the buyer is one of the two parties engaged in the transaction, to speak of this as a "third party" effect would be misleading. Acknowledging this does not, however, make any less forceful the welfare conclusions that are associated with the more typical "third party" sort of externality. A seller's action that causes an agent to have an improved preference results in a spillover benefit from the standpoint of the agent. While the agent must pay for the product that satisfies the changed preference, the act of changing the preference is a cost from the seller's standpoint but not a marketable service.[6] While there will be such instances of improved preferences, they will be too few from an efficiency standpoint, as is true of any practice providing spillover benefits.

A similar line of reasoning applies to sellers' actions that cause agents to be burdened with worse preferences. Because the seller does not have to compensate these agents for the worsened preferences, the seller would be expected to engage in too much of this activity. The often encountered but typically vague sentiment that commercial society changes our tastes for the worse receives support by combining second-order preferences with an application of standard welfare analysis.

Two Objections

Does the existence of markets for changing one's preferences cast doubt on the claim that changing preferences are typically in the nature of spillovers? That such markets exist there can be no doubt. There are health centers that one may join that offer not only the setting in which to exercise but the greater likelihood of preferring to exercise as well. There are countless programs that aim to lessen the desire to smoke, countless books on how to discipline oneself to behave in a way that one would prefer to behave, and countless other examples as well.[7] The existence of these taste-changing markets does not, however, weaken the argument that there is deficiency in the market's shaping of tastes, and might even serve as empirical evidence in its favor. Consider why this is so. The strength of the water purification industry would be expected to be positively correlated with the degree of water pollution that is occurring. The "noise abatement" industry would be expected to grow as the problem of noise pollution worsened. And thus similarly, the extent to which agents would be in the "taste changing" market would be correlated with the degree of market failure in preference production in the economy at large. Were such industries not to arise in reaction to the "problems" that they stood ready to correct, we would be left with an additional sort of market failure. But their existence should not be interpreted to mean that the problems that they correct are not themselves the outgrowth of market failure.

Even granting the above, one might still wish to claim that the argument I make places too much in the sphere of economic analysis and neglects other sorts of social institutions. There can be little doubt that economists have to keep in check a tendency to reduce certain complexities of human existence to their simple models of maximization and that the extension of their modes of thought into new spheres has been a mixed blessing at best. Surely economic actors are not the sole architects of preferences, and surely there likely exist political and cultural paths by which societies might manage to address the shaping of preferences.

But the argument that there is market failure does not presuppose that only sellers affect the preferences of potential buyers. All that it requires is that *some* influence be exercised. The extent to which other social institutions shape our tastes and the extent to which they are to be praised or criticized for their performance in this realm are important questions, but not questions that will be taken up here. Writing as an economist, it is the market alone that has come under the microscope, and the market that has been found wanting.

A Graphical Restatement

Figure 3.3a portrays the imposition of a worse preference ranking on an agent. A seller's marketing efforts have resulted in a drop from point A on IC2 to point B on IC1. The agent would feel indifferent about the prefer-

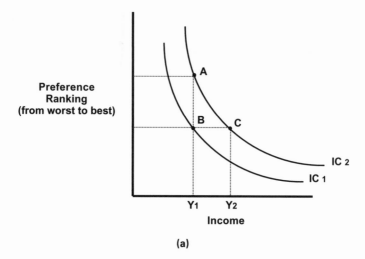

**Preference
Ranking
(from worst to best)**

(a)

Fig. 3.3.

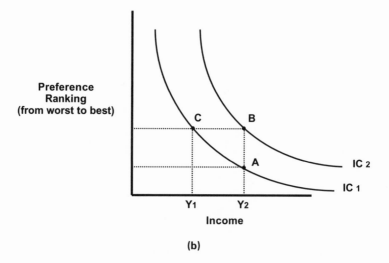

**Preference
Ranking
(from worst to best)**

(b)

ence-altering action of the seller only if a payment were forthcoming sufficient to move the agent to point C on his original indifference curve. For this to occur, the agent would have to receive a payment of Y2 minus Y1 to compensate for the worsened preferences. Clearly, if such payment had to be made to a significant number of the agents whose preferences were adversely affected, the cost of altering preferences would rise and a lower amount of "preference changing" would be optimal from the seller's standpoint.

Figure 3.3b illustrates a case where the effort of a seller has changed an agent's preference ranking for the better, moving her from point A on IC1 to point B on IC2. Were the agent to hand over to the seller Y1 minus Y2, she would return to her original indifference curve. Were the seller's marketing efforts regarded as "preference improving" by a significant number of agents, the subsidies received by the seller would lower the cost of creating these preferences, and a greater degree of preference change in favor of the seller's product would be predicted.

There is an alternative way to model market imperfection in preference production. In figure 3.4a is shown the demand for, and supply of, a change in preference (A pref B) to (B pref A). The demand for this preference change has nothing about it that is unusual. As with most goods and services, the lower is the price, the greater are the number of agents who would be willing and able to purchase this preference change. With no property rights in preferences and no opportunity for sellers to charge a price for successfully changed preferences, a price of zero would prevail. At this price one hundred agents would demand the preference change, while twenty such changes would be supplied. Consistent with the earlier discussion, there has been an underproduction of this desired preference change.

Several points deserve to be emphasized. First, as with any shortage, the introduction of smoothly functioning markets would simultaneously raise quantity supplied and lower quantity demanded. And as noted earlier, the price (monetary or otherwise) of securing an "improved preference" may inhibit its voluntary acquisition. In the figure, an equilibrium occurs at sixty; a market price would simultaneously encourage quantity supplied and discourage quantity demanded.

Second, the shortage that is manifest at the price of zero is unlike most shortages in one significant respect. The act of "supplying" a preference change involves at the same time its being "received" by someone. For the usual shortage caused by a below-equilibrium price, the recipients of the product all value it at least at its going price. In the present case, with the supply imposed randomly, it is entirely possible that some of those receiving the preference change actually disvalue such a change, that is, are not among those who would demand such a change at a price of zero or above.

Third, in figure 3.4a it is being assumed that some positive amount of the preference change is supplied at the price of zero, that is, that the act of changing preferences is sometimes undertaken ("supplied") even when the act is not directly marketable. Not to be ruled out, however, is the possi-

Change from "A pref B" to "B pref A"

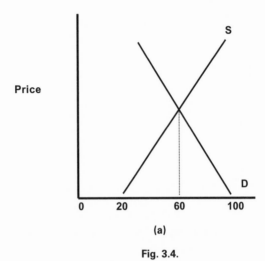

Price

| 0 | 20 | 60 | 100 |

(a)

Fig. 3.4.

Change from "A pref B" to "B pref A"

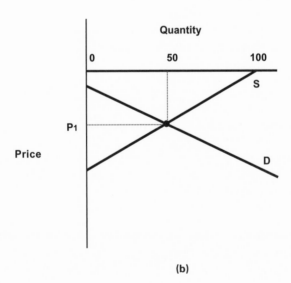

Quantity

| 0 | 50 | 100 |

P1

Price

S

D

(b)

bility of a supply curve intersecting the vertical axis at a price greater than zero. In such an instance, none of the preference change in question would be forthcoming at a price of zero.

Figure 3.4b applies the ideas just discussed to a preference change that is unpreferred by everyone. Demand exceeds zero only when the purchase price is negative. One hundred such preference changes occur (are "supplied") at the prevailing price of zero, to the regret of each person undergoing the preference change. Were there to be functioning markets, a negative price of P1 would prevail. At this negative equilibrium price, sellers would find fewer such preference changes worth supplying since they would have to compensate those undergoing the preference change. In addition, there would be just as many agents willing to "receive" the change in preference as there were such preference changes offered.[8]

Ronald and Margaret Reconsidered

When a welfare assessment was earlier attempted with just two agents in the picture (Ronald and Margaret), no clear conclusions were possible. Given the initial endowment of wine to Ronald and desserts to Margaret, whether marketing efforts harmed or benefited the agents depended on whether they did or did not want to increase their tastes for the other's product. By expanding the number of marketing options available to each agent it will be possible to see how inefficiency can be attributed to the forces of persuasion even in such a primitive economy and even when the marketing that is occurring is beneficial.

Tables 3.1 and 3.2 provide two variations on the earlier considered case in which Ronald and Margaret each benefited from the other's marketing efforts. Ronald, it will be recalled, received a daily allotment of wine and Margaret a daily allotment of desserts. Ronald, it will also be recalled, suffered from a condition that made the consumption of any more than a single wine each day a risky venture. Margaret received a daily allotment of desserts but suffered from diabetes and was thus unable to partake of more than a single dessert each day with impunity.

For each variation shown in tables 3.1 and 3.2, Ronald and Margaret must each select from among three possible courses of action rather than just two. Marketing is no longer an either-or decision, but rather a question of degree. So instead of promoting sales or not promoting sales as the options that are available, the choices are "None," "A Little," and "A Lot." Two other simplifications have been made. Rather than post in each cell Ronald's preference ranking and attained bundle, there appears, in the interest of simplicity, the rank that each agent assigns, with the number on the left pertaining to Ronald and the number on the right to Margaret.

Thus, for example, each assigns a rank of 9 (the lowest possible) to the upper left outcome where no marketing at all occurs. Clearly, in both tables it appears that *any* degree of marketing is better than none. It is also worth noting that a strict symmetry prevails in this analysis, with each agent in each of the examples having the same pattern of rankings as the other.

The four cells at the upper left of table 3.1 portray the optimistic interpretation of marketing that was acknowledged when figure 3.1 was earlier discussed. In this example, Ronald and Margaret each find the strategy of engaging in "a little" advertising to be optimal regardless of what each believes the other will do. The middle box is hence the predicted outcome, with each agent attaining the fourth-best rather than the ninth-best state. In this example, the persuasive effort of each agent results in a superior state of affairs for the other, as Ronald is pulled away from his alcohol and Margaret away from her desserts.

In the present example, however, this seemingly desirable outcome is less compelling than before; for it is a Pareto-inferior state of affairs. Had each agent engaged in more marketing, each would be better off still, ending up with the second-best rather than fourth-best outcome, with Ronald moving still further out of alcohol and Margaret still further out of desserts. Each finds it not worth indulging in this additional advertising since each is unable to extract payment for the spillover benefits provided

TABLE 3.1.

		Margaret's Marketing		
		None	A Little	A Lot
Ronald's	None	9, 9	6, 7	3, 8
Marketing	A Little	7, 6	4, 4	1, 5
	A Lot	8, 3	5, 1	2, 2

TABLE 3.2.

		Margaret's Marketing		
		None	A Little	A Lot
Ronald's	None	9, 9	5, 8	6, 7
Marketing	A Little	8, 5	2, 2	4, 1
	A Lot	7, 6	1, 4	3, 3

the other. Though marketing has left both Margaret and Ronald better off than they would have been with no marketing, neither has seen their preferences *sufficiently* altered.

Table 3.2 provides still another possibility. Given the ranking of states that are shown, each agent would find it optimal to market "a lot." This shares with the just-considered case a feature that tends to disguise the market's failure when it comes to the shaping of tastes, namely, an equilibrium that each rates superior to the total absence of marketing. In this case, however, the persuasive forces are not exclusively welfare enhancing, but rather "go too far." Although Ronald has benefited from drinking less than his full endowment of wine, he finds that his taste for desserts is excessive. And similarly, Margaret feels that her tastes have moved too much out of the sugar rich. Each agent is enjoying his or her third-best, rather than second-best, state of affairs.

I have presented this case to emphasize that the spillovers from persuasion, unlike most spillovers, can be benefits over some ranges and costs over others. In the case presented here, each agent's decision to do "a little marketing" is improving the well-being of the other initially, but eventually a point is reached after which the taste changes induced by still more marketing are harmful. What these latter two examples have been intended to demonstrate is that even when people prefer the taste changes that marketing induces, my basic argument for market failure is not undercut. Since consumers have no enforceable property rights in their preferences, it is simply unlikely that the equilibrium outcome of taste-changing processes is optimal. It is, on the other hand, not at all unlikely that the outcome would be judged superior to the outcome that would follow from the abolition of persuasive forces.

A Competing Critique

The ability to shape one's tastes might appear to be an asset, but a case for concluding the opposite was made by Robin Hahnel and Michael Albert (1990). It was their conclusion that the agent's control over her first-order preferences when combined with market power on the part of sellers would result in a greater distortion than if preferences remained outside the agent's control. These conclusions are worth some examination, for they clearly run counter to the implied message of this writing. According to Hahnel and Albert, rational agents "will diminish their desires for commodities whose terms of availability they believe will become more difficult and augment their desires for commodities whose terms of availability they believe will become easier by changing consumption and work activity choices in earlier time periods so as to change their future human characteristics and, thereby, their future preferences" (1990, 93).

Let there be two products, X and Y. Suppose that at time 1 there is perfect competition in both markets and that the equilibrium price and quantity of each product is $1 and 100,000 respectively. Further suppose that there are 10,000 agents with identical tastes, each having an income of $20 and each purchasing 10 units of each product per time period. In figures 3.5 and 3.6 appear demand and supply in each market (D1 and S1, respectively) and the initial equilibrium in each at point A. Figure 3.7 shows each agent's income constraint and utility-maximizing bundle, again designated as point A.

Suppose that industry X becomes monopolized in period 2, while industry Y remains perfectly competitive. Assume that the new monopolist raises the price of X to $1.25 and that quantity demanded falls to 80,000 (8 per agent) as a result. This is shown at point B in figure 3.7 (D2 can be ignored for the moment). Since less X is being produced, resources are freed up and the supply of product Y rises, price falls, and quantity demanded consequently rises. This is summarized by point B in figure 3.6, the price having fallen to $.83 and quantity having risen to 120,000.[9]

These shifts are summarized by means of an agent's income constraint as it appears in figure 3.7. With income unchanged at $20 (again, a simplifying assumption) the price rise brought on by monopolization in industry X has shifted the X intercept from 20 to 16. The price fall that follows in industry Y has raised the intercept on the Y axis from 20 to 24. Monopolization has led to an inefficient product mix, given the agent's unchanging tastes, and by adjusting from 10 units of each to 8 of X and 12 of Y, the agent has moved from point A to point B. She would have become worse off since the indifference curve on which B lies (not shown because of the crowdedness of the figure) is below the curve on which A lies.

Hahnel and Albert reason that early anticipation of the monopolization of product X would cause agents to act to dampen their tastes for this product, since it is destined to rise in price, and develop their tastes for Y, since it is destined to become cheaper. If agents' tastes were indeed malleable and if they were successful in "reshaping" their tastes, then demand for X would have decreased. Assume that the new monopolist still finds $1.25 to be its optimal price. Consumption of X per agent now falls to 7, as shown by point C in figure 3.5. It can be concluded that quantity of Y would rise but, absent more information, is not possible to conclude what would happen to price since money is freed up that raises demand for Y, and resources are freed up that raise the supply of Y. To simplify, price is shown as remaining constant. To simplify still further, incomes are

Market for X

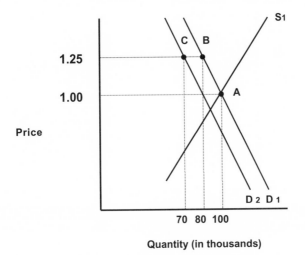

Fig. 3.5.

assumed unaffected, from which it follows that the representative agent is able to purchase 13.5 units of Y. Rather than moving from A to B in figure 3.7, as would have been true had preferences been unchanging, the agent's preferences have changed, and she now maximizes utility at point C. (The changes in preferences is indicated by the fact that the indifference curve on which point C lies intersects the indifference curve on which A lies.)

Hahnel and Albert treat greater quantity shifts that follow from the agent's ability to alter her preferences as evidence of a greater welfare loss.

> In an economy in which production responds to market demand, this implies the production of goods for which individuals are over-charged will be even less than had individuals not adjusted their preferences. As a result the misallocation, which would have occurred in any event due to the overcharge, is aggravated by the process of rational individual adjustment. (1990, 180)

Thus, the fact that the consumption of monopolized product X has fallen from 10 to 7 when preferences are endogenous rather than just to 8 units as would have been true had preferences been unchanging is taken to sig-

Market for Y

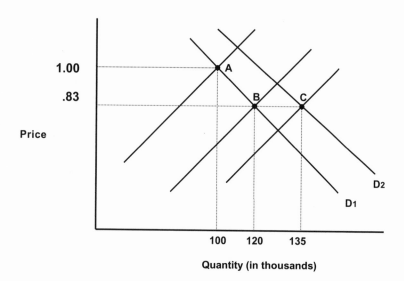

Fig. 3.6.

nal a greater welfare loss. Monopoly's distorting effects are concluded to be greater than previously realized. This conclusion requires, however, that changes in rates of output from the competitive ideal be allowed to serve as a proxy for changes in agent well-being, and closer examination reveals that this assumed link is not valid. Indeed, since the model assumes agents to be in full control of their preferences, it is implied that the welfare loss of monopolization is *less,* not *more,* than if preferences were exogenous.

To see this, refer to table 3.3. State 1 refers to the situation prior to the monopolization of industry X. In this state the choice of bundle A or bundle B would have cost the agent her full $20. Because A was chosen, and the agent was content with the overall state of affairs, it can be assumed that she had the second-order preference shown. For had she been unhappy with her choice of A when B was also available, she might have worked to reshape her first-order preference.

The monopolization of industry X and resulting price change removes option A from the choice set, as figure 3.7 reveals. State 2 is like state 1 except for the choice. At this stage, the agent's preferences are

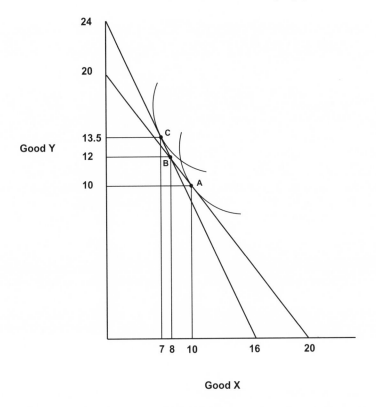

Fig. 3.7.

assumed to be outside her control. Since A is now outside the attainable set, B is selected despite the unchanging first-order preference for A. State 2′ is a restatement of state 2, in terms of the bundles that are now available, B and C. The choice of B signals that it is preferred relative to C. That the agent would seek to change her preference were she able signals that this preference for B is not the one she would choose. That is, she has a second-order preference for C. State 3 is the one that would be expected to prevail if preferences are within the agent's full control. Given the second-order preference that is shown, she would seek to prefer C over B, which would lead, if successful, to the selection of bundle C.

To appreciate the error that Hahnel and Albert make, it is only necessary to contrast the ranking of the states shown with the quantity of monopolized good X in each:

Quantity of good X $1 > 2 = 2' > 3$
Ranking of states $1 > 2 = 2' < 3$

Hahnel and Albert incorrectly choose to allow the first line above to serve as a proxy for the second. The inefficiencies associated with monopoly make the analogy a reasonable one for the comparison of states 1 and 2 (and 2', the restatement of 2). That is, the monopolization of an industry causes a fall in the selected quantity of the monopolized product. With the monopoly leading to Pareto inefficiency, this is a worse state of affairs.

But to allow quantity changes to continue to serve as a proxy when the agent adjusts her preferences in reaction to the higher price of the monopolized product is incorrect. While the quantity of X is lower at C than at B (7 units rather than 8), this cannot be taken to signal a further welfare loss. A comparison of states 2' and 3 in table 3.3 should make this clear. Though the same second-order preference prevails in each, in 3 the agent has the preference she indeed prefers and chooses accordingly (7 units of X), while in 2' she has her unpreferred preference, which leads to the selection of 8 units of X. For the agent to exercise full control over her preferences may exacerbate the decline in the production of the monopolized good, but this further decline would not heighten the welfare loss. On the contrary, it would be the consequence of a "skill" that permits the cushioning of this loss.

Perfect Competition to the Rescue?

While it is true that Hahnel and Albert brought the phenomenon of second-order preferences into their analysis, they traced the damage of changing tastes to the voluntary efforts of consumers themselves. It was not the malleability of tastes, per se, that caused a welfare loss, but this malleability when joined with imperfect competition. Indeed, they detected no failure in preference formation in the ideal world of perfect competition.

TABLE 3.3.

State	Second-Order Preference	First-Order Preference	Choice
1	(A pref B) pref (B pref A)	A pref B	A
2	(A pref B) pref (B pref A)	A pref B	B
2'	(C pref B) pref (B pref C)	B pref C	B
3	(C pref B) pref (B pref C)	C pref B	C

> If private enterprise market systems were totally flexible and efficient in meeting people's desires, why should they not be totally flexible and efficient satisfying people's preferences for alternative desires themselves? Why shouldn't a system that gives people what they care about, in proportion to the degree they care about it, give people the desires as well as the goods they want? (1990, 160)

Not considered is the point that allowed very different conclusions to be drawn earlier in this chapter. With no enforceable property rights in first-order preferences, the preferences that emerge from the market's workings would not be expected to be optimal. But while the earlier argument made no explicit mention of market power as a sine qua non of suboptimal preferences, it was formulated in a way that was far from perfectly competitive. Sellers, after all, were assumed always to have motives for attempting to raise the demand for their products. Would the argument hold if the pristine world of perfect competition prevailed?

Such a world in which sellers passively respond to demand might be judged so utterly mythical as to not merit inclusion in a discussion intended to have practical implications. I would disagree. Strong free-market advocates tend to build their case with reference to precisely such an idealized world.[10] Demonstrating the relevance of the critique being offered to this idealized world and not just to the "fallen" world of reality can only serve to strengthen the argument. And if it be granted that an agent's tastes are at least partly dependent on what is available, it turns out that this world would also be expected to suffer from the inefficient creation of tastes.

Some years ago I lived in downtown Philadelphia. Hot dog vendors were plentiful throughout the area. While not corresponding perfectly to perfect competition (can any industry?) they came close. Their products were virtually identical, as were their prices. Vendors did not engage in anything worthy of the name "marketing." Despite this, I recognized that they affected my preferences, and affected them for the worse. On the occasions that I would buy a hot dog, it was more often than not an impulse purchase. Prior to actually seeing the seller in front of me I had, on such occasions, no thought of a hot dog nor any desire for a hot dog of which I was aware. Now had this hot dog vendor not been there, precisely how my life would have been different is of course (counterfactuals being what they are) impossible to say. But I do recall thinking that I would have been no worse off and probably even better off.

If my introspective efforts were correct, it must have been the case that the mere availability of the hot dogs changed my tastes and, it so happens, changed them in a way that I found unfavorable. Regardless of whether or not the vendor was there, I happened to have, at that particular time in my life, a second-order preference to abstain from hot dog consumption. This is summarized in table 3.4. Line 1a describes my situation when I passed a vendor's particular corner on a day that he was absent. Line 2 describes the changed state of affairs when, by his presence, I preferred his product and purchased it. Line 1b represents a competing interpretation of the vendor-less world. My preference is not at all different, but my choice of actions, by necessity, is. But as argued earlier, such an interpretation is inconsistent with my claiming that, all things considered, I enjoyed his absence.[11] For by the interpretation shown in line 1b, my preference for his product is independent of his presence, and thus having him there, regardless of my having a second-order preference to abstain, would be preferable to the alternative.

Taking the standpoint of the vendor for the moment, is it appropriate to say that he has altered my tastes to his advantage? Suppose that he happened to select this particular corner only after being assured, by the previous vendor, that an adequate level of sales were "a sure thing." Certainly from the vendor's vantage point he is doing nothing whatsoever to influence sales. Merely by being there he manages to meet preexisting demand. But something of an illusion is operating here. From the fact that whenever a hot dog vendor is present, the demand for his product would exist, it does not follow that in the seller's absence, an equivalent demand would have gone unfulfilled. In a way certainly not intended by Say, supply may "create its own demand" when mere "exposure" to a product creates a demand to buy. While marketing efforts that accompany imperfect competition undoubtedly influence tastes, the existence of a problem does not presuppose such imperfect competition. The competitive market, as well, would be expected to be deficient in the shaping of tastes in the absence of recognized ownership of tastes or in the absence of other social mechanisms for guiding the decisions of sellers.

To acknowledge that perfect competition would fall short in the delivery of preferences does not, however, tell us anything about its *relative* performance. Are there reasons for believing that idyllic perfect competition outperforms its real-world imperfectly competitive counterparts and that perfect competition is thus uncompromised as an ideal toward

TABLE 3.4.

	Second-Order Preference	First-Order Preference	Choice
1a	($1 pref H) pref (H pref $1)	$1 pref H	$1
1b	($1 pref H) pref (H pref $1)	H pref $1	$1
2	($1 pref H) pref (H pref $1)	H pref $1	H

which public policy should always be directed? On initial consideration, it might appear so. Perfect competitors, after all, only influence desires (and hence demand) through their decisions to make products be available. Imperfect competitors go further than this.

I can recall when working for Pepsi-Cola during my college summers how ability to command shelf space could make huge differences in sales. To situate the product at eye level rather than at floor level mattered significantly, as did placing displays at the end of frequently traveled aisles rather than off in some less traveled cul-de-sac. But unlike the hot dog seller, we at Pepsi had a differentiated product and spent vast sums to influence people's tastes. Advertising and marketing confronted shoppers well in advance of their shopping expeditions.

And Pepsi-Cola is not in any way exceptional. Advertising has been on the rise for a century.[12] And as Robert McChesney suggests, the decision of the U.S. Supreme Court to extend the First Amendment protection of free speech to advertisers has likely fueled this trend over the past quarter century (1999, 268). The new avenues discovered have less to do with the application of new technologies than with the erosion of implicit social prohibitions against marketing. As McChesney reports, even a relatively old medium, the movie theater, is just now getting into the act, as "over one-half of the twenty-seven thousand U.S. movie screens now show advertisements before films, more than [double] the number of U.S. theaters that showed ads in 1993" (1999, 40). And that nearly antiquated advertising form—outdoor postings—have risen as well, one new trend being "'street furniture,' where municipal governments let private interests provide bus shelters and newsstands permanently draped in the firm's advertising" (McChesney 1999, 41). This was just one of the developments that led the *New York Times* to conclude that the United States is experiencing "an onslaught of ads that accost Americans at every turn" (Cooper 1998, A1, qtd. in McChesney 1999, 41). Nowhere has the insinuation of advertising stirred such controversy as within those previously advertising-free zones, the public schools, and McChesney notes that "Channel One, an advertising-supported television program for use in schools, is now shown in . . . 40 percent of the total number of schools" (1999, 47), a development contributing to the conclusion of *Business Week:* "Corporations are flooding schools with teaching aids—and propaganda" (Wechsler 1997, 68, qtd. in McChesney 1999, 47).

While it is tempting to conclude that these developments have been instrumental in worsening the problem of unpreferred preferences, there are two reasons for doubting any such conclusion. First, it should be recalled that, Galbraith notwithstanding, it is not the creation of tastes that poses a problem but *inefficiency* in the creation of tastes. That advertising and marketing are on the rise might indeed make more salient the suboptimality of markets as preference shapers but, somewhat surprisingly, would not be expected to worsen the overall situation. To influence preferences more would indeed result in more frequent occurrences of preferences being worsened but also more frequent occurrences of preferences being improved. While a shift in the cigarette industry from perfectly competitive to oligopoly might indeed create a net increase in unpreferred preferences through its marketing and advertising, an equivalent shift in the health food industry would likely have the opposite effect.

Second, to the extent that advertising does indeed convey information that would be lacking in a perfectly competitive setting, it works to improve preferences. Let there be two products, A and B, and suppose that prior to advertising the agent has a preference for A and prefers this preference over the alternative. If information succeeds in communicating information and results in the agent preferring B, it would be expected to change the second-order preference as well. In other words, an agent's altering her preferences (and choices) based on new information would be expected to lead her to prefer having this new, better-informed preference.

In ending this chapter, it is worth recalling a major point raised by Harry Frankfurt. By his account, it was the ability to reflect on and to evaluate one's preferences that set human beings apart from all other living creatures, and freedom of the will is, according to Frankfurt, the freedom to shape these preferences as one wishes. Market failure in the shaping of tastes would thus appear to be unlike most others. It is more than just giving us too much of one product or too little of another. Rather, it amounts to a failure to facilitate the very human function of shaping one's preferences, the very human function of exercising a free will.

As Chapter 2 served as prologue to the arguments presented in this chapter, Chapter 4 will serve as an extended postscript. The discussion to this point has treated the second-order preference as stable. What if it is not? Might an agent be well advised to adjust the second-order to conform to the first? Might the strong case for market failure weaken? And what if the actions of sellers alter the second-order as well as (or instead of) the first? On such extensions shall the next chapter concentrate.

CHAPTER 4

Fortifications, Extensions, Clarifications

A Redefined Servant's Role?

Only one solution has thus far been considered for resolving a conflict between one's preference orders. If a person smokes in response to a preference to do so but simultaneously has a second-order preference to not smoke, then the assumption has been that a welfare gain will be achieved only if she is able to alter her first-order preference. Once she succeeds in experiencing a preference to not smoke (to have, that is, the preferred item from her second-order preference ranking) then she will indeed cease smoking and will be better off according to a straightforward application of economic welfare analysis. But what about the possibility of altering her second-order ranking instead? Might she not be well advised to come to peace with her inner demons by learning to embrace the preference that she in fact has, rather than living in a state of restless dissatisfaction? The philosopher Elizabeth Anderson certainly seems to suggest so. As she states, "There is no guarantee that second-order desires are characterized by any less conflict than first-order desires. And why should one accord more authority to a desire, just because its object is a desire rather than some other state of affairs?" (1993, 136). In the paragraphs to follow, I will demonstrate that there is indeed a reason to accord more "authority" to the former.

In chapter 2 the point was made that acting "as if" one had a preference that included the welfare of the other ("as if" one had one's preferred preference) might allow one to overcome a prisoner's dilemma and reach a more highly ranked element in one's unchanging first-order preference ranking. The strategy now under consideration might bear some resemblance to this but differs in the following sense. Changing one's second-order ranking does not assure the attainment of a more highly ranked element in the first-order ranking, but rather permits the agent to "feel better," as it were, about her selection.

In table 4.1 are shown three combinations of second-order ranking, first-order ranking, and choice, where N = not smoke, and S = smoke. Suppose that the agent is very much in the grip of a preference to smoke and believes that, at least in the short run, it is not possible to develop a preference to not smoke. There would thus be only states 1 and 2 for the agent to consider. Since (S pref N) is the only first-order ranking possible, S is the only rational action possible. Second-order rankings are hence all that differentiates these states, and there would appear to be no unequivocal way to rate either 1 or 2 as the superior.

To illustrate, suppose that the agent has preference (S pref N) but must choose N (a timely example given the greater limits placed on smokers in recent years). What can be said about the agent's welfare if she were to learn to live with the impossibility of S by changing her first-order ranking to (N pref S)? Such a "sour grapes" strategy may seem intuitively attractive but is impossible to defend within the neoclassical paradigm. Once the preference changes, we have a "whole new person," and as surely as interpersonal comparisons are impossible, so too are comparisons across essentially "different people" within the same body.

For the smoker summarized by conditions 1 and 2 in table 4.1, the second-order ranking occupies the position, for welfare-comparison purposes, that the first-order ranking occupied in the more traditional case just considered. It is, so to speak, where the agent "ends." In this case, moreover, the "first-order preference and choice" occupy the position, for comparative purposes, previously occupied by just the "choice." This is a critical point worth some elaboration with a more general example. Let there be two goods, A and B. It must be true that

(A pref B) and A

is preferable to

(A pref B) and B.

That is, "having a preference and fulfilling it" is better than "having a preference and not fulfilling it." Now the same general exercise can be carried to the next level:

TABLE 4.1.

Condition	Second-Order Preference	First-Order Preference	Choice
1	(N pref S) pref (S pref N)	S pref N	S
2	(S pref N) pref (N pref S)	S pref N	S
3	(N pref S) pref (S pref N)	N pref S	N

[(A pref B) pref (B pref A)] **and** [(A pref B) and A]

is preferable to

[(A pref B) pref (B pref A)] **and** [(B pref A) and B].

As can be seen, the second-order ranking stands where the first-order ranking did in the first example (to the left of the *and* in bold type), while the first-order ranking and choice together stand where just the choice stood in the first example (to the right of the *and* in bold type). For the same reason that no welfare judgment is possible in the standard neoclassical case when an agent's preferences change while choice does not, no welfare judgment is possible in the move from 1 to 2 in table 4.1.

Suppose next that the conflicted smoker finds it just as possible to alter her first-order ranking as it is to alter her choice of activities. It follows that condition 3 in table 4.1 would also be a possibility. It is clear that 3 ranks above 1 as surely as a traditional neoclassical agent becomes better off in going from having [(N pref S) and S] to having [(N pref S) and N]. Thus, it becomes somewhat easier to understand why the move from 1 to 3 has an intuitive advantage over a move from 1 to 2. To the extent that welfare theory overlaps with common sense, the first of these moves is an obvious welfare gain, while the second move is not.

This explanation is hard to reconcile, however, with some instances where 2 is accorded a *higher* ranking than 3. Some striking examples of this can be found in particular social movements when members of marginalized groups attempt to rid themselves of a sense of inferiority imposed by the dominant culture. The gay and lesbian movements of the last three decades provide examples of this. Table 4.2 is identical in formal features to table 4.1. Where N previously appeared, F = female sexual partner now appears, and where S previously appeared, M = male sexual partner now appears. The active gay male who suffers internal conflict is summarized by condition 1 in 4.2, similar in nature to the earlier considered condition 1. The agent has a preference that he acts on but would prefer were different.

One curious difference between this and the earlier considered cases is

TABLE 4.2.

Condition	Second-Order Preference	First-Order Preference	Choice
1	(F pref M) pref (M pref F)	M pref F	M
2	(M pref F) pref (F pref M)	M pref F	M
3	(F pref M) pref (M pref F)	F pref M	F

the likelihood that a contemporary gay person, if described by condition 1, would be far more likely to wish to move to 2 rather than to 3, the general belief being that learning to accept one's sexual desires is better than changing these desires. By itself, this favoritism of 2 over 3 (relative to 1) does not contradict any conclusions that were reached in the smoker's case.

There is, however, one likely ranking that is hard to reconcile with the model as thus far developed. The smoker's move from 1 to 3 was an unarguable welfare gain. Why, then would the movement from 1 to 3 be regarded within the current gay culture as generally undesirable? It would be an accurate generalization to say that a gay person having a second-order preference ranking to be straight would rarely wish to see this higher-order preference be acted upon. Rather, this is the ranking he would be more likely to wish see changed.[1]

More generally, it is necessary to recognize that nothing prevents an agent from critically assessing his second-order rankings. The philosopher whose ideas were summarized in chapter 2, Harry Frankfurt, was not oblivious to this complicating possibility. But after acknowledging that "[t]here is no theoretical limit to the length of the series of desires of higher and higher orders," he went on to say, "When a person identifies himself *decisively* with one of his first-order desires, this commitment 'resounds' throughout the potentially endless array of higher orders."[2]

As reasonable as this generalization may be, it would clearly not be valid in the case of the conflicted gay individual here under discussion. The preference of 2 over 3 suggests the existence of a *third*-order preference ranking. While the agent may prefer to have a second-order preference for M, he is, when at 1, "stuck" with a second-order preference for F. To alter this second-order ranking, as occurs at 2, is to be experiencing the preferred second-order ranking that allows the agent to identify more fully with the first-order ranking that moves him to act. And this new complication makes suddenly relevant some reflections on preferences that were offered many years before Frankfurt's version appeared.

Aristotle's Categories

The mainstream economic vision of rational action bears a similarity to the vision of rationality offered by Socrates, for whom "bad" choice could only result from a less than full grasp of the facts. In the writings of Aristotle, in contrast, the sorts of internal conflict being explored here were much in evidence.[3] In book 7 of the *Nicomachean Ethics* Aristotle contrasts three types of people: the temperate, the incontinent, and the self-indulgent (1973, 145). Letting I = act in accord with impulses, and E = exercise restraint, the combinations of second-order ranking, first-order ranking, and choice for these three types of agent are summarized in table 4.3.

Second-order rankings provide a particularly clear way of highlighting the differences between these types. For "Temperate" the first-order ranking is (E pref I), and the chosen action is thus E. For both "Incontinent" and "Self-indulgent" the first-order ranking is (I pref E), and the selected action is I. "Temperate" and "Incontinent" share a second-order ranking to exercise restraint, while "Self-indulgent" stands alone in having a second-order ranking to go with his impulses.

There may appear to be nothing here particularly different from what has already been discussed. "Incontinent's" second-order ranking, first-order ranking, and choice closely resemble the profile of "Conflicted" that appeared early in chapter 2. "Temperate" and "Self-indulgent," in contrast, are each content with the preference that they have. But clearly something new has been added to the picture. The name "Temperate" accords well with an agent who is at peace with her preferences, while the name "Self-indulgent" opens up a whole new issue.[4] It seems that Aristotle, while not implying the existence of a *third*-order ranking on the part of the agent, was claiming that second-order rankings were capable of evaluation. The "Temperate" agent's second-order ranking was judged favorably, while the "Self-indulgent" agent's second-order ranking was not.

If this interpretation is correct, it would seem to follow that the higher-order preference structure stands somewhere between Aristotle's belief that preferences can be objectively evaluated and the mainstream economic belief that they cannot be.[5] This is summarized in table 4.4. In the second line appears the first difference between the three. The second-order ranking approach would have to be aligned with the mainstream

TABLE 4.3.

	Temperate	Incontinent	Self-Indulgent
2nd-order	(E pref I) pref (I pref E)	(E pref I) pref (I pref E)	(I pref E) pref (E pref I)
1st-order	(E pref I)	(I pref E)	(I pref E)
Choice	E	I	I

TABLE 4.4.

	Neoclassical	Second-Order Preference	Aristotle
1. Can bundles be ranked?	Yes	Yes	Yes
2. Criterion for ranking	Subjective	Subjective	Objective
3. Can preferences be ranked?	No	Yes	Yes
4. Criterion for ranking	NA	Subjective	Objective
5. Can 2nd-order pref be ranked?	NA	Yes	Yes
6. Criterion for ranking	NA	Subjective	Objective

economic approach by this criterion since for each, the relative goodness of something is determined by the preference of the choosing agent. For Aristotle, in contrast, there is a criterion that transcends the individual's ranking. With line 3, the second-order ranking approach shifts its loyalties. Contrary to the neoclassical approach but consistent with Aristotle, evaluation of preferences is possible. In line 4, the second-order approach is unlike either of the others. It differs from the neoclassical approach by permitting an evaluation of the agent's preferences. It differs from the Aristotelian approach by having the agent be the sole evaluator of her preferences.

The entries that appear in lines 5 and 6 are a repeat of lines 3 and 4, and from this it follows that a rethinking is necessary as to what distinguishes the earlier considered "Temperate" from Aristotle's "Self-indulgent." For as discussed in the last section, as surely as the second-order approach recognizes the agent's capacity to evaluate her preferences, there is nothing stopping us, on a formal level, from permitting the agent to evaluate her second-order preference. While Aristotle might be said to have *required* an evaluation of the second-order preference and to have made that evaluation independent of the agent's opinion, the second-order preference model itself can at least recognize that such an evaluation is possible.[6] Just as second-order preferences have made possible a new way of thinking about first-order preferences, to recognize the very possibility of third-order preferences makes it apparent that similar questions can be raised about second-order preferences.

A Moving Target: Shifting Second-Order Preferences

Acknowledging the existence of preferences beyond the second order may appear to compromise severely the major claim of the last chapter, namely, that the market fails in the shaping of tastes. For no longer does the second-order stand forth as the Archimedean point. Frankfurt simply claimed that discord between the second order and orders above it is rare. We might go further still with this sort of defense by noting that matters generally regarded as "economic" in nature would be less likely to yield conflict above the second order than other sorts of preferences. To prefer to prefer not to smoke does indeed appear to be the end of the discussion, as does a preference to prefer to spend less, a preference to prefer to eat fewer calories, and so on.

As tempting as a defense of this sort might appear, it is undeniably ad hoc in nature. But such a defense is not even necessary. Briefly put, with ownership of preferences (of whatever level) unrecognized, market forces would breed more discord than is optimal. As a first possibility, suppose that a seller's efforts succeed in changing both the first-order and the second-order rankings (and, were they to exist, any rankings of still a higher order.) A creative chef, to take one example, if able to alter tastes in a way that brings new customers, might be causing agents who previously had neither a first- *nor* second-order preference for some new creations to suddenly find themselves experiencing both. Clearly, in a case such as this the normative conclusions would be as impossible as is currently true in received theory whenever the first-order ranking changes.

As a variation on the above case, suppose that while the efforts of the seller change both the first- and second-order rankings, the agent has a contrary third-order ranking that remains intact. Were this to occur, welfare conclusions would be every bit as possible as when only the first order was variable, and the market would be expected to be inefficient in the taste-shaping processes for essentially the same reasons. Consider a promoter of beef who succeeds in changing a vegetarian's tastes toward his product and at the same time causes this convert to fully embrace his new preference. The promoter has still lowered the convert's overall well-being if the vegetarian tastes still hold sway at the third order and above.

As just suggested, scenarios such as this seem rather unlikely at the level of everyday consumption activities. But such conflict can be observed in certain deep conflicts over personal identity, as was discussed earlier in this chapter. This now brings us to a third case that makes more demands both analytically and normatively. What can be said about instances in which a seller succeeds in altering the second-order preference (and all higher orders), but either fails to change the first-order preference at all or changes it in such a way that the agent still has conflict between the first and second orders?

Let there be three classes of home furnishings: L = low quality, A = average quality, and H = high quality. Let the differences in quality be clearly reflected in the prices charged. Suppose that initially the agent chooses the low-quality furniture, that this is indeed his preference, and that he is fully satisfied with this preference. This is summarized in line 1 of table 4.5.[7]

Had the "flipping" of the second-order preference ranking been accom-

TABLE 4.5.

Second-Order Preference	First-Order Preference	Choice
1. (Pref for L) pref (pref for A) pref (pref for H)	(Pref for L)	M
2. (Pref for H) pref (pref for A) pref (pref for L)	(Pref for A)	A
3. (Pref for H) pref (pref for A) pref (pref for L)	(Pref for L)	L
4. (Pref for A) pref (pref for H) pref (pref for L)	(Pref for H)	H

panied by a change in the first-order ranking such that the preferred preference prevailed, it would, as already noted, not be possible to draw any conclusions. But line 2 shows something other than a *complete* turnaround occurring. While the marketing efforts of sellers have caused the agent to move from having a second-order preference for the low quality to having a second-order preference for the high quality, the agent's first-order preference has not quite "kept up." The agent has been transformed from having a first-order preference for the low quality to having a first-order preference for the average quality, but has seen his second-order preferences change still further. While finding it optimal to now purchase the average-quality furniture, this agent would prefer to have a more sophisticated preference for the very best.

Welfare assessments to this point have ranked states occurring over time. An agent having a second-order preference that does not change but a changing first-order ranking was an agent becoming better or worse off. A before-and-after comparison was central to the normative analysis. Now, however, no such comparison is possible, for the earlier noted reasons that are a part of traditional welfare analysis. Since the agent's second-order ranking has changed, we cannot say whether the agent's welfare has improved or worsened. This is true regardless of what has happened to his first-order ranking. Given the second-order preference shift, however, we can isolate a market inefficiency by comparing an efficient period 2 first-order ranking with the ranking that market forces would bring into being.

In the process of changing the agent's second-order ranking, the seller's actions have changed the first-order ranking away from the low-quality furniture and toward the average quality. This change is, of course, a good one. Given the agent's new second-order preference for expensive furniture, she is better off preferring the average quality than preferring the low quality. Her tastes have moved in the direction of her changed higher-order ranking, albeit not as much as would be optimal. Inefficiency in the extent of the taste change follows from the fact that the change is in the nature of a positive externality. For the seller has taken steps that have shifted the buyer's tastes in a desirable direction (from the buyer's standpoint) and has received no compensation for doing so. As a consequence, the seller would be expected to find it worth shifting tastes less than is optimal from an efficiency standpoint.

It is indeed conceivable that the seller's actions would fail to shift the first-order ranking at all. This is represented by a movement from line 1 to line 3 in table 4.5. From the seller's standpoint, the marketing efforts are in vain (at least as regards this one hypothetical buyer). They have caused a change in the buyer by shifting his second-order ranking but have not changed the preference that moves him to act. Both before and after the marketing actions, it is the low-quality furniture that the agent prefers and purchases. Note again that it is not possible to conclude that the buyer has been harmed by the seller's overall actions, since the second-order ranking *has* shifted. Since there is no market for preference shifts, however, it can be concluded that there has been an insufficient number of favorable shifts occurring.

Lines 2 and 3 each describe an instance where shifts in the buyer's second-order ranking away from the low-quality furniture and toward the high-quality were harmful events. They differ only in that some shift of the first-order ranking occurs in the one case but not in the other. Line 4 represents another possibility, one in which the first-order ranking shift, when considered in light of the new second-order ranking and when compared with line 1, must be judged as too substantial. The seller's marketing actions have had some effect on the second-order ranking, causing the agent to prefer a preference for the average-quality furniture. No longer does the buyer regard low-quality furniture as his ideal, nor is the high-quality alternative that which he would prefer preferring. His first-order ranking, however, has shifted farther away from what it formerly was. He now prefers purchasing high quality over the other alternatives. Once again, a direct welfare comparison is ruled out since line 4 includes a different second-order ranking than line 1. However, given the new second-order ranking that prevails, his first-order ranking has changed more than is optimal from an efficiency standpoint. The seller's actions that shifted the agent's first-order ranking were beneficial, an example of a spillover benefit, but the continued shift in taste toward the high-quality furniture is an instance of a spillover cost and would thus be expected to occur too often if property rights in preferences go unrecognized.

To summarize, though my argument for market inefficiency in the shaping of tastes is most easily presented in a context that holds the second-order ranking constant, the argument is no less valid if this ranking is itself assumed to shift. All that is required for such a conclusion is the assumption that the second order and first order do not move in tandem. Were they to do so, no welfare conclusions would be possible. But if they do not, then the change in the first-order ranking following a second-order shift would tend to be inefficient in degree.

Autonomy

Even if conflicts between the second order and still higher orders are rare, their mere possibility raises a new question. By Aristotle's account, a second-order ranking could be evaluated by criteria wholly independent of the agent's opinion. For the conflicted homosexual, the second-order ranking could be evaluated by that agent's third-order ranking. Different as these two accounts may be, they each offer a clear means by which to evaluate second-order preferences. But what about the most common case that emerges from the Frankfurt model? If it is true that an agent "ends" at her second-order ranking, or, alternatively, that she has third and still higher orders consistent with the second order, is there any basis for still according such a second-order ranking less than full normative significance? Thought of differently, must any other conditions hold for the second-order ranking to be deemed "genuine"?

One response to such a question might be that it really does not matter and that for normative purposes a second-order ranking's status does not depend on how it came into being. Such a response would be in close accord with what mainstream economists have to say about the *first*-order preference ranking. And it was precisely Galbraith's failure to fully confront this issue that placed his critique well outside the neoclassical discussion. The ability of General Motors to convince the 1958 car shopper that tail fins were preferable to more traditional offerings was for General Motors to create a preference. But as defenders of received theory pointed out, this placed General Motors in a role not unlike the economics professor trying to create a particular preference in his students.[8] It was thus the belief that the source of a preference did not affect its legitimacy that played a large role in the mainstream's dismissal of the Galbraithian critique of the forces of modern marketing.

The utilitarian influence on the thinking of welfare economists has contributed to the relative neglect of "autonomy" as a concept worthy of careful consideration. And since utilitarianism is a consequentialist sort of moral philosophy, "autonomy" tends to be approached strictly as a potentially utility-enhancing characteristic on those occasions when it does receive consideration.[9] Among philosophers, it remains a much more examined concept. Gerald Dworkin warns against any specification of autonomy that "makes it impossible or extremely unlikely that anybody ever has been, or could be, autonomous" and cautions that "a theory which required as a condition of autonomy that an individual's values not be influenced by his parents, peers, or culture would violate this condition."[10]

By some accounts, the critical test of an agent's independence is whether she "identifies" with the desires that she has, not whether she herself is responsible for their presence. Thus the agent with a thirst for water would be described as "autonomous" by virtue of having a second-order preference for such a desire. But as should be clear, this particular first-order desire cannot be understood as having been selected by the agent. For no matter what her second-order preference might have been, this desire would be present.[11] But if the second-order preference itself is to figure into any evaluation of an agent's autonomy, what conditions would be required? It is not difficult to think up examples in which an agent comes to have a particular second-order ranking through either the manipulation of information by others or through systematic methods of persuasion. Dworkin requires only that the formation of the second-order ranking transpire with what he chooses to call "procedural independence," wherein minimal conditions are met in the formation of the second-order rankings (Dworkin 1989, 60–61).

Susan Wolf requires the existence of a "sane deep self" as a precondition for declaring an agent as autonomous. To have such a "sane deep self" requires, by her account, that the agent be able to revise herself, "to get rid of some desires and traits, and perhaps replace them with others on the basis of . . . deeper desires or values or reflections" (1989, 148). This clearly implies the existence of a second-order preference ranking, but Wolf specifies elsewhere that the "sane deep self" must have a second-order ranking that would follow from a sensible and accurate evaluation of oneself, full and accurate information, and no deliberate deception by others.

These are rather stringent conditions that are not implied by the expanded model of rational choice that is being offered here. To see this, let A represent the set of all potential second-order rankings, B represent the set of potential second-order rankings for which the highest first-order ranking is attainable, and C represent the set of all potential second-order rankings that might follow from the agent having a sensible and accurate evaluation of herself, having full and accurate information, and facing no deliberate deception.

A "sane deep self" would have a second-order ranking belonging to both sets B and C. Nowhere does Wolf claim that membership in one class entails membership in another. But by offering this "sane deep self" as a precondition to the attainment of autonomy while also treating autonomy as an attainable state, Wolf implies that the situation appearing in figure 4.1a is the rule. In this figure sets B and C are shown to overlap, suggesting the existence of second-order rankings that agents would not only arrive at following full and unbiased information, but would be able to act upon so as to make the most preferred ranking within this ideal second-order ranking a reality.

This seems an unlikely occurrence for most agents, with the situation summarized in figure 4.1b seeming far closer to reality. Unlike in figure 4.1a, sets B and C have no common members. The second-order rankings that emerge from full information would be such that one's realized first-order rankings would never be one's perfect ideal. And those second-order rankings that would make possible the attainment of the best first-order ranking would not follow from full and accurate information. To illus-

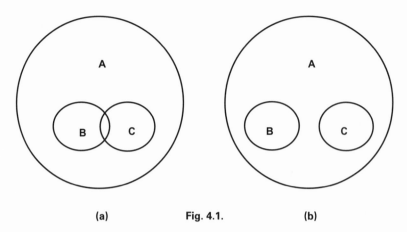

(a)   **Fig. 4.1.**   (b)

trate, a second-order ranking belonging to B might have as its most preferred ranking "a slothful existence" preferred to any other sort of existence. To experience such a first-order ranking is not unimaginable but is unlikely to be a preferred preference for one having "all the facts." In contrast, C might include a second-order ranking that places at the top a preference to live a charitable, forgiving life, a noble ideal but an unlikely preference to attain. It is, in short, quite possible that a sane person with a well-informed second-order ranking is unable to realize her "preferred preference." To say such a person is not in possession of a "sane deep self" is to overlook the basic economic insight that scarcity is an existential fact, as true for preferences as for goods.[12]

Another question now arises, however. Does an agent "possess" *his* first-order preference ranking when the one he experiences is not the one that he prefers? For example, is the preference to smoke that the regretful smoker experiences "his" or is it alien just by virtue of the fact that it is other than what he wishes it to be? Resolution of this somewhat arcane question is quite critical if the normative analysis of the previous chapter is to have any weight. For an agent's welfare is dependent on what she "has" or "possesses" relative to what she would like to "have" or "possess."

Frankfurt reveals a slight ambiguity in answering this question of ownership, noting, "The unwilling addict identifies himself . . . through the formation of a second-order volition, with one rather than with the other of his conflicting first-order desires," and thus "makes one of them more truly his own and, in so doing, withdraws himself from the other" (1971, 13). In other words, while each desire the agent experiences "belongs to" the agent, the desire that moves him to act may or may not be "most truly his own."

In reexpressing this in the "relational" language of preferences, the translation is quite imperfect. For it does not follow from the fact that [(N pref S) pref (S pref N)] (i.e., that the agent has a second-order preference to not smoke) that (N pref S) is "most truly his preference." It is what he truly *wishes* his preference to be. But as discussed in chapter 2, if the preference is for S, it would be logically contradictory to allege the simultaneous existence of a preference for N within the agent. To be stuck with a first-order preference he would prefer not to have is simultaneously to *not* have the other (preferable) preference. Thus it would be inaccurate to characterize the conflicted agent as one who does not possess "his" preference (the preferred one) and who is instead forced to possess one not belonging to him. For it is very much "his," albeit not the one he most desires.

Merger Mania: Reducing the Two Rankings to One

"Two selves" models differ from "two rankings" (first- and second-order) models in one important respect, noted in chapter 2. The rankings in the two-selves model are over *identical* elements, but this is not true when a first-order ranking is being compared with a second-order ranking. To acknowledge this difference raises another question. Might it be possible to present an agent's second-order ranking in a way that guards against the mistake of interpreting this ranking as simply that of a "second self" within the agent and guards against the just-discussed habit of speaking of an agent's unpreferred preference as "not really his"? For if it is true that an agent at any moment has both a preference ranking over elements in her choice set and a preference ranking over potential rankings of these elements, what is to prevent the merging of these simultaneous rankings into a single ranking?

In the case of the two-selves models, it is not possible, in principle, to arrive at a single ranking since the conflicting selves have competing rankings over an identical set of elements. If for one part of John apple pie is preferred to cherry pie, while for another part of John it is the reverse, it would not be possible to speak of the unconditional John's having a single ranking. To weight the two selves equally would require that the sum of the items that are preferred by each "self" within him is preferred to the sum of the items that are not preferred. It would follow that "apple pie and cherry pie" is preferred to "apple pie and cherry pie," a conclusion that makes a mockery of what *preference* entails.[13]

The competing rankings in the two-selves model are over identical elements, but this is by definition not so when a second-order ranking is compared with a first-order preference ranking. If the elements of the respective rankings are so radically distinct, then why has no attempt been made to combine the two rankings into one ranking, each complex element in such a ranking consisting of a preference ranking of elements and a particular element?[14] A major reason, I would suggest, is nothing more than clarity and convenience. The second-order ranking is less cumbersome to introduce when constructed solely of rankings of elements. Acknowledging this, however, should not deter an attempt to repackage the discussion, particularly if doing so has the potential to open up new avenues by drawing attention to matters that are obscured when two orders of ranking are employed in the analysis. In the course of this discussion, it will become apparent that a "preferred preference" is valued (1) intrinsically and (2) instrumentally. In addition, the conditional nature of the "preferred preference" will become more obvious. Unconditional second-order rankings of A and B presuppose the presence of both A and B in the agent's choice set. If when A and B are both options [(A pref B) pref (B pref A)], does this second-order preference necessarily hold if A ceases to be an option? As will be shown (lending support to informal earlier assertions), this agent's second-order preference may or may not change as a consequence. That is, it is possible that [(A pref B) and B] will be preferred to [(B pref A) and B] and also possible that the latter will be preferred to the former.

In table 4.6 are displayed three potential rankings of "complex elements." Each complex element contains (1) an "element" (e.g., an apple, a cigarette, "the act of not smoking") and (2) a ranking of elements. In each ranking of complex elements shown, a strict preference relation applies, with each complex element preferred to whatever complex elements appear beneath it. The numbers that appear on the left refer to the corresponding complex element and do *not* refer to relative position. (Only in the first of the three cases shown do the rankings coincide with the numbers assigned to the complex elements.)

For each of these rankings 1 ranks higher than 3, which in turn ranks higher than 4. The ranking of 1 over 3 is nothing more than a starting assumption. The agent would prefer "preferring to not smoke and acting upon that preference" to "preferring to smoke and acting upon that preference." The ranking of 3 over 4 is not an assumption but is true by

TABLE 4.6.

First Ranking	Second Ranking	Third Ranking
1. (N pref S) and N	1. (N pref S) and N	1. (N pref S) and N
2. (N pref S) and S	3. (S pref N) and S	3. (S pref N) and S
3. (S pref N) and S	2. (N pref S) and S	4. (S pref N) and N
4. (S pref N) and N	4. (S pref N) and N	2. (N pref S) and S

definition (i.e., "preferring to smoke and smoking" is preferred to "preferring to smoke and not smoking"). It was earlier noted that this often meets with resistance, and it was suggested that this is likely the result of defining preferences too narrowly. Now from the ranking of 1 above 3 and 3 above 4, it follows that 1 must rank above 4, that when not smoking the agent would rather have a preference to not smoke than a preference to smoke. From this it follows, as noted above, that even if the "element" is held constant (in this case "not smoking"), it is possible that having one particular preference is rated better than having another.

Now while for each of the rankings shown 1 ranks above 3, which ranks above 4, the relative position of 2 varies. In the first ranking, this "complex element" occupies the second position, in the second ranking, the third, and in the third ranking, the fourth. Figures 4.2a and 4.2b help to clarify via indifference curves the "wild card" nature of element 2. What distinguishes this from the smoking example is that an element is now a particular combination of two goods and a complex element consists of one such element along with a particular utility function.[15]

For simplicity, let the mix of goods represented by points A and B be the only alternatives available to the agent. In figure 4.2a, given the utility function that prevails, A is preferred to B. In other words, since A lies on a higher indifference curve than B, it is preferred and would be chosen. In figure 4.2b, a different utility function prevails, as indicated by the differently sloped indifference curves, and B is preferred to A. Assume that the agent prefers the second described state of affairs to the first. In other words, assume that [(B pref A) and B] is preferred to [(A pref B) and A].

In the smoking example, [(N pref S) and S] ranked second, third, and fourth best, respectively, in the rankings shown. An equivalent outcome is true here, and somewhat easier to see.[16] A utility value of 30 has been assigned to the indifference curve on which point B lies in figure 4.2b. By starting assumption, the utility value associated with point A in 4.2a must be less, since [(B pref A) and B] is preferred to [(A pref B) and A]. A value of 20 is shown. Furthermore, it follows that the utility level associated with point B in figure 4.2a must be less still, since it lies on a lower indifference curve. This is shown as equal to 10. Now the only conditions that can be placed on the value assigned point A in 4.2b is that it be less than 30. The precise amount could *(a)* exceed 20, in which case [(B pref A) and A] would occupy the second place in the ranking of the four points, *(b)* fall between 10 and 20, in which case it would occupy the third position, or *(c)* be less than 10, in which case it would occupy fourth place. To summarize, the ranking of three of the four elements is known. All that is known about the fourth element is that it ranks below one of the elements, namely [(B pref A) and B].

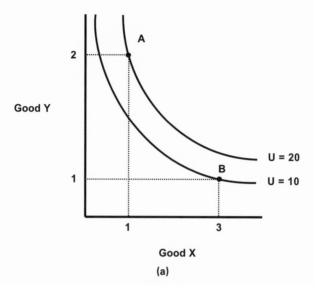

Fig. 4.2.

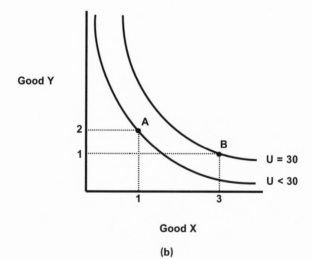

The intent of this exercise has been to put in clearer perspective the wild-card nature of complex element 2. Roger McCain offers ranking 1 as *necessarily* true.[17] A first step in uncovering the meaning behind the three rankings will be to review his reasoning. According to McCain, 2 is preferred to 3 for the same reason that 1 is preferred to 2. Since 1 and 2 have a "ranking of elements" in common, goes this reasoning, 1 is the preferred since it has the preferred "element" (N instead of S). By the same reasoning, 2 was concluded to be better than 3, since they share the "element" S and 2 has the better "ranking of elements," (N pref S) instead of (S pref N).

The analogy is unsuccessful. In the case of "complex elements" 1 and 2, it is indeed true that the shared "ranking of elements," (N pref S), *necessitates* that the complex element that also contains N is preferred to the one that also contains S. But no similar reasoning applies in the comparison of 2 and 3. Given that "element" N is not an option and that "element" S is thus the only possibility, the agent may or may not prefer (N pref S) relative to (S pref N). To say without further qualification that he has a second-order preference for (N pref S) only requires that if S and N are *both* available, (N pref S) would be preferred to (S pref N).

This returns us to the task of seeking an interpretation of the three different rankings in table 4.6. Consider the way in which complex elements 2 and 3 are ranked. The first ranking places 2 above 3, while for the second and third rankings the reverse is true. In the case of the first ranking, the ranking of 2 above 3 might be understood as a variation on Mill's noted claim that he would rather be Socrates dissatisfied than a pig satisfied. Letting S symbolize the "normal life of a pig," Mill asserts that even if constrained to S he would rather have the preference ranking of Socrates, (N pref S), than a preference for a pig's life, (S pref N).[18] In contrast to this, for both the second and third rankings, if saddled with S the agent would prefer having (S pref N) as her preference to having (N pref S).

For the smoking example as well, 2 being preferred to 3 can be imagined, as can 3 being preferred to 2. If "not smoking" were not an option (an admittedly odd occurrence), a truly "politically correct" agent might still prefer having a preference to not smoke while one not quite so driven by principle might find preferring to prefer smoking the more attractive way to confront the situation.

Table 4.6 reveals one other pair of complex elements, 2 and 4, that do not maintain the same ranking with respect to one another across the three rankings shown. For the first and second rankings [(N pref S) and S] is preferred to [(S pref N) and N], while for the third ranking it is the reverse. Unlike what was true with the comparison of complex elements 2 and 3, the present pair (2 and 4) have neither an element nor a "preference for an element" in common.[19] As one possible way of interpreting this difference, assume that initially "complex element" 1 prevails. An agent having the first or second ranking would be more willing to shift into smoking while still preferring to not smoke than she would be willing to continue to *not* smoke while at the same time having a preference to smoke. For this agent, how she "feels" about smoking (i.e., her preference with regard to smoking) is more important than whether or not she smokes. An agent with the third ranking, on the other hand, is more willing to shift into the unpreferred preference (S pref N) while continuing to not smoke, than to retain the preferred preference (N pref S) while at the same time smoking. For such an agent, "actions speak louder than preferences." There is a final paradox to note. An agent with the third ranking would prefer sacrificing *both* (N pref S) and N to sacrificing just one, a result drawing attention again to the value that can be placed on symmetry between preference and activity.

Matters would grow considerably more complex if more than two elements were in the choice set. Despite this, the exercise has served two purposes. First, it has demonstrated that introducing second-order rankings into the analysis does not require the abandonment of the "single ranking" assumption. To speak of a first-order ranking and second-order ranking has been pedagogically convenient but not logically necessary. In addition, this exercise has demonstrated that a second-order preference ranking could be, but need not be, unconditional in nature. One's preferences over preferences can vary with the composition of the set of available activities or bundles.

This recasting of the discussion from two preference rankings to one, besides allowing the fresh perspectives just considered, allows some previously considered subjects to be reinvestigated. Burton Weisbrod's model is particularly ripe for some further analysis. Weisbrod, it will be recalled, specified two conditions that had to be met for a ranking of what are here being called complex elements to be possible. In his words once again, "[O]ne type of utility function, and the expected consumption bundle it generates, may be said to be preferred to another, and the expected consumption bundle it generates, if and only if (a) the two expected consumption bundles are different and (b) the same consumption bundle is preferred no matter which utility function is used to evaluate the two bundles" (1977, 993). By replacing "utility function" with *ranking of elements* and "consumption bundle" with *element,* it is possible to fit these specified conditions to the current discussion.

It was earlier demonstrated that the second condition was incorrect since its acceptance would rule out the most basic point of much of this book, namely, that humans have the capability to evaluate the state of acting with respect to one preference ranking relative to the state of acting with respect to another. That a different "bundle" (or "element") might follow from each preference ranking did not alter this conclusion. With the aid of complex elements we are now in a better position to take on the first of Weisbrod's two conditions as well. And this, too, will be seen to be incorrect.

According to this first condition, a pair of complex elements cannot be ranked if the consumption bundle (or element) associated with each is the same. Returning to the earlier example, this implies that if the opportunity to smoke was outside the agent's choice set, it would make no difference to her whether or not she preferred to smoke. That is, it would not be possible for complex elements 1 and 4 in table 4.6 to be ranked, as they clearly, in fact, are.[20]

But what if Weisbrod's first condition were not rejected while the second one was? For an agent having second-order preference ranking [(N pref S) pref (S pref N)], only the following ranking of complex elements would appear to be possible:

[(N pref S) and N] indifferent to [(S pref N) and N] preferred to [(N pref S) and S] indifferent to [(S pref N) and S]

This is an unusual ranking. As emphasized when Weisbrod's condition (b) was refuted, if the agent has a second-order preference to "not smoke," it follows that she prefers the first complex element ("having a preference to not smoke" and "not smoking") to the fourth ("having a preference to smoke" and "smoking").[21] If we adhere to condition (a), it further follows that if the agent must not smoke, she would be indifferent as to which preference prevails (i.e., she would be indifferent between the first two complex elements) and similarly, that if she must smoke, she would be indifferent as to which preference prevails (i.e., she would be indifferent between the latter two complex elements). Looking at this from another perspective, by this particular ranking, the agent's preferences over her activities are fully separable from her utility function. Her preference to abstain from smoking holds regardless of the utility function she happens to be experiencing.

By some interpretations of what it means to prefer one thing to another, however, this ranking undoubtedly holds some appeal. An argument in its defense might be along the following lines. "This agent prefers having a preference to not smoke simply because having such a preference *causes* her to not smoke. It is really 'not smoking' that is the ultimate source of well-being. If refraining from smoking could be achieved while having a preference to smoke (by keeping the option to smoke outside the choice set), this would be just as good."

By such an interpretation, the basis for one's preferences over preferences is strictly instrumental in nature. The above ranking shows the agent preferring to not smoke regardless of which preference she happens to be experiencing. An analogy might be the following. Let U = university education, H = high school education, M = many abilities, F = few abilities. Suppose that for the agent:

(U and M) indifferent to (H and M) preferred to (U and F) indifferent to (H and F)

In this example, it is "many abilities" (however attained) that is preferred to "few abilities." The agent prefers having the university education strictly as a means to the attainment of "many abilities" and is indifferent between this state of affairs and the attainment of "many abilities" with just a high school education.[22] If able to choose between the university education and the high school education, he might go with the former only because that makes the attainment of "many abilities" more likely.

The analogy with the preference example is unsuccessful in at least two respects. First, while a university education might indeed be valued in a strictly instrumental sense, preference rankings, when thought of as dispositional states, have a broader function, as earlier suggested. A preference ranking, in other words, can be understood as a reflection of a psychological state that can be valued intrinsically.[23] Thus an agent having an "other things being equal" preference to prefer to not smoke would not be indifferent between the first complex element, [(N pref S) and N], and the second complex element, [(S pref N) and N], but would prefer the former to the latter. And similarly, [(N pref S) and S] would be preferred, not indifferent to [(S pref N) and S].

Second, and more significantly, the preference for the second element over the fourth, while making sense in the education example, *is logically contradictory in the earlier example,* and did not appear in the four rankings that are shown in table 4.6. For if one's first-order preference is (S pref N), then it necessarily follows that [(S pref N) and S] pref [(S pref N) and N]. To claim otherwise, as already argued, is to ignore a core assumption of the maximization model. Having a preference to smoke does not just "cause" one to smoke. It results in the agent who experiences such a preference being better off by doing so.

As an earlier quoted passage suggests, Amartya Sen is fully in accord with this point. The unhappy meat-eater went along with his preference for meat despite wishing that he had a preference for vegetables. Sen made the point strongly by having the agent feel "repugnance" toward the vegetables that he would prefer to prefer. But it would have been just as formally correct to describe the agent as remaining a meat-eater even while finding vegetables to be enjoyable, as long as meat was more enjoyable still (and a choice had to be made between the two).

That there is resistance to this conclusion is undeniable, and why this might be so is worth exploring. Two types of objection can be distinguished. The first claims that agents are not blindly obedient to their preferences. One raising such an objection might note, for example, the clear existence of recovering alcoholics who report experiencing a preference to drink that they act to counter because of the long-term consequences drinking would have. As already noted, if an act (or bundle) is defined narrowly rather than in an "overall" sense, it would indeed be correct to say that such agents act against their preferences. But the meaning of preference in the context of rational choice is always intended to be "overall" in scope. A recovering alcoholic would be said to have a preference to drink in this overall sense only if he prefers the full scope of the future contingent on his drinking relative to the full scope of the future contingent on his refraining. By this distinction, one who refrains despite "preferring" to drink would be described as one having an "intrinsic" preference to drink (which he acts against) but an overall preference to refrain (which he acts upon).[24]

There is a second objection that poses a greater challenge by drawing attention to the paradox of agents deliberately restricting future choices. While multiple-selves models may seem well equipped to make sense of such self-paternalism, the present model might seem less able to explain such acts. If we admit the reality of self-paternalism while rejecting two-selves models in favor of second-order ranking models, aren't we forced to accept the claim that agents act so as to keep themselves from "choosing what they prefer"?

Reports of Ulysses-like actions to restrict oneself are not uncommon. Tim Brennan, for example, no supporter of multiple-selves models, provides the following rationale for self-constraint that such models offer: "After a light dinner, a dieter may lock the refrigerator and tell a friend to hide the key until tomorrow. The dieter knows he will have a preference later in the evening for more food but, just after finishing dinner he believes he should not snack later even if he then will desire to do so" (1989, 192). Letting N stand for "not eat" and E stand for "eat," this sort of argument may rest on the following line of reasoning. "If the agent is free to choose later in the evening, he will choose what he prefers. Thus, if it is the case that (E pref N), then the choice will be E. Despite this, [(E pref N) and N] is preferable to [(E pref N) and E]. As a consequence, actions that the agent might take now to rule out E as a possibility can leave the agent better off."

By this explanatory strategy, preferences are reduced to mere "causes" of choice but do not serve as explanations that preserve the rational nature of the choosing agent. As I have previously proposed, an event such as Brennan describes can be understood within the rational choice model as an attempt to mold future preferences (George 1984, 96–100). The act of ruling out nighttime snacks would be understood to cause the agent to indeed not snack but, as importantly, would be understood to change, if successful, the agent's preference ranking from (E pref N) to (N pref E). By this approach, self-paternalism becomes understandable as a tool for altering future preference rankings as well as a tool for making future choices.

This "sour grapes" phenomenon served as an organizing principle for much of Jon Elster's work, and its credibility is substantiated by even the most modest introspective efforts (1983, 109ff.). An agent who prefers grapes to apples experiences such a phenomenon when she finds her first-order preference changing in favor of apples following the removal of grapes from her choice set. To the extent that this mental habit applies, a deliberate strategy of self-imposed constraints can alter the experience of not engaging in the activity.[25]

The story of Ulysses, as usually told, provides an unusual case. While restrained, Ulysses' desire to heed the call of the Sirens was the same as when he was unrestrained. The sour grapes rationale for restricting one's choice set appears not to apply, and this will for present purposes be treated as a very special case. Letting S = succumb, and R = resist, this may indeed be characterized as that rare instance when the agent (Ulysses) is not able to do what he prefers except by foregoing his free agency. In other words, by not restraining himself, it would be the case that [(R pref S) and S], while after restraining himself [(R pref S) and R]. Being in the grip of an unpreferred preference is not at issue here. Rather, Ulysses might be described as one unable to choose what he prefers, even when it is ostensibly in his choice set. The act of maximizing with respect to his first-order preference ranking requires in this mythical case a very creative exercise in free choice, and this sort of case will be treated as lying outside the scope of the present topic of concern.

This brings us to the conclusion of chapter 4 and the conclusion of the more theoretical part of the book. The working assumption to this point has been that consumers maximize utility and that firms maximize profit. The central message has been that with the integration of second-order rankings in the theoretical model of a market economy a serious short-coming emerges. But this shortcoming has been in relation to a textbook ideal. Is there a shortcoming to be identified relative to alternative real-world possibilities? The remaining chapters will not attempt to construct solutions to the problem that has been identified. That would be a monumental task requiring talents beyond what I can currently offer. These chapters will instead attempt to provide some evidence that unpreferred preferences are a worsening problem, largely due to the erosion of customs and laws that served to shape preferences. Absent an understanding of second-order preferences, such practices are increasingly viewed as constraints on one's freedom to choose.

CHAPTER 5

Market Failure or Human Imperfection?

Let's face it, the idea that advertising creates artificial desires rests on a wistful ignorance of history and human nature, on the hazy, romantic feeling that there existed some halcyon era of noble savages with purely natural needs.

—James Twitchell

It is Twitchell's sentiment that will form the backdrop for the book's remaining chapters, a sentiment the growing power of which should not be underestimated. Not to be taken lightly is the accusation that welfare theorists may have been guilty of stacking the deck when they coined the term *market failure*. For this expression manages to push into the background a critical question, namely, "Failure relative to what"? By the newly proposed evaluative criterion captured in the epigraph, markets would be said to fail not when they fall short of the textbook ideal, but rather when they fail to compare well with other real possibilities. And as one observer has noted, "[T]he market has assumed mythological status, becoming a totem to which all must pledge allegiance or face expulsion to the margins."[1]

In this chapter I will offer some reasons for suspecting that the mismatch between the preferences that are experienced and the preferences that are preferred, while indeed an inevitable part of the human condition, has been worsening over this century as social institutions that have served to alleviate the mismatch have weakened. In the chapters following this one, some particular case studies will be offered. The focus will be overwhelmingly on the United States, with other nations and cultures making only occasional guest appearances. Contributing to this constricted focus are the limitations that I bring to the project. Also contributing is the cultural imperialism of the United States. One hears continual reminders of the spread of the American ways of life, particularly since the collapse of the Soviet empire. To focus on century-long changes in the United States is to focus on changes, whether for good or ill, that are occurring or will occur in other parts of the world as well.

Avoiding the Panglossian Temptation

By some accounts, the very occurrence of a change is clear testimony to its efficiency. Taken to an extreme, such a position leads to what has been called the "Panglossian temptation," the belief that we always live in the best of all possible worlds. This sort of reason for rationalizing change cuts across ideological boundaries and, while useful for scoring rhetorical points, represents a very limited and misleading view of social change.[2] As history reveals, changes sometimes occur that by any normative criteria are changes for the worse. A serious understanding of social evolution does not rule out such unfortunate occurrences, and it is incorrect for proponents of change to assume that the efficiency features of what they propose ensure its inevitability.

If the description of Americans offered by both Daniel Bell and William Leach as unusually accepting of the "new" is correct, the United States is particularly well suited to enthusiastically embrace change (Bell 1976, 34; Leach 1993, 4). Americans might be described in a way that appears on the surface contradictory, namely, as advocates of a rule of thumb that urges one to "rigidly reject the rigid rejection of change." This would suggest that in the United States, to a greater extent than in other parts of the world, market structures might be found displacing other social mechanisms regardless of whether or not such changes represent social improvements.

Such suboptimal change is particularly possible in a society that is experiencing economic growth. This may on initial consideration seem odd, since one might expect those characteristics that are associated with economic growth to be the same characteristics that encourage the discovery and correction of inefficiencies. But consider as an analogy the suboptimality that is possible for a firm with some degree of market power. Since above-normal rates of return on investment are the norm for such enterprises, their managers can incur unnecessary costs without jeopardizing their future as long as stockholders continue to do better than they could expect to do elsewhere. Similarly, in an economy undergoing rapid growth, the replacement of efficient social practices with inefficient ones might go undetected if people on average experience improvements in their economic situations.

This can be summarized by means of the prisoner's dilemma. Let table 5.1 represent the initial situation facing a representative agent. Suppose that she, like everyone else, can either refrain from influencing the preferences of others (don't) or engage in preference influencing behavior (do). Let the columns represent similar decisions made by "everyone else," and the numbers in the box represent the single agent's utility levels.[3] The numbers that are shown suggest the potential for a prisoner's dilemma. Regardless of what "everyone else" does, the agent is clearly better off if she seeks to influence others' preferences. If everyone else is refraining from such activity, the agent can realize a payoff of four rather than the payoff of three she would experience were she to refrain. If everyone else is instead engaging in such activity, she can realize a payoff of two by doing likewise, but a payoff of just one if she does not. Though the rational choice model in its simplest form leads to the prediction that "do" will be the dominant strategy, the evidence is strong that societies often manage to avoid such "destructive rationality."[4] The payoff in the upper left cell in table 5.1 is underlined, on the assumption that customs exist that inhibit the temptation to push one's product. The representative agent, as well as everyone else, has succeeded, I am suggesting, in avoiding the prisoner's dilemma.

In table 5.2 appears the same dilemma, the only difference being that payoff amounts have doubled. Let this table pertain to a later time historically when real economic growth has occurred. Suppose that the norms restricting preference manipulation have eroded and that for the single agent shown, and for everyone else as well, the rationales for stifling the urge to persuade others to purchase one's product have eroded. All would now be engaging in persuasive efforts, and each as a consequence would have a payoff of four (the underlined entry) rather than the six that would be possible were restraints still in place. If the agents were to have tables 5.1 and 5.2 in front of them, they could clearly see that they would have been better off if they had all agreed to refrain. But this information would not, of course, be available. What the agents *would* be aware of is that over the historical period in question (1) they had become economically better off, moving from a payoff of three to a payoff of four, and (2) they had all instituted more competitive practices. Clearly, it would be difficult to have seen that these practices had actually been harmful. Moreover, by the

TABLE 5.1.

		Everyone Else	
		Do Not Influence Others' Preferences	Influence Others' Preferences
Agent	Don't	<u>3</u>	1
	Do	4	2

propensity to reason *post hoc ergo propter hoc* there would be the very real possibility that some of the gain in economic well-being would be attributed to the adoption of these destructively competitive practices.

This has been a highly stylized account, and whether or not it applies to the real economy within the United States is a question that only historians could answer. It has been offered as a reminder that the introduction and spread of inefficient practices is a very real possibility. Pangloss to the contrary notwithstanding, overall growth can disguise inefficiencies that might be more easily spotted in an economy not undergoing an overall rise in its level of prosperity.

The Market's Advance

There can be little doubt that social practices have always existed that have served to help agents in their preference-shaping efforts. Across cultures and across time, personal relationships have typically been such that one has felt no obligation to give to others that which, if given the opportunity, they might be most likely to select for themselves. Thus, anyone cooking for a friend with a weight problem might plan the event while keeping in mind the friend's preference to prefer less food. Addictive snacks might be ruled out, as might be particularly tempting desserts. Actors in the market, in contrast, would take the overweight person's expressed preference for these things as sufficient reason to provide them.

This is not to say that *only* nonmarket interactions are sensitive to second-order preferences. As Margaret Radin argues, even instances in which the market prevails as the main distributive mechanism, nonmarket relationships between seller and buyer have been known to "interfere" with pure market outcomes (1996, chap. 7). A bartender may tell a heavy drinker that he's had enough, sometimes because the law requires such a warning, but sometimes because the bartender is a friend of the heavy drinker and is, for his friend's sake, refusing to meet his demands. Simi-

TABLE 5.2.

		Everyone Else	
		Do Not Influence Others' Preferences	Influence Others' Preferences
Agent	Don't	6	2
	Do	8	<u>4</u>

larly, an art dealer may discourage a potential purchase of a painting, not with any long-term financial gain in mind but with an aesthetic sense that overrides her business sense. But even while recognizing that markets do not logically require the neglect of second-order preferences, their advance has likely contributed to such neglect. And several trends stand out.

The Demise of Production for Self

The market's crowding out of "production for self" has a long history. Consider a hypothetical eighty-year-old urbanite who spent her first years on a farm. Such a person likely witnessed the market's role in her own food provisioning rise in several distinct steps. In the 1920s, production for self may have dominated virtually every stage of the process, as food grown on the family farm provided full sustenance. Forced off the farm during the turbulent 1930s, her family would have become more reliant on the market, but the initial reliance would have likely been limited in scope. The legacy of production for self as well as a still limited selection of prepared foods might have resulted in her family's choosing to purchase basic ingredients that they would have then "worked on" until a finished meal resulted. By the end of World War II, establishing her own household, the woman would have begun a new shift from the purchase of raw ingredients to the purchase of prepared foods as technological changes gave markets an ever widening role in the food preparation process. And by the 1990s, long retired, our hypothetical person might be enjoying her share of the "restaurant revolution" that has been in process for at least twenty years in the United States. No work time whatsoever is required of the restaurant diner, as the "renting of cooks" fills in for one's own time in the kitchen.

While it may be difficult to isolate other products for which such a clear step-by-step procedure away from production for self and toward the market has prevailed, it is not difficult to come up with other similar shifts. The purchase of finished articles of clothing has replaced the purchase of raw materials, marketed entertainment has replaced "self-produced" entertainment, and, perhaps most strikingly, purchased transportation (trains, autos, planes) has replaced self-produced transportation (walking). The very nature of economic advance has brought with it ever greater reliance on the market.

Government's Retreat

A second force, of more recent origin, is the retreat in governmental efforts to alter market outcomes. The claim that government has fallen in *popularity* within the United States over the last three decades is hard to contest, but it does not necessarily follow that this fall in popularity has been translated into action. If measured by government expenditures, however, the decline in relative size is very real. Federal expenditures have hovered between 20.0 and 23.6 percent of annual GDP since the mid-1970s, reaching their minimum level of 20.0 percent in 1998 (*Economic Report* 1998, 374, table B-79). When it is considered that transfer payments have been on the rise as the Social Security program matures, the drop is more striking still. Netting out all transfer payments, and adding in state and local governmental purchases, between 1960 and 1992 total government purchases ranged from a low of 19.8 percent of GDP to a high of 23.8. Since Clinton's first year in office (1993) the figure has fallen below this range and dropped all the way to 17.5 percent by 1998.[5]

To allow these figures to stand as sufficient evidence that government is indeed "shrinking" might rightly meet with some disagreement. For such a conclusion would rest on the assumption that government purchases stand as an accurate reflection of government economic presence, and this would be a mistake. At the introductory level, students are often taught that the economic functions of government can be usefully divided into five categories: (1) monetary transfers to entitled parties, (2) provision of public goods, (3) maintenance of competition within industries, (4) correction for spillover effects, and (5) stabilization of the macroeconomy.

The categories that involve by far the greatest expenditures are the first two, and it is noteworthy that the rising dominance of markets has likely had less effect on these than on the latter three categories. When it comes to monetary transfers, there is no obvious tension between the belief that markets are highly efficient and the belief that government ought to act to alleviate the inequalities that it creates. While welfare payments to the poor may have declined during the last two decades, the much larger transfer payment program, Social Security, has not budged.

When it comes to the second category, the provisioning of public goods, it is tempting to assume that the still flourishing "privatization" efforts are lessening this sort of spending. But to "privatize" does not usually mean substituting private spending for public spending. It means substituting private employees for public employees while still having government do the purchasing with the tax dollars it receives. If as dollar-efficient as advocates of privatization maintain, such shifts might lower taxes slightly but do not at all lessen the need for governments to do the purchasing and for tax dollars to finance such purchases. All that would have changed is that government would now be more apt to pay private firms than to pay government workers.

It is the latter three categories listed (maintenance of competition, correction for spillovers, and macroeconomic stabilization) that have been most affected by the rise in the stature of markets, and since none of these are particularly costly, their decline has not resulted in any dramatic spending reductions. To "deregulate" has sometimes been recommended as a means by which to put the unemployed back to work,[6] and sometimes as a means of allowing efficient firms to flourish without the fear of antitrust action. More often, however, the deregulation that has been under way since the 1970s in the United States has consisted in the easing of regulations originally enacted to correct for potential spillovers. It needs to be emphasized that the arguments for such deregulation have been nuanced and sophisticated, with the point usually being that spillover costs, though regrettable, are not something that governmental actions can be expected to correct. But at the wider societal level the economist's retreat from the advocacy of regulation has been a likely contributor to the greater acceptance of market outcomes and to a vision less inclined than previously to notice weaknesses.[7] And the desire to deregulate has been as real among the Clinton Democrats as it has long been among the Republicans. Early in a recent *Economic Report of the President,* the point was made that "[t]he administration is . . . committed to reducing the burden of government regulation and ensuring that the benefits of new regulations justify their costs" (1998, 24). By an historical untimeliness, the failure in the market's ability to shape tastes, an externalities phenomenon par excellence, is attracting attention at precisely the time that efforts to correct for externalities are in retreat.

An Eroding Time Buffer

This now brings us to a third long-term trend, implied by the first trend already discussed (production for sale replaces production for self). As greater reliance has been placed on the market, the time separating an agent's binding decision about future consumption from the consumption activity itself has shortened. And as David Hume observed over two centuries ago, humans "are always much inclin'd to prefer present interest to distant and remote" and it is not easy "for them to resist the temptation of any advantage that they may immediately enjoy" (qtd. in Lasch 1991, 58).

To be sure, there was an "immediacy" in the situation facing the hunters and gatherers who occupied the globe for many millennia prior to the relatively recent dawn of agriculturalism. But facing the severe constraints that they did, such earlier peoples did not have the luxury of seeking to alter their preferences. The early hunter who sighted a deer that he proceeded to kill not only preferred the deer but had better prefer this preference as well. Any other first-order preference would have resulted in severe hunger if not starvation.

With the rise of agriculture, it is debatable how long it took for material living standards to rise at all significantly. It is not debatable, however, that a separation emerged between one's consumption planning and the consumption itself. To elect to plant this type of seed rather than this other was to place a clear restriction on what could be reaped and consumed several months later. With specialization and trade, however, one's "productive" decisions placed constraints on future purchasing power without restricting to the same degree the nature of what one might ultimately consume. Such consumption choices were only binding when the time came to spend one's earnings.

Two points deserve brief emphasis. First, it is not logically necessary that one is made better off by separating the time between purchase decision and consumption. For example, a compulsive person may benefit from decreasing this interval. The casual evidence does seem to suggest, however, that a lessening of time between purchase and consumption more often leads to worse preferences than better. Second, that there has been a rise in personal discontent following the rising propensity to shop is at least partly evidenced by the fact only in the latest edition of the manual of psychiatric disorders (*The Diagnostic and Statistical Manual*) has compulsive shopping been officially recognized as an illness (Twitchell 1999, 251). While it is tempting to attribute this development to the rise in advertising and marketing, this explanation overlooks the fact that sellers of capital goods as well as financial institutions can advertise and market just as readily as can sellers of consumer goods. What sets consumer goods apart is that to decrease the time between decision and consumption is to decrease the time between decision and the attainment of well-being contingent on the decision. In contrast to this, a spontaneous decision to invest, as opposed to a decision a day in advance of the literal act of investing, hardly affects at all the relative closeness of the well-being contingent on the decision. In either case, the payoff remains far in the future.

Political Redefinitions?

While it may indeed be the third trend's effect on preferences that is most difficult to assess normatively, it is the trend considered second—the retreat of government—that stands apart from the others when viewed from a different perspective. Changing relative costs more than changing beliefs can explain the rise of markets and the shortening of time between consumption decision and actual consumption. In contrast to this shift, the more recent retreat of government's oversight role has had much to do with changing beliefs about government's overall responsibilities, beliefs that are greatly influenced by a voter's broad vision of what is in the overall social good.[8]

Table 5.3 situates certain groups in relation to where they tend to be on matters of freedom in the economic sphere and freedom in the noneconomic sphere of life. While rather abstract, this way of differentiating American political groupings provides a useful means of summarizing certain contemporary positions. The appropriateness of locating a group within a particular box is historically contingent and would only make sense as long as the group's ideals fail to take hold. Conservatives, for example, would only advocate "more" economic freedom for as long as there was less freedom than they favored. But it is a reasonable generalization to see the groups named in the table as remaining in the cell in which they appear at least since the Great Depression.

In the lower left cell are located traditional conservatives. Those fitting this description have, without question, advocated less social control of the economy since at least the time of Roosevelt's New Deal. Suggestions for such "decontrol" come in many guises; lessening of existing regulation, opposition to new proposed regulation, easing of antitrust efforts, and discouraging of unionization efforts, to name just a few. Achievement of any of these goals works toward the fulfillment of the most sought after goal of all, lower tax rates. In further describing such traditional conservatives as also advocating *more* social control in the noneconomic realm I am not suggesting that they have necessarily favored a more active *government* in this sphere of life. Such a conservative might wish to see minors kept on shorter leashes, adults less inclined to engage in extramarital sex, and neighbors resisting the temptation to party loudly late into the night, but would be inclined to advocate reliance on the family and on informal social censure to accomplish these ends.[9]

Located in the upper right cell are the traditional liberals. To describe this group as advocating more social control in the economic sphere is only to say that pure laissez-faire has been judged undesirable and that the

TABLE 5.3.

		Noneconomic Affairs	
		More Social Control	Less Social Control
Economic Affairs	More Social Control	Communists Traditional Catholics	Traditional American liberals
	Less Social Control	Traditional American conservatives	Anarchists Libertarians

degree of governmental involvement in economic affairs is usually judged as insufficient. It is negative freedom that such liberals seek to limit, a type of freedom that has long been central to the conservative economic vision. The liberal advocacy of *more* freedom in the noneconomic realm has had a different legacy than their economic positions. It remains, however, as valid a generalization of traditional liberals today as of their forebears in the 1930s. The heavy hand of the state has been viewed as something worth removing in some instances, with abortion and sexual practices being the most encountered examples. The equally heavy hand of tradition is as frequently isolated as the culprit in need of exorcism—traditions that might make a woman feel duty-bound to remain within the home or that might inhibit behaviors that should, according to the liberal viewpoint, remain strictly personal matters.

The entries in the upper left box comprise an odd grouping, and this should serve as a warning of the very abstract nature of this classification. To say that communists and traditional Catholics[10] would be in agreement on the surrender of personal liberty in both the economic and noneconomic spheres says nothing about the means by which they would advocate that their suggestions be realized and nothing about what authorities they believe should enforce the surrender of liberties. Besides sharing a belief that individual freedom is excessive, however, these groups share a lack of popular support within the United States. While this is obvious in the case of the communists, it is less so in the case of traditional Catholicism, but it is a valid generalization to say that the Vatican's economic liberalism and social conservatism does not enjoy wide acceptance among American Catholics. According to Michael Cuneo, for many American Catholics the trend has been toward economic conservatism since the onset of the Cold War and thus a general drift toward the lower left box.[11] That there has also been a drift toward the two boxes on the right is also apparent. Between 1987 and 1997, the percentage of American Catholics agreeing that "one can be a good Catholic without obeying the church hierarchy's teaching on birth control" rose from 66 to 72, while the percentage agreeing that "one can be a good Catholic without obeying the church hierarchy's teaching regarding abortion" rose from 39 to 53 (D'Antonio 1999, 12).

Finally, in the lower right box appear anarchists and libertarians. The former of these has never gained a serious base of support in the United States, while the latter has. Indeed, of all third parties with a well-articulated political philosophy it is the libertarians who have most influenced public debate and social policy in the United States over the last quarter century.[12] And even while remaining marginal when judged by party membership, libertarians have exerted a strong influence on traditional conservatives and traditional liberals alike, a point stressed by Christopher Lasch:

The political alignments of the seventies and eighties indicated that a defense of values loosely identified with the counterculture was quite compatible with a defense of business and the free market. Neoliberals declared themselves probusiness at the same time that they endorsed the sexual revolution, championed gay rights and women's rights, opposed the death penalty, and applauded the Supreme Court's decision in *Roe v. Wade.* The free-market element in the Reagan coalition displayed much the same pattern of economic conservatism and cultural liberalism.[13]

Postmodernism is currently used to describe a bewildering range of viewpoints and sensibilities.[14] There is, however, one component of a postmodern perspective that gives a richer sense of the shifts in liberal thinking. As judged by Terry Eagleton, the postmodernism that he observed in his native England "flirts with the naive libertarian belief that power, systems, laws, consensus, and normativity are themselves unequivocally negative" (1996, 56). In his view "its idea of freedom is often enough the 'negative' conception of it espoused by classical liberalism" (42), leading to "dreams of a human subject set free from constraint, gliding deliriously from one position to another" (28–29). This description fits well with the predictions made two decades before by the American sociologist Daniel Bell. Far from serving as an antidote to capitalism's "logical contradictions" that he had described just a few years before, Bell viewed this spreading sensibility as a regrettable carrying forth of "the logic of modernism to its farthest reaches" (1980, 51), where "reason is the enemy and the desires of the body the truth" (288). And the still burgeoning information revolution has only served to strengthen the popular appeal of this sensibility. Jedidiah Purdy notes a new brand of libertarianism captured by the magazine of high-tech sophisticates—*Wired*—that "exchanges the gray woolens of conventional, economically minded libertarianism for the shimmering colors and romantic rhetoric of a technologically enhanced Friedrich Nietzsche. The magazine heralds a nascent political culture, a Nietzschean libertarianism" (1998, 86).

A recurrent theme that appears in writings on the psychological particularities of the postmodern age is the "dissolution of the self." As Calvin O. Schrag has put it,

> Questions about self-identity, the unity of consciousness, and centralized and goal-directed activity have been displaced in the aftermath of the dissolution of the subject. If one cannot rid oneself of the vocabulary of self, subject and mind, the most that can be asserted is that the

self is multiplicity, heterogeneity, difference, and ceaseless becoming, bereft of origin and purpose. (1997, 8)

Postmodernists might accept this description while rejecting Schrag's critical evaluation of it. The psychologist Kenneth Gergen, for example, traces the conflict facing modern humanity to the dramatic rise of human contacts we each have. Following from such a rise in contacts is an increase in the desires and wants that the postmodern person experiences, but more significantly, a rising probability that one will experience conflict over what one desires (Gergen 1991, chap. 3).

Missing from the Gergen account is any consideration of the role that the spreading power of the market has had in what he describes. But more seriously, nowhere does he consider the possibility that there might be a unified agent that is able to evaluate its preferences. Gergen's recommendations have nothing to do with shaping one's preferences. Rather, one following his advice would learn to be at peace with having "different selves." By this account, for one to wish to gamble large sums when embedded in one cultural setting while at the same time deploring gambling when in another need not present the problem that it long has. To decenter oneself is to become many selves, none of which gets in the way of the others. Much as Daniel Bell anticipated, immediate desires appear to have been accorded a more respectable status. By the postmodern account, it is more difficult for a person to feel in a position to criticize her tastes, as such "self-criticism" becomes conceptually problematic. With second-order preferences not considered, it is never *oneself* criticizing one's desires, but just some busybody contending self.[15]

From this follows a postmodernist response to critics of the commercial realm that reflects what has been described as "the odd alliance in defence of the market and consumer culture between the New Right and the post-modern left" (O'Neill 1998, 95). Jim Collins well represents this postmodern position: "The commodity status of both popular and Post-Modernist texts appears to be their "original sin" according to [some], that which makes them inferior works of art, somehow tainted by the filthy lucre one must pay in order to appreciate them" (1989, 124). It is "patronage" such as was enjoyed by artists of centuries past that Collins offers as the alternative. And while such patronage is represented as a vehicle by which the elites alone exercise influence over production, the market is held up as a truly democratizing alternative that offers such artistic influence to all wishing to exercise their purchasing power. The postmodern proclivity to defend the popular culture as reflected in market forces thus fails to consider whether the market properly speaks for the public that it serves, and fails to consider whether the public expressing itself politically would opt for a different sort of cultural product than their market decisions reveal them to prefer.[16]

The use of postmodernist ideas by economists has been primarily within the "rhetoric and economics" movement (see, in particular, McCloskey 1985), which by one account has "invested so heavily in the *techne* of persuasion that [it] rarely ask[s] what it means to exist in a condition of having been persuaded" (McGee 1985, 14, qtd. in Schrag 1997, 137). Kevin Quinn and Tina R. Green (1998) suggest that this avoidance of the subjective partly explains why the rhetorical movement within economics has not come to be associated with any particular position regarding the market. By one early account, hermeneutics is good conversation in which each conversant is obligated to bring the listener as close as possible to what was being communicated without "taking in" the other (Booth 1974). For later commentators, in contrast, there were no restrictions placed on what might be said other than that no claims be made that could be shown to be falsifications. In a sense, the focus on rhetoric has coincided with and possibly further legitimized uncontrolled preference shaping, as the persuasive efforts of advertising are being conflated with "good conversation." Absent any sensitivity to second-order preferences, to convince the other to purchase one's product occupies the same rhetorical position as does arguing a political stance that represents one's disinterested belief.

While postmodernism has been strongest within the academic humanities, it has had some influence within the social sciences, including economics. It is tempting to locate the "multiple selves" theorists within this tradition, especially when account is taken of my earlier argument that the multiple-selves models are deficient precisely because they preclude normative assessment of internal conflict. This overlap may be something of a coincidence, however, and by chance certain economic theorists may have crossed paths with postmodernists despite having overall worldviews that are not very similar.

In the chapters that remain, a closer look will be taken at particular spheres in which I will be arguing the formation of unpreferred preferences has been intensifying in recent years. The different causes for the intensification of the mismatch between first-order and second-order preferences that have been the focus of this chapter will figure differently in the cases considered. Having ended this chapter with a consideration of postmodernism, it will be useful to turn first to a realm where its influence has been most notable, namely, that of entertainment.

CHAPTER 6

The Critic's Retreat

Cultural critic Michael Lewis recently noted with dismay a trend that has been under way for at least the past decade. According to Lewis, the critic's assessment of books, movies, and live performances has been losing ground to a formidable rival, one that fits more comfortably with our market-centered society.[1] It is popular opinion that has come to matter more, as usually measured in units purchased or dollars spent. As a critic himself, one might suspect that Lewis has something of a bias in evaluating this trend, but he is not alone in his expression of concern.

According to William Leach, "The brokering style—repressing one's own convictions and withholding judgments in the interest of forging profitable relationships" has been ascendant for a century and represents a defining feature of market-dominated economies (1993, 11). If the evidence suggests that the injection of a little more violence into a movie will benefit sales, then a movie director with a brokering style would not hesitate to make such an injection. Similarly, if the evidence suggests that ambiguous movie conclusions spell bad box office, such a director would not hesitate to substitute a happy ending even if he believed that this does not do full justice to the writer's intent. As communications theorist Robert W. McChesney has commented, "There is little incentive in the system to *develop* public taste over time."[2] And the phenomenon is not limited to the media. A similar consumer sensitivity might be expected, for example, of the restaurant owner who adopts a brokering style. Were the evidence to suggest that an unoriginal menu would do more to attract customers than a menu reflecting the standards that such an owner herself believed in, she would not be at all hesitant to let the former prevail.

It is tempting for anyone troubled by this "brokering" mentality to claim the moral high ground and treat these developments as instances of monetary greed trumping other criteria of worth. But this would be a mistake. The brokering style is not inherently amoral, and the shift from expert opinion to gross sales as the measure of worth is not inherently inconsistent with a concern for others and a desire to do what is right. For the broker's habit of not allowing her own values to influence what she offers might be best understood as reflecting a contemporary ethical belief that sellers should not dictate to potential consumers what they ought to have but should instead offer whatever it is they "most want."[3] The problem is that this contemporary moral belief is oblivious to second-order preferences. And while an expert critic would rarely be expected to be moved by an unpreferred preference when offering a review of a movie or a restaurant, the clientele for food and entertainment often are. Indeed, entertainment and eating are likely the two spheres of life where personal dissatisfaction with one's choice is most frequently expressed.

The Television Wars

Perhaps nowhere is the "brokering style" as strong as in the fiercely competitive television industry, where ratings serve as the broadcaster's main (if not exclusive) criterion for success.[4] Whether or not there is a serious mismatch between first-order and second-order preferences depends upon how the customer is defined. If monetary exchange is treated as the sine qua non of a market relationship, then the problem would have to be described as minimal or nonexistent. For the buyer by this interpretation would be the advertiser, and as with any purchase by producers, no mismatch would be likely. Companies prefer advertising their products and are in all likelihood perfectly content with their preferences.[5] But it is of course the viewer who we usually regard as the "customer," with payment being not in money but in time spent watching commercial messages.[6]

Probably the most often expressed discontent about viewing choices consists of one person—usually an adult—being unhappy about the viewing habits of another—usually a child. It is possible to treat this as a conflict between a first-order and a second-order preference, but this would be a different sort of conflict. The parent would have a second-order preference not over her own potential rankings but over those of her child. She would prefer, let us say, that Johnny, not she, prefer watching one hour of television rather than four.[7] Except for a deregulatory extremist, objections would not be made to the claim that society has a stake in regulating television for the sake of minors. It is much harder, however, to offer credible complaints about what is offered in those contexts where protection of children is not the issue. This is not to say that no attempts are ever made. Some have taken the quality of the programming aimed at adult audiences to be symptomatic of the "dumbing down" of American culture. But for such critics the problem is traced not to the inherent workings of the market but to much broader social forces.[8]

Several other criticisms have located the problem within the industry itself. There is, for example, the argument offered by media critic George Gerbner that violence in television is common because it sells in global markets, not because that is what maximizes American viewership.[9] Then there is the argument that less desired shows prevail because these happen to be the ones that succeed in turning viewers into purchasers of products. By this interpretation, the better, genuinely preferred shows would so captivate viewers that they would become insufficiently attentive to the advertising message. As still another explanation, there is the occasionally heard but increasingly less relevant claim that it is the oligopolistic nature of television that is the problem. One subscribing to this explanation would see insufficient competition as the problem and would believe better shows that would be watched more frequently would follow from an increase in competitive pressures. Finally, cost consciousness is sometimes suggested to be the problem, as the most-wanted shows are reasoned to be too expensive to be profitable for the broadcasting networks to provide.[10]

Each of these explanations for the perpetuation of unwanted shows are attempts to understand why people's stated preferences, when polled, appear not to be reflected by what is offered. And each clearly assumes that any superior menu of shows would elicit greater viewership. Such an assumption, however, does not square well with the model presented in chapter 3. Whether output of a particular good would rise or fall following full enforceability of property rights in one's preferences depends on the nature of the particular good. Rare is the person who believes that she is consuming too much lettuce. If in the present-day economy the mere presence of lettuce influences preferences or if the efforts of lettuce growers to market their product influences preferences, we would have a case where sellers are not being properly compensated for a beneficial preference change that they are creating. Following a new definition of property rights that allows compensation to the instigator of such favorable changes, costs would fall for suppliers, and the equilibrium quantity of the product, lettuce in the present case, would rise. For the sellers of cigarettes it is obvious that the opposite holds. The preferences created by these sellers are most often worse than what they replace, and if sellers had to pay compensation for the unfavorable shifts that they cause, the equilibrium quantity of cigarettes would fall.

Casual evidence strongly suggests that television has more in common with cigarettes than lettuce, at least as regards preference ideals.[11] The actions of broadcasters appear to often create desires to watch what some of the viewers would rather be without. It is much harder to think of cases where the reverse is true and where the broadcasters are creating improved preferences without being compensated. Full property rights in preferences (or less formal social institutions that respect second-order preferences) would in all likelihood give rise to less, not more, television watching.

The failure to appreciate this has allowed those defending the current system to dismiss reformists' claims by pointing to the fact that better shows simply "don't sell." Consider, for example, the observation of one television critic: "Despite cries from community groups everywhere for less violence on TV news, none of the dozen or so stations that promoted the new policy in 1994 saw ratings increase" (Seplow 1996, A1). Or consider another critic's posing the question of whether the networks ought to continue to offer what they do or "heed those who keep insisting, despite contrary evidence from the Nielsens, that there is a national consensus for tranquil TV?" (Rosenberg 1997, C8). Clearly, nothing is allowed to speak for an individual but her post facto response to a show's availability.

This becomes particularly clear in the attempt of Bill Baumann—a station general manager in Florida—to clean up the local news program by de-emphasizing the omnipresent coverage of crime (Winerip 1998). All parties to the struggle that ensued shared the belief that size of viewership ought to serve as the criterion for evaluating any changes that were made. The news director at a competing station was unimpressed with the proposed reforms, reasoning, "Crime is what the audience wants," and rhetorically asking, "Who am I to second-guess the audience" (qtd. in Winerip 1998, 32). Baumann, in contrast, was described as believing that "TV news is so crime-laden that a lot of viewers find it ridiculous and turn it off" (Winerip 1998, 35). The possibility that a different sort of news show might generate preferred preferences that involved *less* watching was completely outside the discussion. The lead-in to the article cited the viewers as the biggest obstacle to attempts to take the high road, and readers were left with the impression that Baumann was, to say the least, tilting at windmills.

"Delayed Broadcasts": Public Television

If my reasoning is accepted, it places public television in the United States in a rather different light. The quality of the offerings of public television relative to the competition is a source of pride for these stations and emphasized during their fund-raising drives. This is at the same time, however, a source of some embarrassment. For public television has often been criticized as "elitist," with the relatively small audiences and the subject matter itself being offered as evidence in support of such a description.[12] Even those who don't believe "elitist" is inherently objectionable are inclined to agree that public television has been captured by the relatively better educated and higher-income segments of the population, and that the major portion of the population that has not attended college is pretty much ignored.

I will not argue for or against this general position but will consider an interesting implication that follows from the introduction of second-order preferences to the discussion. Regardless of whether those with the responsibility to select material for public television are sensitive to public opinion via the ballot box or via private donations, there is one very significant difference that sets public television apart from its rivals. A great deal of time separates the expression of a preference regarding what will fill a particular time slot from the actual presentation of the show. And as noted in the last chapter, this suggests that the preference moving an agent to act is more likely to be a preference that he prefers. Moreover, this paradoxically suggests less time spent viewing rather than more. Contributors to PBS, for example, might reveal a strong preference for, say, a documentary show when actual consumption lies in the future. That is, assurance that this particular show will occupy the Thursday 9:00 P.M. time slot over the next year might be noted to result in more call-in contributions than would something more along the lines of what commercial networks offer. But with consumption still far off, the preference that moves an agent to act is more likely to be a preference that is preferred by the agent.

For commercial television, in contrast, preferences are expressed at the very time that the show is "consumed." While one can easily discover what will be airing a week or even a month in advance, there is no convenient basis for precommitting. There is thus a greater chance that the preference revealed will be a less preferred preference, and as discussed earlier, such a preference would be likely to carry with it more, rather than less, watching. The familiar duo, sex and violence, "sell" in the sense that they can grab the attention of the channel surfer. The very same person who might have donated money to PBS because of what it promised to offer, might register a consumer "vote" for a network or cable show more adept at creating preferences to watch on short notice. If my account is correct, characterizing public television in the United States as serving a small elite while the rest of the population opts for commercial television might contain a grain of truth but would be obscuring a more interesting possibility. PBS might serve people in a way that responds to preferred preferences that happen to carry less time "glued to the tube."

The Demise of "Delayed Eating": The Rise of the Restaurant

It may appear that the "public" nature of PBS is critical to the above analysis, and that the problem with commercial television derives from its profit-maximizing orientation. This conclusion would be not quite accurate. Inefficiency in the shaping of tastes has much more to do with the spread of market mechanisms than with the spread of private ownership. And with the spread of market mechanisms the time between one's consumption decision and one's actual consumption tends to diminish. In recent years, food provides one more interesting example. A feature distinguishing eating in from eating out bears a striking similarity to a feature distinguishing public from commercial television. For each of the former (eating in and public television) a fair amount of time separates the expression of a preference from the consumption activity itself. For each of the latter (eating out and commercial television) the separation in time is considerably reduced. There are, of course, striking differences as well.

First, television broadcasting can be differentiated by the locus of ownership (public versus private), while *both* sorts of food provisioning have long been strictly private (supermarkets as well as restaurants). Both public television and eating in, however, are less thoroughly "in the market" than are their counterparts. In the case of public television it is government that provides an immediate sense of a clear difference, but as just noted above, it is really the delay between one's decision as to what show to support and the actual time that this show airs that is significant. In the case of food consumption, a similar lag occurs, as one's decision to eat at home separates market decision from consumption itself.

Second, with food consumption complications of class are less likely to complicate the analysis. Food stores come in many varieties, as do restaurants. A shift away from cooking at home and into restaurants is just as true for a higher-income person substituting trendy restaurants for gourmet food stores as it is for a lower-income person substituting fast-food restaurants for discount supermarkets. And that there has been a general trend in this direction there can be little doubt. Restaurant spending comprised 20 percent of food spending in 1960 compared with 40 percent by 1996.[13] Between 1984 and 1994 sales of food away from home increased at an annual 2.5 percent inflation-adjusted rate compared with just a 0.4 percent annual real rise in sales of food destined for home consumption (Price 1996, 30). Differences between the quality of home-cooked food and restaurant food is much harder to generalize about, but there is one anomalous trend that seems consistent with this shift.

It has been reported that average weight in the United States is rising, as are cases of obesity. This trend attracted media attention primarily because it ran counter to the expressed determination of so many Americans to maintain healthy weight. The shift out of home cooking and into restaurants can shed some light on this trend. As researchers for the U.S. Department of Agriculture noted, "The increased popularity of dining out presents a barrier for Americans to continue improving their diets," as "food purchased away from home generally contains more of the nutrients overconsumed and less of the nutrients underconsumed by Americans" (qtd. in Fernandez 1998, A20).

Statements such as these are often dismissed by economists because of their paternalistic tone. For those in the health sciences, the mere fact that health suffers serves as sufficient evidence of a "problem," while for economists the sacrifice of some health is more often treated as just a nonmonetary cost rationally factored into whatever decision agents make. But with second-order preferences brought into the analysis, the possibility of a problem becomes clear. When in a restaurant, one's purchase decision is soon followed by the food itself, unlike what is true when one buys packaged food. It follows that when one eats out, there is an increased likelihood that one will be in the grip of an unpreferred preference to eat fattening foods than would have been true if one had bought the ingredients for that meal days prior.

But what if it were necessary to order restaurant meals one week in advance of actual consumption? And what if orders were placed with a full understanding that they were binding and that no substitutions were possible when the time to enjoy the meal actually arrived? How would eating habits change? For many people, I would suggest, lower calories would follow. And this would be a welfare improvement if these agents had second-order preferences to prefer this and if the precommitment indeed resulted in first-order preferences being shaped accordingly.

While nothing quite like this has emerged on the market, there are related sorts of precommitment food ordering strategies that have. A year ago I decided something had to be done about my steadily rising weight. I went to a weight reduction clinic and managed, over a six-month period, to reach my goal of shedding twenty pounds. Each week I would meet with a counselor who would go over a standardized menu for the week to follow, a menu including both foods purchased directly from the weight-loss company and foods purchased at any food market. After the planning and brief pep talk there would be the weekly weigh-in to see if the goal of a one- to two-pound weekly weight loss was being achieved.

What stands out about the plan is the tight structure for precommitment that it provided. Weekly trips to the supermarket, it will be recalled, permit better shaping of future tastes than do restaurant visits. The process is simply taken further with this particular weight-reduction center. One's weekly decision is witnessed by another, *all* discretion for the week is given up, and one must answer to a counselor at week's end. In my own case, the taste shifts were striking. Not only did I announce that I was not going to stray beyond the week's menu, but conforming to this menu was much more pleasurable than it might have been had no one been "watching."[14]

Despite wanting to inform potential clients of its success as a weight-loss technique, the company's official pronouncements did not like to note that it *freed* people from choice and by so doing shaped them as they wished to be shaped. Instead of presenting itself as an antidote to too much "freedom to choose," the program seemed to present itself as a vehicle for making more intelligent food choices. The problem facing the dieter, in short, was presented as a problem of insufficient information, not unpreferred preferences. A brochure thus claimed that healthful restaurant eating is, "like everything else, . . . a matter of awareness—learning how and what to order," and so the organization's founder herself announced that "healthy weight management is . . . about making smart choices for yourself." Even an organization that appeared to specialize in the successful molding of tastes felt the need to rely on the dominant rhetoric of informed choice in communicating what it had to offer.

One practice in particular stands out as anomalous if a client's fees are to be understood as simply compensation for counseling and "information" provided (food charges are separate). At the initial visit I elected to become a "lifetime member," a status that would allow me to attend sessions, visit counselors, and purchase the center's food for as long as I might wish. The stated fee was $350, half of which would be refunded if I managed to be at my stated weight goal one year after first attaining it. There appear to be both psychological and legal reasons for this particular way of packaging the weight-loss incentive. As stated, a reward is being offered to those clients who succeed in meeting their goals. But what if the stated fee for joining had instead been $175 with the proviso that the client would have to pay an additional $175 should she fail to reach her goal? In one sense this represents a better deal for the client. For now she would have access to the $175 that is instead, under the present system, held by the weight-loss company. Despite this clear advantage, however, something about this alternative way of "packaging" the arrangement makes it seem unfair.[15] For if she *fails* to achieve what she intended, the client is being asked to pay twice what she otherwise would. Clearly, in other spheres the procedure is precisely the opposite. One gets money back not if one is satisfied with the one's purchase but if it *fails* to perform as advertised![16]

This can only begin to make sense if it is "changed preferences" more than "information" that one is purchasing, and if one way to increase the likelihood of having the preference change is by hiring someone to enforce a peculiar sort of "one-way contract." This weight reduction company stood ready to collect $175 from me if I failed to reach my stated goal. This, I can say firsthand, has exerted a favorable influence on my eating habits. With weight gain more expensive than it was previously, I am in possession of a preferred preference, namely, a preference to keep my weight down.

Summary

The focus in this chapter has been on two particular spheres of human activity, eating and television watching, for which the problem of unpreferred preferences has been a growing one. Two forces have been isolated as the cause of this development. One of these, the lessening of time between choice of what to eat or what to watch and the act of eating or watching itself, has been primarily the result of changes having more to do with technological change than with changing social institutions. The other, the increasing reliance on box office and decreasing reliance on expert opinion as a means for both buyers and sellers to make evaluations, has been more the result of the populism that has come to characterize the contemporary market economy. The consequence of these separate forces has been the increased occurrence of unpreferred preferences. In the chapter ahead, the focus will shift to a sphere of life that, though still remaining apart from the market in many respects, shares with market activities a rising neglect of second-order preferences. In the sexual realm, preferences matter more than ever, but second-order preferences do not.

CHAPTER 7

Sexual Choices: The First Order's Rise and the Second Order's Fall

With the exception of the political scientists, economists have not been as inclined as other social scientists to bring sexual behavior into their discussions. This is in part due to the abstract nature of the subject that makes us more inclined to speak of "good x" and "good y" than to lower the level of abstraction and allow potatoes, airline tickets, or sexual activity to serve by way of example. It is also true that activities associated with human intimacy have remained more resistant to the market's lure than have most other activities. To take just one example, the explicit view of marriage as a financial transaction has actually been in retreat in much of the world, and probably more now than in the past it is unacceptable to announce that financial prospects played a major role in one's marital decision. And, marriage aside, though "sex for sale" has taken some curious new turns, there are few indications of any rise in the percentage of income being used to procure sexual services.

Yet, even granting all of this, there are two ways in which the "sexual" should interest economists qua economists more now than ever. First, throughout the last century the act of selling goods relied increasingly on the sexual to gain the attention of prospective consumers,[1] a trend that shows little sign of abating. Second, and of more immediate significance, the language and behavior surrounding sexual choices bear ever more resemblance to the model of choice that dominates the economics profession. No money changes hands, but "freedom to choose" is firmly in the discussion. And just as surely, questions about preferences regarding one's preferences do not often arise.

In attempting to link all of this with the claim that an appreciation of second-order preferences has been eroding within contemporary culture, it is necessary to proceed with great caution. For the "sexual revolution" is an event having multiple sources. What is more, the nature of the conflicts between first-order and second-order preferences changes as cultural values change. As indicated by the recent survey *Sex in America,* personal dissatisfaction in the United States today is more often directed at the highly constricted nature of one's choice set than at one's preferences.[2] And on those occasions when dissatisfaction with one's preferences is expressed—at least by the middle-class, middle-aged audience at whom the survey appears to be mainly directed—it is desires for too *little* sex rather than too *much* that are usually the problem. As the authors choose to emphasize early on, the belief that others engage in much more sexual activity than oneself "can badly affect self-esteem, marriages, relationships, even physical health" (Michael et al. 1994, 1). This is not an entirely new development, for as Rollo May noted a quarter century ago, "The Victorian nice man or woman was guilty if he or she did experience sex; now we are guilty if we *don't*" (1972, 15).

As thorough and well executed as the *Sex in America* survey is, the very possibility that someone who prefers to engage in sexual activity may prefer to prefer otherwise receives no attention. So thorough has been the burying of the Victorian sensibility that the very real possibility of wishing to have fewer or different urges just isn't raised. In addition to this shortcoming, the authors note, "In the past fifty years, America has been remade from a society where sexual matters were covert and unmentionable to one in which sexuality is ever present" (Michael et al. 1994, 6) and go on to ask, "Why and how did the[se] changes take place?" (7). Yet they never consider that the market's increasing influence may be a contributing factor. In the sections to follow some attempts will be made to correct for these shortcomings.

The Demise of Victorian Constraints

Well prior to the start of what we would usually refer to as the "consumer society" there arose reactions against Victorianism, particularly among the highly educated members of society. Politically, as already noted, such critics were not of the conservative bourgeoisie and were often at home among the most radical segments of society. With the reliance on the sensual in the selling of goods still in its infancy, capitalism's critics were inclined to associate many sexual inhibitions and constraints with the economic achiever outlined in the work of Max Weber (1930, chap. 4).

Among the less ideological advocates of a freer attitude toward sex, respected social scientists, particularly anthropologists, formed a strong contingent. The social function of taboos was nonetheless still appreciated. As Havelock Ellis stated:

Unthinking people sometimes talk as though taboos were effete relics of the past which it is in our power to cast away altogether. A little reflection might serve to show not only that they are far too numerous

and too deeply rooted to be torn up at will, but that we should be in a
sad case without them; indeed, that human society could not survive
their loss. (1931, 77)

This differs markedly from contemporary popular attitudes. While few
would object to anyone placing limitations on the sexual options he might
exercise, the very notion that a "taboo" might be the cause of such a preference does not sit well today. One's choice ought to be strictly "self-selected,"
freely made after the costs and benefits are rationally taken into account.

Such a shift is not altogether inconsistent with Ellis's position on
taboos. In spite of his stressing the potential importance of those that prevailed in any particular society, their erosion is something that he treats as
an unquestionable good. Something of a social evolutionist, he implies
that the fading of a taboo must be the fading of a taboo for "a good reason." Thus, responding to the erosion of sexual inhibitions in his day, he
confronts the possibility of planned social countermoves with pessimism.
"There has been a furious activity in making new laws and regulations,
without a due recognition of the fact that old taboos can only be replaced
by new taboos, and that mere enactments . . . to be effective must themselves become taboos, printed on the fleshy tablets of the individual citizen's heart" (Ellis 1931, 93). Ellis fails to consider that spontaneous social
change for the worse is possible and suggests that enacting laws to replace
faded taboos could only backfire as, for example, previously ignored
pornography became "surrounded by the halo of the forbidden" (108).

This provides a textbook example of the argumentative strategy that
Albert Hirschman associates primarily with economic conservatives,
namely, the dismissal of a strategy of intervention with the warning that it
is likely to result in precisely the opposite of what was intended (1991,
chap. 2). For Ellis is claiming that rather than a "sour grapes" effect following the reduction of pornography's availability—one no longer preferring what is no longer available—the opposite effect, "the grass is
greener," would occur as agents would desire the forbidden pornography
more than they did when it was available.

While the weakening of sexual inhibitions has been ongoing since
Ellis wrote, it was probably during the 1960s that changes occurred most
rapidly. And within only a few years concerns were being expressed about
what the overall effects of increased freedom in this realm of life might be.
Rollo May anticipated a widening conflict between first- and second-order
preferences, noting with critical hindsight only a few years into the "revolution," "What we did not see in our short-sighted liberalism in sex was
that throwing the individual into an unbounded and empty sea of free
choice does not in itself give freedom, but is more apt to cause inner

conflict" (1972, 17). The common mental sorting habit has been to associate sexual liberation with the "traditional liberal" rather than with the "traditional conservative," but in the above passage it is the social, "libertarian" side of liberalism that May is criticizing. It took an economist, Ezra Mishan, to see the links between market freedom (the libertarianism of conservatives) and sexual freedom (the libertarianism of liberals): "In a civilization as vulnerable as ours is to the many corrupting influences of commercial enterprise, we should have the prudence to resist the invitation to 'crash through the sex barrier' " (1972, 159).

In the quarter century since May and Mishan issued these warnings, the sexual revolution has taken some interesting turns. Some of the more extreme changes that reflected "an unbounded sea of choice"—most notably "open marriage"—indeed proved "empty" and faded from the scene. The spread of the "one-night stand," whether proving empty or not, was slowed or reversed by the spread of AIDS. But these conservative shifts had more to do with the exercise of enlightened self-interest than with the reemergence of taboos, and social conventions that constricted behavior continued to weaken in some spheres. And what are probably the two most widespread and well known movements of the past quarter century—the women's movement and the gay movement—have provided, all things considered, additional pressures to lessen our sexual inhibitions. A libertarian position has dominated the gay movement, both in the sphere of personal behavior and in the commercial sphere of pornography. With regard to the women's movement, matters are more complex and worth some special consideration.

The Path to Gender Equality: Restraining Men or Freeing Women?

Beliefs and positions described as "feminist" by those holding them focus on issues of many different sorts and, moreover, are not in full agreement. My topic of concern is sexuality in the paragraphs to follow, and I will, of necessity, be painting with a broad brush in suggesting that the changes that have occurred, as morally defensible as they might be in an overall sense, seem to reflect less cognizance of second-order preferences than did customs and institutions that they replaced.

The early significance of that now antiquated word, *liberation*, is somewhat telling in its own right. No matter what the particular feminist position one considers, a major goal was, and remains, the attainment of equal status with men. To be sure, there is one tradition of feminist thinking that believes there to be inherent differences in the thinking and abili-

The University of Michigan Press

AND PUBLICATIONS DISTRIBUTION SERVICE
839 Greene Street
FOR ALL ORDERS INQUIRIES AND PAYMENTS

JAMES M BUCHANAN
GEORGE MASON UNIVERSITY
FAIRFAX VA 22030

		ORDERS OR RETURNS FOR AM...
		PRESS OR ACUMEN, CHICAGO...
		REPRESENT AUP AS OF 01/0...
		WEBSITE OR CALL 734-764-...
		INFORMATION.
1	11220	+PREFERENCE POLLUTION
2. Temp. Out of Stock — Delay
3. Not Yet Published
4. Not Yet Published — Cancel
5. Not Our Publication
6. Publication Cancelled
7. Temp. Out of Stock — Back Ordered — Will No Ship
8. Back Ordered
9. Cancel
10. No Paper — Hardbound Available

The University of Michigan Press
AND PUBLICATIONS DISTRIBUTION SERVICE
839 Greene Street
FOR ALL ORDERS, INQUIRIES, AND PAYMENTS:
P.O. Box 1104, Ann Arbor, Mi 48106-1104 TEL. (734) 764-4392
OUR FAX # IS (734) 936-0456

Customer No.	Salesman	Invoice Date	Pg. No.	Invoice Number
M1008815		11-02-01	1	330255

Terms	Ship Via (F.O.B. Shipping Point)
NET 30	4TH CLS/BOOK RATE

S
O JAMES M BUCHANAN
L CTR FOR PUBLIC POLICY CHOICE
D GEORGE MASON UNIVERSITY
   GEORGE'S HALL/4400 UNIV DR
T FAIRFAX VA 22030
O

Quantity	Title No.	Description / Item P.O.
		*****COMPLIME
		AS OF 12/31/01, WE WILL
		ORDERS OR RETURNS FOR AMS
		PRESS OR ACUMEN. CHICAGO
		REPRESENT AUP AS OF 01/0
		WEBSITE OR CALL 734-764-
		INFORMATION.
1	11220	PREFERENCE POLLUTION
		GEORGE 0-472-11220-1

INVOIC

ALL DISCREPANCIES MUST BE REPORTED WITHIN 45 DAYS

The University of Michigan Pre
AND PUBLICATIONS DISTRIBUTION SERV
839 Greene Street
FOR ALL ORDERS, INQUIRIES, AND PAYMENTS:
P.O. Box 1104, Ann Arbor, Mi 48106-1104 TEL. (734) 764-4392
OUR FAX # IS (734) 936-0456

Customer No.	Salesman	Invoice Date	Pg. No.	Invoice Nur
M1008815		11-02-01	1	33025

Terms	Ship Via (F.O.B. Shipping Point)
NET 30	4TH CLS/BOOK RATE

```
S   JAMES M BUCHANAN
O   CTR FOR PUBLIC POLICY CHOICE
L   GEORGE MASON UNIVERSITY
D   GEORGE'S HALL/4400 UNIV DR
T   FAIRFAX VA 22030
O
```

Quantity	Title No.	Description / Item P.O.
		*****COMPLIM
		AS OF 12/31/01, WE WILL
		ORDERS OR RETURNS FOR AM
		PRESS OR ACUMEN. CHICAGO
		REPRESENT AUP AS OF 01/0
		WEBSITE OR CALL 734-764-
		INFORMATION.
1	11220	PREFERENCE POLLUTION
		GEORGE 0-472-11220-1

INVOIC

ALL DISCREPANCIES MUST BE REPORTED WITHIN 45 DAYS

STATUS
1 Out of Print — Cancel
2 Temp. Out of Stock — Cancel
3 Temp. Out of Stock — Back Ordered
4 Not Yet Published — Back Ordered
5 Not Yet Published — Cancel
6 Not Our Publication
7 Publication Cancelled
8 No Rights
9 Substitute Hardbound
10 No Paper — Hardbound Available

ties of the sexes and another tradition that believes any observed differences to be socially created.[3] But regardless of one's position on this matter, the search for equality has largely consisted in gaining for women those privileges historically reserved for men.

Rarely is the possibility raised that equalization might be better achieved in some spheres if instead men were required to face the constraints historically faced by women. And this appears to be particularly true in the realm of freely entered into sexual relations. Women have not, by and large, sought to institute taboos on men's behavior similar to what they themselves have historically faced. Rather, the goal has been the lifting of those taboos that in the past applied exclusively to women. The male prerogative to engage in affairs outside the marriage used to be coupled with social censure for women following a similar path. Over at least the last thirty years, a much greater degree of equality has been achieved, not by censuring the man who strays, but by ceasing to censure the woman. In retrospect it might seem hard to imagine a movement to lessen male "freedom to choose," but it is not difficult to find historical examples where precisely such denials of free choice defined the method by which equality and justice were achieved. To take just one example, the Emancipation Proclamation did not seek to achieve racial equality by declaring race as irrelevant to the issue of who could and who could not be a slave. Rather, it withdrew from the privileged group the right to own slaves.

The point just raised is, of course, a generalization, and it is worth considering a particular shift in acceptable behavior that *did* entail the curtailment of acceptable behaviors for men rather than the expansion of opportunities for women. Until relatively recently, for a man to sexually force himself upon a woman qualified as assault or rape if the parties were strangers but not if they were married or in a relationship. Today, such actions are more likely to be judged as criminal regardless of whether or not a relationship prevails. What seems clear is that the women's movement has sought, with varying degrees of success, to achieve greater respect for a woman's first-order preferences. Should she prefer to engage in sexual activity with a man, she should be free to so choose. But if she happens to not prefer this option, this preference should be fully respected as well.

And yet, curiously, over this same historical period in which respect for the preferences of others has been rising in the sexual realm, respect for second-order preferences has been in decline. To see this, let there be two elements in the agent's first-order preference ranking, N = not engage in sexual activity, and E = engage in sexual activity. Consider the following statements:

1. If (N pref E) and N are currently true, it is wrong for someone to impose E.
2. If [(N pref E) pref (E pref N)] and (N pref E) are currently true, it is wrong for someone to impose (E pref N).

I strongly suspect that the percentage of the population agreeing with the first statement has risen over the last twenty-five years. The second statement bears a formal similarity to the first, with a second-order preference standing where a first-order preference previously stood, and an element from this second-order ranking standing where an element from the first-order ranking previously stood. Despite this, contemporary pronouncements suggest that support for the second is *decreasing*. As in the marketplace, people have more freedom to seek to change the tastes of others. Men and women alike face far less social censure for wearing sexually tempting clothes now than in the past. Unlike as recently as thirty years ago, male and female college dorm residents are not restricted from inviting dates back to their rooms and as a consequence have gained clear advantages should they wish to seduce. These same trends away from concern with second-order preferences can be seen within the marriage relationship. An attempt to persuade a married person to become one's lover does not carry with it the social opprobrium it once did. Rather, in respecting each person's "right to choose," contemporary society's focus is on the choice of an *action* (an element of the first order) but not at all on the choice of a *preference* (an element of the second order).[4] This contemporary focus is reflected in parts of the earlier-considered *Sex in America*. The authors elect to title one of their thirteen chapters "Forced Sex," yet *seduction* is a word not even appearing in the index. They do raise a point suggesting that our culture's relative neglect of second-order preferences may be in part responsible for a particular male-female difference of interpretation.

> We find that large numbers of women say they have been forced by men to do something sexually that they did not want to do. But very few men report ever forcing a woman. The differences that men and women bring to the sexual situation and the differences in their experiences of sex sometimes suggest that there are two separate sexual worlds, his and hers. (Michael et al. 1994, 221)

Men may be defining force strictly with regard to the elements in the first-order ranking. In contrast, the women mentioned in this passage may have their second-order rankings in mind. A male may have "forced" a first-order preference on her that she wished to be without, but the conventions of the day nearly require that one locate forceful acts with regard to the elements of the first-order ranking if one wishes to be taken seriously.

Within the institution of marriage, changes have also been occurring that suggest less appreciation of an agent's tastes for particular tastes. In the 1970s no-fault divorce was the rage, replacing laws that had required as a precondition to the dissolution of a marriage that one spouse present clear and compelling evidence that the other had committed at least one prespecified damaging act. The criticisms currently directed at no-fault focus mainly on situations in which husband and wife face significantly different earnings prospects. In such cases, goes the argument, the financially advantaged spouse gains from no-fault, enjoying the right to do what is in his or her interest at much lower cost, while the spouse facing less rosy earnings prospects lacks the bargaining power that existed prior to no-fault.

More difficult to question is no-fault divorce when both parties desire to end the marriage. While critics have focused on the social costs that even such "friendly" dissolutions of the union might have on innocent parties, they have not raised the possibility that a truly binding commitment might make the marriage itself more pleasurable. For it seems not at all far-fetched to suggest that a binding marriage commitment might facilitate a useful "sour grapes" response. Suppose that at some future date the marriage is going through difficult times. While being single might become preferred to being married if no binding commitment had been made, the perception that becoming single was not an option might reverse this ranking. And if the couple had married with each preferring to prefer to remain together, come what may, they would clearly be better off.

The opposition to no-fault that has arisen in recent years usually comes from conservative quarters. Maggie Gallagher, for example, writes,

> The therapeutic ideal, by reducing love and marriage to means of personal growth, makes both temporary by definition. It is a rational, utilitarian, practical ethic, deeply American and consumerist. It encourages us to view marriage as a disposable spiritual consumption item and to view our spouses as particularly valuable vehicles for personal growth, to be traded in when they have served their purpose.[5]

Though not obviously conservative in tone, blurbs on the back cover from William J. Bennett, Robert H. Bork, William Kristol, and William F. Buckley Jr. leave little doubt about the political leanings of Gallagher's readership. But some who would situate themselves on the left have been voicing opposition to easy divorce as well. Sylvia Hewlett and Cornel West, for example, have advocated legislation that would make it harder to end a marriage.[6] This has not, however, been a position that many on the left have found it possible to accept. As one writer in the Democratic Socialist paper remarked, such advocacy is "certainly . . . troublesome . . . to many leftists and feminists but a staple of the cultural right" (Hogan 1998, 7). Here, in particular, we may have an instance where "traditional liberals" are more likely to be comfortable with a strongly libertarian position than are "traditional conservatives." To limit one's freedom to leave any "relationship" smacks of the strong arm of the state interfering with one's freedom to choose.

Pornography's Advance

The institutions that have been the focus of the discussion to this point have been institutions in which the market figures only peripherally. In concluding this chapter it will be worth briefly considering a sphere in which this is not at all the case, the steadily growing trade in movies, magazines, and books whose apparent purpose is to arouse their customers sexually, variously labeled *pornography* by some and, less harshly, *erotica* by others.

The arguments that are raised in favor of prohibiting or restricting the pornographic are most inclined to invoke third parties as the group in need of protection and tend to apply only to that material that is violent in nature. Such movies, books, and magazines have been implicated in the objectification and degradation of women—a widespread spillover borne by an entire gender—and have been implicated as a contributing factor in the commission of rape as well.[7] In England, the Williams Report on pornography went further still, isolating a third category of people bearing spillover costs, namely, those who from an aesthetic or moral standpoint took offense at the public display of pornography for sale (Assiter 1989).

While practical efforts to curb or limit pornography have overwhelmingly chosen to focus on third-party effects, this has not always been the case at the less applied and more academic level. But even here, concern with the "first party" (the buyer) has been slight relative to concern for the "second party" (the seller). As we move to a less abstract level of analysis, this becomes somewhat understandable. The "seller" who garners concern is not typically an owner but rather the marginalized prostitutes, peep-show personnel, and telephone sex personnel for whom other employment opportunities are scarce and who are not infrequently the victims of violence at the hands of their "customers."

Potential harm to the *consumers* of pornography has been much less part of the discussion in more recent years. Looking a few years back one can find expressions of concern. Margaret Mead saw the pornographic as expressing "the signature of nonparticipation—of the dreaming adolescent, the frightened, the impotent, the bored and sated" (qtd. in Dean 1996, 80). In a similar vein, Ezra Mishan observed, "For complex reasons, associated with the pace and pressure of modern life, all too many adults who find themselves unable to attain ordinary sexual fulfillment are tempted by the new supercarnal erotic art to withdraw further from the potential reality of experience, set by biological limitations into the gaping jaws of fantasy, so isolating themselves further from affectionate communication with others."[8] In the years since Mead and Mishan wrote these passages, the romantic novel has come to serve a secondary function for women ever closer to what *Playboy* and *Penthouse* long served for men. As Alison Assiter has remarked about this genre, "Women find these novels gripping . . . because they are erotic. . . . If the pattern . . . has changed over the last ten years . . . it is in this respect: the sexuality has become more overt" (1989, 115). Assiter's comments pertain to Great Britain and were made a decade ago, but they would apply at least as well to the United States and more strongly than ever in the years since she wrote.

Feminists have been strongly divided on these developments. While some have argued forcefully that pornography is harmful to women, this position has been shifting in recent years (see, in particular, Strossen 1995; Dean 1996). According to Carolyn Dean, "American feminists opposed to pornographic images have replicated older concerns about sexuality as polluting, contagious, and self-fragmenting, as if impermeable, integral female subjects are the new combat veterans of a war whose generals have dehumanized them and seduced them into acting against their own best interests" (1996, 69). As the tone of these remarks reveal, Dean herself wants nothing to do with this project, and she goes on to argue that "censorship represents an effort to ward off threats to the concept of stable sexuality . . . embedded in normative heterosexual expression" (70). And even while acknowledging that "anti-pornography discourse now focuses more on women's 'addiction' to pornography" (92), she herself does not seem to accept such a possibility.

Despite the existence of such organizations as Sexaholics Anonymous and Sex and Love Addicts Anonymous for heterosexuals and Sex Compulsives Anonymous for gays and lesbians, it remains extremely difficult for many to take them at all seriously.[9] With shortened life expectancy or lowered health status not inextricably linked with sexual activity as it is with excessive substance abuse, the temptation to dismiss any claims of addiction as mere faddishness are strong. Absent any awareness of second-order preferences, such a reaction is not at all surprising.

This is not to suggest that claims of sexual addiction are alone in failing to meet the standard criteria of addictions. In the next two chapters two other activities will receive consideration. Gambling problems are, however measured, on the rise and will be the focus of chapter 8. So too are problems of consumer credit, the topic of chapter 9.

CHAPTER 8

Risk Taking: The Rise of the Gambler

Over the past thirty years has occurred a dramatic rise within the United States in legalized gambling. In just a fourteen-year period, from 1975 to 1989, the amount wagered in state lotteries rose fivefold, from $22 per capita to $108 per capita (Clotfelter and Cook 1990, 105). And this rise in state-sponsored gambling has not come at the expense of the private gambling sector. As state lotteries grew in number and flourished, private sector gambling rose significantly as well. By the mid-1980s, $166.4 billion was being wagered annually at legal establishments, a 26 percent rise in just a five-year period (Clotfelter and Cook 1989, 20). The 1990s witnessed a considerable rise in states permitting casino gambling. While legal in only Nevada and New Jersey as recently as 1988, by 1994 casinos were authorized or operating in twenty-three states (Goodman 1995, 2). Visits are estimated to have doubled, from 46 to 92 million, over just a three-year period (Goodman 1995, 3).

It would be inaccurate to suggest that a 180-degree shift has occurred in the public's attitudes toward gambling. Doubts there surely are and occasional calls for the scaling back of the legalization juggernaut. Why? What comes to the mind of gambling's opponents when they seek to restrict a freely made agreement to gamble? Historically, third-party concerns have been most prevalent, with the abusive gambler being portrayed as one who imposes costs on those near and dear, as spouse and children go ill-fed and ill-clad as gambling losses mount. Concerns about third-parties more distant from the gambler are also occasionally raised, as lenders face unpaid bills, taxpayers face increasing social support burdens, and everyone faces rising crime rates brought on by insurmountable gambling debts.[1]

Less frequently suggested is the possibility that the gambler himself is the one suffering from his behavior. To be sure, gambling addiction has been receiving more consideration in recent years, but for the general public it is less easy to envision just how a wager entered into voluntarily can be harmful, assuming that information regarding odds is properly provided. This stands in contrast to the other classic vices, most notably smoking, drinking, and overeating. Since these activities impose clear *physical* costs on the consumer himself, no appreciation of second-order preferences is required to conclude—albeit without the strong support of economists—that the one indulging excessively in any of these activities is "harming himself."[2] Third-party effects in the case of smoking and drinking might legitimize legal interference but are at least widely understood as merely the tip of the iceberg when it comes to an assessment of the harm being done. With gambling, the iceberg's tip is all that is noticed. Absent second-order preferences, it is difficult to find a basis on which to criticize freely undertaken gambling activities.

Pre-1900: Gambling's Rise and Fall

Reliance on lotteries within the United States as a means to finance public goods spending goes all the way back to colonial times. According to Clotfelter and Cook, "[M]odern lotteries are a restoration of a device for exploiting the widespread interest in gambling . . . for the sake of funding worthy activities" (1990, 106). A similarity between past and present lotteries there obviously is, but there is an important difference as well. Government-sponsored lotteries were sufficiently infrequent in the early years to minimize the risk of creating habitual gambling habits. As Kathleen Joyce notes, "Lotteries were run for specific purposes, such as construction of a hospital or a road, and they ceased operation once the required funds had been raised" (1979, 146–47). As economists have long recognized, unless an unusual sense of altruism or civic-mindedness prevails, reliance on voluntary contributions will result in an underprovision of public goods. The power to tax was considerably more limited in the eighteenth century than it is today, and the offering of lotteries likely elicited "contributions" not otherwise forthcoming. The voluntariness of the lottery might have been a way of presenting a tempting and attractive buy that had the effect of righting this allocative inefficiency.

Bake sales provide a roughly comparable example. These occasional events are overwhelmingly comprised of foods that are tempting and that are far more likely than not to be desserts. There may be a number of reasons for this. The bake sale likely goes back to a time when one could rarely find baked items for sale in organized, ongoing markets. In addition, baked desserts probably had a much longer shelf life than baked main courses. Also to be considered, however, is the persuasive powers of baked dessert items. Any hesitance to give to a worthy cause is more easily broken down when a chocolate cake rather than a baked potato awaits the donor.

Does the fact that a lottery ticket and a chocolate cake are "temptations" say much about whether the preferences people experience to buy these items are unpreferred? If preferences for impulsive actions and impulsive purchases only tend to become unpreferred after continual and chronic occurrence, then the very rarity of the old-style fund-raising lottery and fund-raising bake sale might have served to keep preferences for these items in reasonable check. This would not be an instance of one wrong—the creation of an unpreferred preference—righting another—the failure to contribute to the provisioning of public goods—but rather would be a case of a skillfully engineered and welcomed short-run preference righting the underprovision of public goods.

By the early part of the nineteenth century, a more "privatized" gambling was spreading and creating its share of dissatisfaction. Opposition focused more on suppliers than demanders. Cardsharps became a defining feature of the frontier society and provide a colorful stereotype of this period in American history. Why corruption would be more prevalent in wagering than in the selling of typical goods is not easy to answer. A tendency of gamblers to indulge while far from home might have lessened the probability of "repeat purchases." This suggests that a moral hazard problem might have been particularly acute, with the honesty of the professional gambler not being encouraged by prospects of repeat business. But this would also suggest that providers of other services purchased by travelers would be similarly inclined to cheat, a pattern not reflected in the history that has been passed along. What seems more likely is that unsuccessful gamblers were inclined to rationalize their losses by attributing them to the dishonesty of providers.

Something similar to this has occurred in recent years with the image of the drug pusher that has come to prevail. To criticize someone merely for providing recreational drugs does not sit well with many in our society. Because a drug sale is an act between "consenting adults," the dissatisfaction of purchasers is frequently directed not at mere provision but rather at misrepresentation of what is provided.

When the gambler was subjected to criticism, it was more often for behaving in a socially irresponsible way than for being in the grip of an addiction. What were the specifics of the "social irresponsibility"? For one, the young naive gambler was often portrayed as gambling with someone else's money. It was surely not the norm for the average person to be particularly liquid in mid-nineteenth-century America. Too often, it was money belonging to one's boss that was gambled, and in such instances there was cause for criticizing the gambler himself that had nothing to do with "unpreferred preferences."

While this first reason for opposing gambling focused on specific cases, there was another criticism more general in scope. Gambling, it was frequently argued, "crowded out" real economic investment.[3] The basis for this claim is not hard to see. Real investors take risks, spending money in the hope of reaping benefits. From the standpoint of the individual gambler, there are indeed formal similarities between these two activities. But to view the one as replacing the other is mistaken for at least two reasons. First, just because there is a formal similarity between the subjective experiences of gamblers and investors does not mean that one occurs at the expense of the other. Rather, the costs incurred in gambling may cause a corresponding decrease in spending on other *consumer* activities.

Second, and more significantly, even if the introduction of gambling did have the short-run effect of lowering real investment, it does not follow that the long-run effect will be the same. Gains as well as losses obviously occur. Only to the extent that gambling uses up real resources will other real economic activities diminish, and the value of the resources used up is far less than the amount actually gambled. And there is another consideration. From the early-nineteenth-century classical economists clear up until the present, it has often been alleged that a precondition for a person to save and thus provide the means for real investment is an income level sufficiently above the mean income, and that because of this real investment may be positively associated with income inequality. Since gambling activity contributes to income inequality, it follows that gambling activity might exert a positive influence on the level of real investment.

The Twentieth Century: Gambling's Return

The demise of legalized gambling in the nineteenth century was brought to a halt with the state of Nevada's legalization in 1931. Though different in almost every respect from the state lotteries of one hundred years earlier, Nevada casino gambling shared a feature with the early lotteries that served to keep compulsive gambling in check. Just as the very restricted availability of the early state lotteries might have inhibited the formation of unpreferred preferences, the geographical distance separating gamblers from gambling sites likely had a similar effect. If so, this would have continued a tradition begun in parts of Europe years before. As Goodman notes, "European casinos were traditionally located in remote areas, with favored sites at the distant resorts of the wealthy" (1995, 130). And if geography was not a sufficient deterrent, selective granting of gambling privileges often was. Thus, "In Paris's famous Palais-Royale of the late 1700's, even the bourgeoisie weren't allowed to enter the gambling rooms of the wealthy except for a few days of the year" (Goodman 1995, 130). Las Vegas was long regarded as worth visiting only if one intended to gamble. Its population being small, it was not a likely destination when one visited friends or family, nor was it a likely business destination. It thus follows that considerable forethought would precede any gambling expedition. The gambler could decide well in advance of the event just how much he was willing to risk, and such precommitment served as a safeguard against any truly impulsive gambling.[4]

Beginning in the 1960s, states began to rely on lotteries and other games of chance that provided neither the temporal safeguard (occasional lotteries) or geographic safeguard (gambling at a distant location) that had previously prevailed. An often stated reason for the rise of the lotteries is "financial expediency." Marcum and Rowen, for example, assert, "This process has been driven largely by state legislators' desire for revenues" (1974, 25). Joyce goes further, stating, "Like the earlier periods of gambling permissiveness, the recent wave of legalization has been motivated entirely by state and local revenue considerations" (1979, 151).

It is notoriously difficult to link social changes to particular causes, and here we have no exception. The "need for revenues" might have been what legislators and state officials were inclined to *mention,* but it is doubtful that this can provide a full explanation for the decision of states to legalize certain forms of gambling. One might argue that the historical unfolding would follow a reverse order, with lotteries serving as a steady source of funds in the years *prior* to the development of a regular tax base. When it is considered that the propensity to wager money on lotteries is voluntaristic and hence less predictable than tax revenues, it seems a bit peculiar that the former would be serving as a measure to ensure additional dollars. And history does show that lotteries were adequate for the occasional project in earlier times but were not seen as realistic as a regular source of revenues for state governments.

An explanation other than the "need for revenue" might shed more light on the rise of state lottery systems. As discussed in chapter 5, the private sector has made significant gains relative to the public sector in the last quarter century, at least as much through the resonance of its symbols and practices as through its relative size. Raising revenue by selling a desired service rather than by raising taxes has proven to be more popular. And the act of buying a lottery ticket, like any act of gambling, is a private, asocial sort of action. As Atlantic City businessman Reese Paley put it when making the case for gambling casinos:

> I'd like for people who come here to have a safe space to be as natural as they possibly can. A space where the normal judgments and constraints of their neighbors don't apply. . . . It's for people who have the money and would like to have the privilege. (Qtd. in Goodman 1995, 20)

Though the less exotic lottery falls short of this utopian image, that it serves as a partial substitute for taxation is curious indeed. For the lottery has the advantage of permitting the government to carry out its functions without, as it were, ever having to "coerce" its citizenry. People need not be required to contribute to the funding of public goods but can engage in voluntary purchases of chance. And what is more, governments have in recent years been allowed more opportunities to elicit such voluntary purchases. As recently as 1974, nearly half of Congress opposed television and radio advertising for state lotteries (Joyce 1979, 153). Yet by the early 1990s, not only was advertising of the lotteries firmly entrenched, it was immune from regulation by either the Federal Trade Commission or the Better Business Bureau. By 1994, states were spending over $350 million a year to advertise their lotteries (Goodman 1995, 137).

There is more than just a little irony in all of this. That institution which has earned the strong dislike of strong free-market advocates—government—occupies the peculiar position of offering for sale a service that has often symbolized the excesses of capitalism and moreover, promotes this offering in a way that might make Madison Avenue blush. And still more significantly, the service offered has few equals in embodying the market's shortcoming that is under discussion here, namely, the inefficient shaping of preferences.

Increasing "Privatization"

It would be naive to suggest that there is an imaginable social structure that would fully overcome the problem of unpreferred preferences. There always have been and always will be, nevertheless, accepted practices within societies that have the effect of mitigating the problem. There is no reason to believe that prior to the 1960s the preferences for gambling were "ideal" as judged by the agents who experienced these preferences. But there is evidence that institutional safeguards that helped to inhibit the unpreferred urges to gamble have been eroded.

A shift toward greater "privatization" has been under way in the United States ever since the 1980 election of Ronald Reagan. Privatization most often refers to the substitution of private employees for public employees in the expenditure of public dollars, but sometimes refers to efforts to have individuals provide for themselves what was previously purchased with public funds.

Coincident with the rise in material living standards, there has been still a third type of "privatization" occurring. For there has been a long-term trend toward increasing anonymity (or "privateness") in the market place. In some spheres this is a trend undoubtedly for the better, but for some activities, gambling among them, this new sort of privatization might raise the likelihood that agents will be moved to act by preferences that they would prefer not to have.

Two forces stand out as the major causes of the move toward greater anonymity in the purchase decision. First is the population shift away from small towns and rural communities and toward large, more impersonal metropolises. The contrast between an eighteenth-century purchaser of a lottery ticket and his modern counterpart is rather striking. The former, if experiencing an impulse to purchase more than just a few tickets, would find it difficult if not impossible to keep others unaware of his actions. The latter, in contrast, can buy an unlimited number of tickets from a lottery dealer who is a complete stranger. And should the mere fact of a single unknown lottery dealer being aware of the extent of his gambling habit prove at all unpleasant, the modern purchaser can take his business to any number of different dealers at no great additional cost in time or inconvenience.

In addition to urbanization's raising the degree of privatization through greater anonymity, the rise in economic prosperity has made still more privacy within the reach of most, as rising incomes led to a net migration from city dwellings where density is high to suburban dwellings where it is low.[5] Similar forces are at work in retailing as well. The more upscale the seller, the less publicly announced does one's purchase tend to be. And something much like this has been going on in the realm of casino gambling. Live dealers handling the wagers of several gamblers all at once has a long history. The slot machine, a capital-intensive casino investment, has a much shorter history and brings with it virtual anonymity to the gambler.

A strategy for warding off the occurrence of unpreferred preferences is to make others aware of what one intends and by so doing to shape one's preferences for the better. In my own case, precommitments to finishing an article raise the probability that I will in fact have a preference to write. Somewhat similar to this, being in a setting where others know what I am eating makes it more likely that my preferences will be as I wish them to be. By the same line of reasoning, the "publicness" of table gambling relative to the slots might serve to keep gamblers' preferences as they wish them to be, a safety mechanism that is weakened with the rise of impersonal slots.

This is not to say that anonymity *always* results in a worse preference. Robert Goodman, for example, notes, "More women play slot machines, according to industry observers, because they tend to feel intimidated at traditional table games" (1995, 124), suggesting that the slot machines provide a setting in which *preferred* preferences can occur. And with some players it is possible that the social dynamics of the casino table encourage unpreferred preferences to gamble more than do the anonymous formats.[6]

Each of these possibilities—anonymity giving rise to a preferred preference to gamble more and anonymity giving rise to a preferred preference to gamble less—seem on initial consideration to be consistent with the main thesis developed by Timur Kuran. As suggested by the title of his book—*Private Truths, Public Lies*—it is freedom from the glare of others that most encourages an agent to enjoy internal harmony.[7] But Kuran focused primarily on an agent's preference of what *utterance* she would make. To the extent that such utterances are or are not in accord with the facts, they might indeed be described as either true or false. Thus an agent of some years past may have chanted "I like Adlai" when in the privacy of his own home but chosen instead to announce that "I like Ike" when in the company of Republicans who happen to also be his employers. It seems reasonable to say that his speech preference is more apt to be a truthful expression when by himself.[8]

Such a shift in preference is not necessarily a cause of conflict between the first- and second-order preferences. It is possible that this agent is unhappy with the preference that moves him to announce loyalty to Ike and that both when alone and with his employers he would prefer to prefer truthfully reporting his preference for Adlai. But it is equally possible that both orders of preference change; that the company of his bosses makes him prefer to lie about his loyalties and makes him prefer to prefer lying as well.

While this relation of the Kuran model to my own is noteworthy, there is another difference of more immediate relevance. None of the preferences that I have used to make my argument in earlier chapters were preferences about whether or not to be honest. All of these preferences are thus without any truth content. The agent who prefers to gamble when alone but prefers to not gamble when in the company of others is not becoming disingenuous as a result. Her preferences have simply changed. Truthfulness is irrelevant in assessing the desirability of the shift, but the agent's second-order preferences *are* critical. And it is again worth emphasizing that the increasing privatization of gambling has had the likely effect of causing some to find their preferences moving in a direction that is not at all desired.

Decreasing "Waiting Time"

In chapter 2 the "multiple selves" literature was reviewed and special attention given to hyperbolic discounting functions and the preference shifting that followed from this. As argued then, the reduction in time between one's consumption decision and one's consumption often raises the likelihood that the preference moving the agent will be unpreferred.

It was not conscious marketing strategies that led to this greater prevalence of unpreferred preferences, but impersonal forces leading to greater reliance on the market. The typical seller, in other words, was not presented as one who intentionally alters the time between decision and consumption so as to increase sales. But within the gambling industry, matters are different, and in recent years for casino gambling and state lotteries alike, deliberate shifts in the timing of payoffs have occurred that have likely generated still more unpreferred preferences to gamble.

Marketing trends I will be describing exploit precisely those human discounting proclivities that have long beleaguered the gambling "addict." Though not a gambler, I have had firsthand experience of what has come to be known as the "chase." Writing can be stressful. I reward myself every so often with a relaxing game of solitaire. If forced to agree in advance on how many games I would play at one sitting, I would precommit to just three. But enforceable precommitments are, of course, not possible, and, unless I have managed to win after three tries the preference to stop is replaced by an unpreferred preference to continue. I am an occasional victim of "the chase," albeit a chase that requires no direct monetary expenditures.

By psychologist Henry Lesieur's account, the chase comes in two varieties (1977, chap. 1). The short-term chase self-extinguishes if abandoned after a sufficiently large number of losses. The long-term chase, in contrast, has no time boundaries. To have failed to win on one day would cause a stronger than normal preference to play the next day.

It is into the first category that my mild solitaire addiction nicely fits. Following a loss, the desire to play again increases. That is, were it necessary to pay to play, I would be willing to pay a larger amount the greater the number of successive losses I had experienced. This rising willingness to pay holds, however, over a relatively short period. When an important constraint necessitates that I discontinue play, I feel no more drawn to playing the next day than I would had I won the previous day's chase. In short, the formation of unpreferred preferences continues only over a relatively short time period. My attachment to crossword puzzles is similar. A "chase" of sorts describes my attempt to complete the puzzle appearing in the daily newspaper. If some squares remain blank after fifteen minutes I usually experience an increasing desire to complete the puzzle. By the time the next day's puzzle arrives, however, I am usually not even sufficiently curious about the unsolved words to bother looking at the solution that is right in front of me. In contrast to this, someone suffering from the long-chase syndrome would eagerly await the arrival of the next day's paper.

Without attempting to resolve why some chases are short and others long, it will be helpful to use preference rankings to summarize what is being described. Suppose there to be a gambler facing the need to pay up on a one-thousand-dollar loss in thirty minutes or, if he prefers, to accept another gamble that offers him 40 percent odds of winning one thousand dollars and 60 percent odds of losing one thousand dollars, and suppose that it would take one additional hour to know the results of this second gamble. Suppose finally that thirty minutes prior to the likely loss of his thousand-dollar gamble, this agent vows that he would rather swallow the thousand-dollar loss than risk losing still more. In other words, the agent has the following preference thirty minutes prior to the conclusion of the first gamble, a preference that he would act on if it were possible to do so:

($1,000 loss in .5 hours)

preferred

(.6 prob. of losing $2,000 in 1.5 hours + .4 prob. of breaking even in 1.5 hours).

If this agent did not discount the future even slightly, this ranking would follow since the expected value of the top item is minus one thousand dollars, while the expected value of the lower item is minus twelve hundred dollars. But given that the agent favors a dollar today over a dollar tomorrow, it is not obvious that the ranking would be as shown. And more significantly, there is a good deal of evidence that this ranking would be reversed as the time between decision and the actual payoff decreases.

To illustrate, suppose that the thirty minutes pass, the loss is a fait accompli, and a decision must be made on whether to enter into another game. And suppose in addition, in keeping with the reported experience of so many (including myself in the realm of solitaire), that the agent's preference is suddenly reversed. Rather than choosing to drop out, he chooses to place another bet because his preference now is

(.6 prob. of losing $2,000 in 1 hour + .4 prob. of breaking even in 1 hour)

preferred

(Immediate loss of $1,000).

Within the private sector, certain changes have permitted a reduction in time between outcome and knowledge of that outcome, but it is in the realm of the state lotteries that some truly dramatic changes have occurred. Through the lens offered by Clotfelter and Cook the shift toward more immediate gratification appears as an unmixed blessing.

> As late as 1973, the only significant lottery product was a sweepstakes game conducted in much the same way as colonial lotteries; it was essentially a raffle in which bettors bought tickets and waited days or weeks to see if their ticket was drawn. Today this old-fashioned game is virtually extinct, having been replaced by games with quicker pay-offs, bigger prizes, and greater intrinsic "play value." (1990, 108)

A far less sanguine perspective is offered by Goodman. After observing that the reduction in time between playing and learning the outcome occurred in degrees, from weekly drawings to daily drawings all the way to instant jackpots in Massachusetts by 1974, he states, "Instant tickets promised nearly immediate gratification without even the energy required to choose lottery numbers" and goes on to conclude that such instant results "produced a giant leap forward in problem gambling" (1995, 127). Though aware of the relatively low payout ratio of instant lotteries, Goodman attributes this to the use of machines that are "relatively inexpensive, . . . and need little supervision or maintenance" (127). The low payout ratio can be better attributed, however, to the dramatic reduction in time between decision to play and discovery of the outcome.

This is summarized in figure 8.1. Let D1 be the demand for lottery tickets when one week separates purchase from the determination of the winner. Let $1 be the price, 100 the number of tickets purchased, and .01 the probability of having the winning ticket that promises to pay eighty dollars. Suppose that "instant lottery" is suddenly instituted, allowing one to know immediately upon purchase whether one has the winning ticket. Consistent with the evidence noted above, suppose that this causes the demand curve to shift outward to D2. Further suppose that the authorities raise the price to a level that results in the same number of sales as before, as shown by the $2 price at point B in the figure. By bidding up the price of the lottery tickets, the players in this market have lowered the rate of return from 80 percent as prevailed at point A ($80 won after $100 played) to just 40 percent ($80 won after $200 played). Without intending to suggest that this is the sole explanation of the low payout ratio for games offering a quick payoff, it is more suggestive than what was offered by Goodman. As I have constructed the two demand curves shown in the figure, a clear preference shift has occurred. Prior to the reduction in time

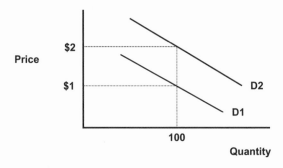

Fig. 8.1

between purchase and knowledge of results each agent had preference ranking [$2 pref (.01 prob. of $80) pref $1]. That is, since there would be no demand at price $2, it follows that each agent preferred holding on to $2 but not to $1. After the reduction in "notification time," the first two elements of the ranking shift (the third element can be ignored). For each agent the 1 percent probability of winning $80 ranks superior to holding on to $2. And the chances seem high, at least according to Tom Cummings, director of the Massachusetts Center for Compulsive Gambling, that there are agents who are unhappy with this preference shift. For the instant lottery, in his words, represents "the most pernicious, vicious, silent, subtle, deadly form of gambling in the state" (qtd. in Goodman 1995, 127).

Whether Cummings would make the same strong statement about the rise of instant credit is debatable. But it too has undergone shifts of a very similar sort in recent years. To the changes in consumer credit practices over this century we now turn.

CHAPTER 9

The Surge of Consumer Credit

The influence that John Maynard Keynes had upon the classical economic interpretation of reality cannot be overestimated. While the two decades that have elapsed since the election of Ronald Reagan have seen a retreat in his particular vision, a majority of American economists do still believe that, absent governmental efforts, there will not necessarily be a demand for borrowed funds that manages to precisely match the supply of personal savings. And a majority would still attribute the spiral into the Great Depression as an event facilitated by an insufficient demand for just such savings.

Following World War II, it was not uncommon for converts to the Keynesian view of the economy to express fears that another painful recession loomed unless strong measures were taken by government. Dramatic deficit financing necessitated by the war, after all, had provided stunningly clear evidence that expansionary fiscal measures could stimulate a sluggish economy. The deficit jumped from not quite $3 billion in 1939 to just short of $48 billion a mere three years later (*Economic Report* 1987, 331, table B73). Not only had the country never faced a deficit of such magnitude before, expressed as a percentage of output, it has never incurred one of such relative magnitude since. Over the same period, the unemployment rate made a remarkable turn around, from 17.2 percent to 1.2 percent (*Economic Report* 1987, 280, table B31).

Despite the striking evidence, it was rightly feared that the public would not tolerate such deficits once the war ended. Deficits to defend the nation did not raise the hackles of fiscal conservatives, a group probably unmatched for patriotism. But governmental deficits for most other pursuits were still not something the fiscally conservative public was ready to accept. When Keynesian-leaning economists considered this and considered as well that the economy had all the potential for a rapid spurt when peace was restored, the prognosis they came up with was not a good one. With the prosperity that loomed, went their reasoning, ever greater levels of consumer savings loomed as well. Investment opportunities were thought to be simply inadequate to mop up the flood of savings that loomed on the horizon, and with anything less than a strong governmental response, inadequate aggregate demand seemed almost certain.

What happened? The evidence suggests that in the years immediately following the war's cessation, pent-up consumer demand was much greater than had been anticipated. Yet even after this delayed demand had been satiated, savings levels failed to return to the level that had been predicted. The precise reasons for this are many. From a sociological standpoint, there was the rise of what would eventually be called the "consumer society." The rise of suburban living combined with advertising's penetration into the new medium of television to create a different consumption ethos. At a more abstract level, the possibility was raised that the effect of economic growth on overall savings rates had been greatly exaggerated and that *relative,* more than *absolute,* income determined savings decisions (see, in particular, Duesenberry 1952, chap. 3). By this account, though the purchasing power of a middle-income family in 1950 might have been equivalent to the purchasing power of an upper-income family in 1900, it did not follow that each would save the same percentage of its income. The evidence instead suggested that the postwar middle-income family was far more inclined to save the same percentage of income as did their "relative" predecessors—the middle-income families of the past.

And not to be underestimated as a contributor to the decline in savings was a process that, though having its roots at the turn of the century, truly began to take off in the decades following the war. I refer to consumer credit, a clear contributor to the decline in savings and, as will be considered in this chapter, a likely contributor to the formation of unpreferred preferences as well.

Credit Discredited: The Early Views

Prior to the twentieth century, a loan was one of those acts between "consenting adults" that was often questioned, controlled, and at times outright forbidden. The most common reason for disapproval was the interest, or "usury," received by the lender. Beginning with Aristotle, and carried forward by the Scholastic theologians, the charging of a price for the lending of money was seen as morally suspect and not like the acceptance of payment for the provisioning of a tangible product.[1] When a product exchanged hands, the one ceding ownership (the seller) was seen as deserving of compensation since full control and use of the tangible good was permanently relinquished. A recipient of a loan, in contrast, was viewed as one not acquiring inalienable ownership of the borrowed money in quite the same way. For when the time of repayment arrived, she was obligated to return to the lender exactly what had previously been lent. By this reasoning, the principal itself constituted full repayment and any interest charge was an unjustified add-on.

In the sixteenth century this argument was rejected by the French jurist Carolus Molinaeus. Usury is not harmful, he reasoned, since "nothing is done . . . contrary to charity, but rather from mutual charity. It is plain that one grants the favor of a loan from his property; the other remunerates his benefactor with a part of the gain derived therefrom, without suffering any loss" (1991, 49). An interesting argument this certainly was, but one that could only apply as stated to *producer* loans. From the standpoint of a business a loan is only rational if it raises the present discounted value of the firm by permitting a greater addition to the present value of the future revenue stream than to the present value of the future cost stream. Molinaeus reasoned that one would never accept a loan unless the interest rate was sufficiently low to permit the increase in present value of the enterprise to exceed the present value of pending interest payments, a two-hundred-year jump on Adam Smith's insight that a trade can only occur if both parties to the trade stand to gain, if, in the modern jargon, the trade is a Pareto improvement.

Molinaeus apparently felt no need to justify the charging of interest on a *consumer* loan, for his argument would not easily apply in that setting. While later economists would reason that, just like a business, a rational consumer would never accept a loan at interest unless the perceived gains outweighed the costs, the argument offered by Molinaeus was not prepared to dabble in utility functions or indifference curves but was based on a loan's effect on concrete physical yields to the participants. It is unlikely that he felt any need to address the consumer loans, for it would be over three centuries before they would become sufficiently respectable to rise out of the underground economy. Not until the late nineteenth century, that is, did the extension of loans to consumers begin to gain acceptance by borrowers and lenders alike.

One might argue that the rise of the wage-labor system well prior to the late nineteenth century represented something bearing a resemblance to consumer loans, particularly if Adam Smith's way of presenting this historical shift is considered. By Smith's account, capital was more than just tangible physical assets. It was, in addition, the forwarding of purchasing power to workers so that they might consume prior to the time that the products they were engaged in producing were completed and ready for sale. In a certain sense, the wage might be thought of as a loan, with the product's value on the market going to the entrepreneur as repayment of principal as well as an interest payment, in the form of profit.

To treat this historical shift away from production for oneself and toward wage labor in this manner, however, would require acknowledging one distinct difference with consumer lending in the modern age. By controlling the amount of the wage (loan) advanced to the worker, the entrepreneur faced little risk of "default," since repayment consisted of nothing more than, say, a week's work. In addition, it was not possible for "borrowers" to overextend themselves. The flow of loans was steady and not something that the worker (borrower) could increase when he had the urge to do so. This historical development, in other words, while understandable as an early introduction of consumer borrowing, had built within it important safeguards against anything that might be termed overborrowing. By always living on money received prior to a product's completion, wage earners, on net, did not change the relative flow of consumption over time, but rather participated in a system that facilitated economic growth.

Despite this relative rise in consumption levels that the wage system may have made possible, however, subsistence was hardly left far behind. Indeed, nineteenth-century economists from the time of Malthus to the time of Marx characterized the working masses as living in exactly such a state, albeit that this state was at least to some extent "socially determined." It is thus not difficult to understand why there was little demand for, or supply of, consumer loans and why they were practically nonexistent. From the working-class consumer's standpoint, to borrow might raise the current period's standard of living but at the cost of accepting a below-subsistence standard in a later period. And from the standpoint of potential lenders, any such loan would be particularly risky, as those just living at subsistence would be prone to renege on the making of loan repayments that required belt tightening of a particularly harsh sort.

Altered Time Flows

But there is another matter that cannot be overlooked. The easy availability of loans for consumption purposes might have contributed to the formation of unpreferred preferences, a problem not likely to be encountered with producer loans. A producer who borrows does not shift her consumption from the future to the present. While it is true that *purchasing power* is shifted into the present, this increased purchasing power is not used by the producer to purchase items that yield immediate pleasure but are instead used to invest in capital goods that are expected to advantageously strengthen future bottom lines. In most cases the borrower expects that the loan will raise net income in at least one future period and lower net income in none. Even in those instances when the loan would cause net income to rise in some periods and fall in others, all affected periods lie in the future. As long as net present value is increased, there is no reason to believe that the loan would have generated preferences within the borrower that he would prefer to be without.

Matters are clearly different with consumer loans. Because they are used to purchase utility-yielding goods directly, they have the likely effect of shifting consumption from the future into the present while at the same time leaving the flow of costs unaffected. This effect is *likely* but not *certain* since there clearly are plenty of consumer items that are not used up until well after the time of purchase. But such "consumer durables" were relatively rare prior to this century. Cash payments to food and clothing merchants and rental payments to landlords yielded utility through the fairly immediate consumption of food, clothing, and shelter. In short, consumer loans then, even more than now, would have had the effect of shifting consumption into the here and now while leaving costs in the future. And for reasons already discussed in the previous chapter, the pushing of costs into the future or the pulling of benefits into the present raises the probability of having an unpreferred preference.

As noted in chapter 5, there appear to be instances when the opposite is true, that is, when the delayed costs might actually allow one to experience a preference change for the better. Consider an agent facing a trip to the dentist for a major root canal procedure. Suppose her to be without dental insurance and thus facing a four-hundred-dollar payment due at the time services are rendered. Further suppose that though she has an unswerving second-order preference to go forward with the procedure, she knows from experience that just hours prior to the event she will prefer to cancel and will. If we define the benefit of the dental services to be immediate pain relief and the monetary to be immediate as well, we might appear to have an instance of (1) an unpreferred preference having nothing to do with an "overdiscounting" of the future, and (2) delayed payment that is, all things considered, beneficial to the agent.

Upon some further consideration, however, it should be apparent that while the second claim is valid, the first might rest on a misinterpretation of cost and benefit flows. The benefits of dental surgery are not just immediate. Though the surgery might eliminate immediate pain, it also might lessen pain in future periods. The option of paying at time of purchase in this case would be better described as an option that creates a time bias. It is not future costs that are being overly discounted (by the agent's own analysis) but future benefits. In such an instance "credit" might actually create a more level playing field. The overdiscounting of future benefits would be neutralized by the overdiscounting of future costs. And it is precisely this consideration that serves to distinguish credit's most early manifestation, installment buying, from the forms of credit that were to follow. To see why, a closer look at each of these historical periods is necessary.

The Rise of Consumer Credit: 1894–1930

Long prior to the foray of reputable institutions into the consumer loan trade there were the "loan sharks." Such figures bore certain similarities to professional gamblers, both in the way that they were often regarded by customers and onlookers alike, and in their choices of places to frequent. The chronic gambler was inclined to insist, following an unsuccessful binge, that the "professional" with whom he had just done business could not have been totally honest. That there was a degree of denial at work on the part of the frustrated loser seems very probable. For in retrospect it likely was hard to imagine that one could have voluntarily entered into a legitimate agreement that could have resulted in such dismal consequences. And similarly, those voluntarily transacting with the loan sharks must often have marveled, ex post, at their having agreed to pay such high interest rates, and by so doing to have so highly discounted what was once the future but had suddenly become the present.

Much as the case made for legalizing gambling has included the desirable side effect of ridding society of an underground, crime-ridden gambling industry, the early appearance of respected institutions that stood ready to provide consumer loans appeared to many to have a similarly desirable side effect, the elimination of the unaffiliated, undignified shark. In 1894, the Provident Loan Society of New York debuted as the first respectable consumer lender, offering loans at what was, relative to the disreputable competition, the stunningly low rate of just 1 percent monthly (Medoff and Harless 1996, 10). Such loan societies grew in number over the next half century and were joined, beginning in the 1920s, by commercial banks as well. But there was a different sphere in which consumer loans grew even more rapidly. The burgeoning retail traders of the period, led by department stores, began permitting purchases on credit as well as the more structured form of buying on installment.

While differences between open-ended credit and installment plans may seem inconsequential, there is an important difference that suggests the latter of these may have been beneficial from a preference formation perspective. As considered earlier, whether the pushing back of costs or the pulling forward of benefits is beneficial from a preference-shaping perspective depends upon what the agent thinks of her preferences prior to the change. And what she thinks of these preferences in turn tends to depend upon what the time path of costs and benefits would be absent the new purchase arrangement. Installment buying differed from credit in applying strictly to the purchase of particularly costly items. One could purchase a new piano, new furniture, or a new car "on installment." One could not purchase a bundle of consumer nondurables in the same way. The burgeoning of consumer durables was a defining feature of the period under consideration. To save and pay cash for such items would be expected to lead, in the aggregate, to too few preferences for such goods. This follows from the fact that anyone purchasing a durable in this manner would bear the full cost at the time of purchase but experience benefits as a flow over the life of the good. The practice of installment buying served as an equalizing device of sorts, allowing the flow of costs and benefits to be spread equivalently over time. We would thus appear to have here a happy coincidence. The offering of installment purchase plans increased sales considerably and at the same time likely shaped agents' preferences for the better.

To be sure, installment plans were not without their critics. As William Leach reports, a sense of noblesse oblige led at least one critic of capitalism's disregard for the poor to treat such arrangements as just one more "plague of the poor" that "robbed [them] of their earnings" (qtd. in Leach 1993, 126). Many middle-class people "disdained" installment buying, at least in its early years (Leach 1993, 300). Precisely why this might have been so is not indicated. Not to be ruled out is a legacy from the Calvinist past that might have discouraged any practices that would tempt consumption by pulling closer pending benefits or pushing farther away pending costs. Were such a rule of thumb in place, even an entirely defensible sort of borrowing as is manifested in installment plans might have failed to make it past the very active censor's control.

Concerns about the installment plan's setting in motion a domino effect would not have been misplaced. For with the passage of time installment purchases took a backseat to less structured charge accounts. Originally limited to the very wealthy, they became much more common in the 1920s, particularly in the department stores, as "consumers were engulfed in a sea of easy credit" (Leach 1993, 299). The higher-end stores are reported to have carried out somewhere between 45 and 70 percent of their business via the charge (Leach 1993, 299), and within a decade hotels, airlines, and restaurants also began to extend credit to their customers (Medoff and Harless 1996, 10).

From antiquity through the Middle Ages, the brunt of the opposition to lending was directed, it will be recalled, at the charging of interest. Would opposition have died had loans been offered at zero interest, at loans, that is, that would have been in the nature of gifts? As Richard Titmuss has argued, the selling of certain items, most notably blood, leads to a far less dependable stock than does the voluntary offering of the same (1972, particularly chaps. 8, 9, 12). The giver, by Titmuss's account, is more apt to have the well-being of the recipient in mind than is one who is seeking to make money by giving blood. It seems likely that interest-free loans, involving as they do a paternalistic element, may have historically carried fewer risks of catering to unpreferred preferences. One giving money without any intent of ultimately profiting would appear to have no motive for ignoring how the borrower regards his desire to borrow. To the extent that blood relations or close friendships lie behind such selfless loans, it is all the more likely that the requests for money would be honored only if the potential donor were convinced that the preference moving the requester was not in the nature of a compulsive, unpreferred preference.

If interest-free consumer loans were thus shielded from the criticism directed at "for profit" loans, what are the implications for the sorts of loans being considered here? Neither installment purchases (already exonerated from preference manipulation criticisms) nor charge accounts at commercial establishments were accompanied by interest charges. Nonetheless, the motivation for granting customers charging privileges was most certainly not altruistic in nature. To grant charge accounts must have been good business.

Does this in turn suggest, however, that sales across an entire retail industry would have to increase for the credit practices to continue? Not to be overlooked is the possibility that the offering of charge accounts is one more instance of competition that was destructive, at least from the standpoint of the competitors themselves. The prisoner's dilemma might have been at work, with each firm finding it to be in its interest to offer charge accounts regardless of what it believed its rivals would do, but also eventually finding that overall sales are unaffected when all rivals do the same.

What seems more likely is that cumulatively the sales of consumer products rose. For comparatively speaking, the sellers of such products had an advantage over the "sellers" of savings accounts and sellers of capital goods. While it is not impossible to offer persuasive reasons why one ought to sock away some funds in an interest-earning account or purchase capital goods (or corporate stock), it is not possible by the very nature of these entities to shift the utility that they might provide from the future into the present. Hence the conclusion; the rise of the charge account brought with it an advantage to the sellers of consumer goods and likely resulted in rates of savings that fell short of what would have been predicted had long-term trends continued. A strong defender of consumer credit noted in 1930, "Just as credit and its availability [underlies] the entire *productive* machinery of the nation . . . so it is now being recognized [that] the credit system sustains the whole system of distribution" as well.[2] A critical difference was clearly overlooked.

The Postwar Deluge

Though the spread of credit practices was considerable from the 1920s onward, a shift occurred soon after the end of World War II that brought about the system that prevails today. The Diners Club appeared in 1949 and was the first "universal" card. Use was no longer restricted to a single establishment—as was the practice when retailers themselves were the issuers—but could now be used wherever Diners Club was accepted. Accepted mainly by restaurants, spontaneous purchases likely remained a rarity with this still rather limited sort of universal card. With the rise of the more general universal card a decade later, however, the rise of impulse purchasing seems indisputable indeed. When a single retail chain had been the issuer of a charge card, the cardholder had to be at one of a relatively small number of locations before a sale could take place. A degree of forethought would typically precede one's ending up in any such well-defined retail outlet. With a card covering many more establishments, in contrast, the spontaneous purchase became more common, as the cardholder was more apt to stumble upon items whose mere presence created a preference to buy.

There was another change that was probably of greater significance still. For with the Diners Club card it was no longer just the buyer and seller who were involved in the transaction. The new participant, a financial institution, was not offering credit as a means of selling what might otherwise go unbought, but was in the business of selling credit, and thus dependent on interest payments as the source of its profit. To be sure, long prior to this change there were financial institutions that made loans to consumers, but a clear difference had arisen. These earlier lenders required clear evidence of the borrower's intended use of the loan and in addition were prone to set up clear payment plans that the borrower agreed to meet. Whether out of self-interest or a healthy paternalism, the relationship included a certain degree of guidance on the lender's part. Indeed as late as the 1950s, the Household Finance Corporation saw fit to offer a jingle that began with the admonition, "Never borrow money needlessly." No such advice would ever be forthcoming as the credit card culture spread through the years that followed.

The increase in credit card debt has been dramatic, going from $2.7 billion in 1969 to $74 billion (inflation adjusted) by 1994.[3] Over just a three-year period at the beginning of the 1990s, the number of Visa and Master-Cards rose fully 28 percent.[4] And accompanying the rise in credit cards has been a dramatic rise in bad debt. In early 1997 it was reported that "credit-card delinquencies soared to a record last quarter, with 3.72 percent of borrowers falling behind in payments" (Baumohl et al. 1997, 64). Bankruptcies have been hitting record levels as well, with 1.2 million Americans filing in 1996, a 49 percent rise in just two years (McGinn 1997, 50).

To explain these events has presented a challenge, since the U.S. economy was by most measures thriving in the 1990s. David Laibson observes that "increasing access to *instantaneous* credit has reduced the effectiveness of commitment devices like illiquid assets."[5] Some have blamed the rise in bankruptcies on a changing ethos that has tended to banish shame while making bankruptcy "just another lifestyle choice" (McGinn 1997, 50). A different explanation has attributed the growing debt and all that has accompanied it to a changing rate of real economic growth. Medoff and Harless, for example, reason that

> Americans are struggling harder and harder to maintain a standard of living that is dictated by habit. That is, they are spending as if their incomes have kept pace with the growth of the 1960s, when in actuality their incomes clearly have not. . . . [Americans] have to borrow in order to support a level of consumption consistent with a lifestyle they have come to anticipate. (1996, 15–16)

From the perspective of strong critics of the modern market economy this is a tempting account since it faults free-market forces for creating too much liquidity via the loan while also faulting it for growing too slowly. There are two considerations, however, that weaken its persuasiveness considerably. First, Medoff and Harless assert that "[t]he 1970s and 1980s were lean years" (1996, 14) and that "[r]eal wages for most U.S. workers either stagnated or fell during this period" (15). But recent considerations of the methods used to calculate cost-of-living changes have led to a growing consensus that inflation rates have been lower and real growth thus greater than originally thought.

Second, and at least as significantly, even if it be granted that the real wage has fallen for some jobs, it does not follow that those holding such jobs have witnessed a fall in their wages. To appreciate why this is so, consider the following example. That the average height of oak trees has not changed over the last half century poses little risk of misinterpretation. Such a statement is meant to convey that ten-year-old oaks now average the same height as did ten-year-old oaks in 1950, that fifty-year-old oaks are the same as their counterparts in 1950, and so on. It certainly does not mean that a 1950 oak sapling that survives today has not experienced growth. For reasons not entirely clear, it is harder to appreciate this same basic point when it comes to income. Even if it were true that real incomes have fallen since 1972, it would not follow that the average income earner earns less now than she did in 1972. Rather, it would be likely that the position she now holds was better paid then than it is now while she has witnessed a movement into a higher-earning position. Assistant professors may make less now than did assistant professors then, but 1972's assistant professors are more likely than not in higher-paying positions today.

Acknowledging this weakens considerably the claim that people are buying more on credit because their incomes are falling. Borrowing does seem a likely strategy for an individual who has grown accustomed to a particular material standard and who experiences a fall in real income. But the decision to take on more debt seems considerably less likely for an individual experiencing earnings *increases,* even if these increases are less than expected.

When it is considered that the rise in consumer debt predated by several years the alleged growth slowdown of the 1970s, still more doubt is created. Writing early in the 1960s, one concerned commentator spoke ominously of "a consumer credit explosion that makes the population explosion seem small by comparison" (Black 1961, 6), backing up his concern with the observation, "During the fiscal year of 1959 nearly 89,000 families failed financially, a 300 percent increase over the past decade and more than the total number of bankruptcies filed during the height of the Depression" (7). Even within John Kenneth Galbraith's classic work of the late 1950s—a work that has come to symbolize a time in which rapid growth and prosperity were seen as historical inevitabilities—rather deep concerns about looming indebtedness are voiced. As Galbraith put it:

> [W]e should expect that every increase in consumption will bring a further increase—possibly a more than proportional one—in consumer debt. Our march to higher living standards will be paced, as a matter of necessity, by an ever deeper plunge into debt. (1958, 200)

And:

> One wonders, inevitably, about the tensions associated with debt creation on such a massive scale. The legacy of wants, which are themselves inspired, are the bills which descend like the winter snow. (201)

Clearly, the unnerving private debt picture in the United States was understood by some as a near inevitability. Falling real income was not a part of the envisioned future in which this rising debt would become a reality.

A Macroeconomic Bias

Among economists serving in official government positions, and most in the public eye as a consequence, the possibility of a "credit abuse" problem is rarely raised. For in this realm macroeconomic concerns loom large, while microeconomic concerns do not, and the criteria for evaluating the state of the economy are rates of employment, inflation, and growth. Rarely considered are such questions as whether producers offer an optimal mix of products or whether buyers behave rationally. In keeping with this perspective, the rise of consumer credit is viewed through a macroeconomic prism, with any psychological complexities assumed away. Janet Yellen, for example, concludes that "the rapid growth in consumer lending by banks, particularly that involving credit card loans, reflects a natural evolution of banking activities toward the household sector and has generally enhanced consumer convenience and produced significant profit for banks" (1996, 818). What about the overextended borrower? Might such a person be in the grip of unpreferred preferences? All that Yellen acknowledges is that there are those for whom "borrowing may be a means of sustaining consumption through a period of household economic distress" (816).

And what might explain the trend toward the offering of loans to those who might have previously been denied the "privilege"? According to the Board of Governors of the Federal Reserve system, "competition, which was keen during the 1980's, . . . focused on efforts to broaden customer bases by increasing the availability of cards to higher risk groups" (1994, 296). Yellen similarly attributes the trend to a "competitive zeal [that] all too often attracts weak or otherwise marginal borrowers" (1996, 817). Yet this same period of "competitive zeal" also witnessed health insurers' *reducing* coverage to particularly risky segments of the population. The practice of not raising doubts about the welfare effects of consumer indebtedness, it should be stressed, is likely at least in part attributable to sound macroeconomic concerns. For as noted earlier, indebtedness can help to ensure a high propensity to consume, which in turn can serve to lessen the need for governmental actions to strengthen demand.[6] But the very possibility of the erosion of customs and practices that might have in the past limited the formation of unpreferred preferences is simply not raised, since these very economists occupying positions much in the public eye choose not to question the standard assumptions of rational choice.

In other, less official realms, there is far less hesitance to question the desirability of the expansion of choice via consumer loans. According to a survey conducted by a consumer advocacy group, "53 percent of all credit card users questioned said they were in debt because of 'overspending'" (Worsnop 1996, 1011). And self-reports of undersaving for retirement are common. In a 1993 survey, 77.2 percent of respondents reported saving too little for retirement, while only 4.7 percent reported saving at more than their target rate (Laibson, Repetto, and Tobacman 1998, 94–95). Echoing this, a 1997 survey found 76.2 percent reporting that they should be saving more, while only 6 percent reported being "ahead" of their savings goal (Laibson, Repetto, and Tobacman 1998, 94).

The sort of advice that usually follows acknowledgments of such "problems," however, typically attributes the regretted behavior to misinformation. Just as teens made fully knowledgeable about the effects of drugs or unsafe sex would never engage in such self-destructive behavior, runs this reasoning, so too will knowledge liberate regretful borrowers from their foolish ways. Thus, "[E]xperts like New York Law School professor Karen Gross argue that debt-management classes should be made a part of the bankruptcy process" (McGinn 1997, 50). That this may do some good is evident, but that there may be a comforting illusion created by the neglect of second-order preferences seems evident as well. In a culture unfamiliar with preferences for preferences, an agent's announcement that he prefers to spend wisely leads to the conclusion that knowledge will lead to wise spending. For agents who really mean that they prefer to prefer to spend wisely, matters are more complex. Knowledge may move forward the project of reshaping the agent's tastes for the better, but such a measure is unlikely to suffice. An ethos that encourages the creation of preferred preferences and discourages the creation of their opposite is surely a critical precondition. And, at least in the realm of consumer loans, this is an ethos in retreat.

Working Off the Debts

If Americans have indeed been living beyond their means as consumer credit has become ever more available, what have been the long-term effects? For the great majority who never declare bankruptcy, what impact did overspending in the past have on present-day economic decisions? One possibility, already noted, would be for the consumption made possible by past debt to be paid for by an adequate lowering of present consumption. Another possibility would be for the debt to be rolled over until eventually the day of reckoning arrives. Whichever path is chosen, or whichever variation on either of these, the decision to consume more than was earned in the past results in lower levels of consumer spending either now or at some point in the future.

Not to be overlooked is the possibility of simply earning more in the present than would have been worth earning had no debt been incurred. The rise in consumer debt, in other words, might lead eventually to a rise in the time allocated to gainful employment. And by most indications, the United States has been witnessing just that over the last quarter century.

For at least a century prior to 1950, there was a steady decline in the average amount of time the American worker devoted to earning an income. According to Juliet Schor (1991), the decline halted around mid-century, and since about 1970, counter to what had been widely anticipated, the trend has been in the opposite direction. As the historian Gary Cross argues, the assumption had long been that productivity advances would continually bring with them significant decreases in work time.[7]

Table 9.1 summarizes the changes uncovered by Schor in the annual per capita allocation of time devoted to paid work (market hours), to production for self (household hours), and to leisure over an eighteen-year period. It was Schor's argument that the rise in work time can be mainly attributed to the strengthening power of employers (1991, chap. 3). By her analysis, businesses tend to benefit from a longer workweek than most workers find optimal, and a longer week has accompanied the lessening of union strength in recent years. As figure 9.1 shows, if free to choose, the average worker presented by Schor would have chosen to work *fewer* hours as hourly income rose over time, reflecting a backward-bending labor supply curve. The result of such a decision would be more time available for household production and for leisure. According to Schor, however, this desire to spend fewer hours at paid employment has been ruled out by employer-imposed work time requirements. As a consequence of these requirements, the average employee is working more hours for pay, as shown by the point off and well to the right of the supply curve in figure 9.1.[8]

The empirical component of Schor's work has not been without controversy. A review article by Juster and Stafford (1990) presents both time-series and cross-sectional data that are not consistent with Schor's findings. A study by Roberts and Rupert concludes that the average worker is indeed working longer hours for pay but also concludes that these hours have come strictly at the expense of household production.[9]

In a follow-up study designed in part to reply to their critics, Leete and Schor (1994) stress that changes in time on the job frequently take the form of a change in the number of paid holidays or a change in the length of vacation time, neither of which is reflected in changes in the allocation of time during a "typical" workweek. Because of this, they point out, trends in time allocation per year rather than per typical week are clearly more reflective of change. Yet virtually all of the earlier studies, largely because of data availability, had focused on trends in time allocation per

TABLE 9.1.   Allocation of Time, Entire U.S. Population

Year	Market Hours	Household Hours	Leisure Hours
1969	1,199	1,227	3,414
1987	1,316	1,157	3,367

Source: Market hours and household hours are Schor's estimates (1991, 36). Leisure hours are author's calculations, based on assumption of 16 hours per day to devote to the three types of activities shown.

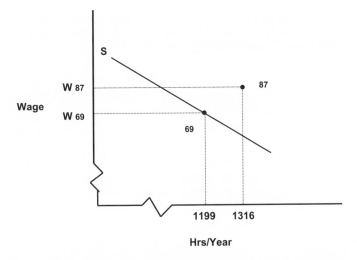

Fig. 9.1.

week rather than per year. Significantly, Schor's original work and Leete and Schor's more recent study stand alone in making use of annual rather than weekly data.

Leete and Schor note another problem with the previous studies. None attempted to adjust for the business cycle in estimating changes in the allocation of time, an omission that can seriously distort the sorts of trends that it was Schor's original purpose to uncover. Clearly, there are far more people working fewer hours than they would wish during downturns in the economy than during upturns. If a later year in a study happens to be a recessionary year, it would easily distort the upward trend in work time that Schor was trying to isolate. With this in mind, in the later study Leete and Schor isolate full-time workers from the rest of the population and conclude that for this subgroup between 1969 and 1989 "[annual] market hours have increased by 138, a 7.7 percent increase" (1994, 32).

As empirically sound as her findings might have been, Schor recognized that her account did not go far enough in capturing the changes that had been occurring. For there were at least two anomalies in need of explanation. First, while one would expect workers being forced to work longer hours to respond by choosing less voluntary overtime, no such trend occurred. For U.S. workers, the average weekly overtime hours for production over the period 1960 to 1969 was nearly identical to the average from 1979 to 1988, at 3.2 hours per week (see U.S. Department of Labor Statistics 1989, 307, table 77). Second, as workers put in more than the optimal number of hours, savings rates would be expected to rise for reasons similar to what led civilian workers to save during World War II. As already noted, no such thing has occurred. By one means of calculation, savings rates went from approximately 8 percent of disposable income in the 1970s to around 4 percent of disposable income by the late 1980s. By another approach, the fall has been less, from an average of about 10.7 percent in the early 1970s to an average of 8 percent in the 1980s.[10]

Schor responded to such evidence by arguing that "overwork" gives rise to an increased desire to purchase products; that earning more than one intended soon causes one's optimal consumption bundle to rise commensurately as well.[11] "Work and spend" is how she has chosen to phrase it, and it turns out that this particular ordering of the verbs is critical if her argument is to retain any normative power, absent the recognition of second-order preferences. Consider why this is so.

Requiring an agent to work more than she intends is harmful according to standard welfare analysis simply because this action restricts her choice set and places her preferred alternative outside this set. But if this restrictive action changes the agent's preferences such that the imposed alternative becomes the preferred, can the agent still be said to be worse off? At a strictly formal level, no. Any preference change creates a "whole new ballgame," making pre- and postchange welfare comparisons impossible. But less formally, the normative ball remains in Schor's court. For there is an intuitive impulse that causes us to treat as illegitimate preference shifts in reaction to injustice.

Consider the "Uncle Tom" syndrome. The loss of freedom caused at least some slaves to prefer that state over a state of freedom. But clearly, though formal welfare theory would be unable to declare one experiencing such a preference change as better or worse off, at an intuitive level there would be agreement with the conclusion that enslavement leaves one worse off. While having one's choice set restricted is far more general, less dramatic, and more morally complex than "being enslaved," it is just as true that coming to like what one has been forced to do does not lessen the exercise of the moral intuition that, all things considered, the agent has been harmed.

"Work and spend" thus at least allows the informal impression to remain that agents have been, on balance, harmed. To substitute "spend and work," as I am proposing, would carry no normative force if agents are defined as ending at their first-order preferences. With second-order preferences, the normative task is straightforward.

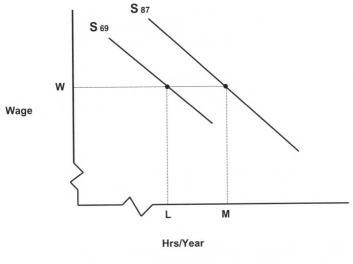

Fig. 9.2.

It is thus a purely empirical question: Are agents who express dissatisfaction with their voluntary allocation of time more inclined to prefer to prefer more or less time devoted to work? The relatively recent introduction of the term *workaholic* does suggest that there are a significant number of workers who would prefer having the preference to work less.[12] If "workaholism" is intended to have something in common with the word from which it appears to derive, *alcoholism,* it becomes apparent that for those afflicted, the Schor interpretation is inadequate. Certainly one who is *forced* to drink heavily is not an alcoholic. Rather, an alcoholic is better understood as one who is acting on a preference that she would rather not have. Such an agent has a preference to drink heavily but a second-order preference to not do so.

Figure 9.2 presents the same shift in labor supply as appeared in figure 9.1. Since the concern now is not in comparing two labor supply decisions over time but in comparing two potential decisions at a single time, only a single wage is shown. Let L stand for "less" and M stand for "more," with the former symbolizing the time that the agent would allocate to work if consumer credit were scarce, and the latter the time in paid employment if consumer credit were plentiful.

The shift in the labor supply curve indicates that the agent's preference has changed from (L pref M) to (M pref L). For her to describe herself as a workaholic would suggest that she has a preference she does not prefer (but which, given that she has it, she rationally acts on). In other words, the agent's discontent could reveal her second-order preference to be

(L pref M) pref (M pref L)

Although she would prefer to have a preference to work less (and to act on that preference), she has instead a preference to work more.

The overworked American of this variety becomes a more complex figure than that offered to us by Schor. She is not the victim of a class struggle, ordered to work more than she wishes or not work at all. Rather, she is one who works as much as she prefers, but is in the grip of preferences that she wishes were otherwise. And the extension of consumer credit might be one more feature of the age that has brought this about.

CHAPTER 10

Conclusion

Theorists within the natural sciences who face the task of drawing a writing to a close are usually not expected to provide blueprints for application. In such cases the testing of hypotheses might lie in the future but direct application is not even possible. One theorizing on the origin of the universe, for example, may be called upon to provide evidence but is never called upon to put her ideas to work.

Social scientists are more often called upon to put their ideas to work. For the "consumers" of these sciences are subjects as well. The implications of new theory hit home with a particular force, and the desire to create a better human environment both prompts the funding of much research and prompts the call to derive practical implications of whatever advances are made. This final chapter will be highly ruminative as I offer some thoughts on how an understanding of the market's neglect of second-order preferences might be channeled into action.

Competing Visions of Change

Processes by which new ideas are channeled into action differ in the degree of prior understanding of the ideas and in the degree of self-conscious planning that they require. Three processes are worth mention here. At one extreme is a strong process of social evolution. In such instances, the fact that a particular social practice allows efficiency gains is sufficient reason for the social practice to arise spontaneously. Were such a process always to occur, the absence of social practices that seek to channel or limit the freedom to persuade would suggest that it must be inefficient to do anything more than we currently are when it comes to respecting agents' preferences for preferences. Such spontaneous spread of efficiency does not, however, always occur, and the preceding five chapters have provided examples of contemporary society in the United States "undoing" many efficient social institutions. This clearly runs counter to a social evolutionary process.

A second process of change requires awareness of a problem before change can occur but requires only individual rather than collective action

155

as the vehicle for this change. While growing up in Detroit in the 1950s our family installed an incinerator to simplify the trash disposal process. Not long after we put it to use, our next-door neighbors gently expressed displeasure at the occasional fumes that resulted. We ceased using it almost at once. Regardless of whether altruism or the fear of alienating friends motivated this action, the fact remains that *knowledge* of the spillover harm had to precede change and that *knowledge* was by itself sufficient to instigate change.

A single example, however, says nothing about how common such unilateral corrections might be. Perhaps the power of community was a necessary precondition and perhaps such voluntary corrections are more common for activities having immediate effects on family, friends, and neighbors than for activities having effects on unknown third parties or on the general population. While the decision to cease relying on the incinerator was indeed voluntary, no such voluntary action is forthcoming when it comes to auto pollution. Since one auto's pollutants are spread over countless unknown third parties, governmental actions are required before any downturn in emission pollution can be realized.

On first consideration it might appear that the shaping of tastes, when approached as an externality, has more in common with the auto example than with the incinerator example. Businesses over the past century have been growing in size and have become less familiar with their customers than in earlier times. It would thus seem to follow that growing awareness about the market's shortcomings in shaping preferences would not, by itself, cause much to happen. This overlooks, however, a feature of our "producer selves" that, though probably weakened by the market's hold on the modern mind, nonetheless suggests that spontaneous reaction might sometimes occur.

The "brokered" personality discussed in chapter 6 may indeed be on the rise. For such a personality, what is produced and sold is nothing more than a means to an income, and abandonment of one product in favor of another hinges strictly on this easily quantifiable measure of success. On first consideration it might seem that while the small merchant of years past who cared about the welfare of his customers may have indeed been influenced by the discovery of second-order preferences, the brokered personality of today would not. As noted earlier, however, to be a profit maximizer does not rule out the possibility that the welfare of customers matters to the seller. If the simplified model of markets is believed, such an other-directed seller might usefully employ profit as a measure of her true contribution to society. Such a brokered personality would not be substituting dollars for the welfare of others in her utility function, but would be simply using the former as a proxy for the latter. And for such a personality, the knowledge of second-order preferences might well influence behaviors unilaterally. Profit, after all, would have become a less reliable proxy, and the act of "doing good" would not be inextricably linked to "doing well."

Nowhere does this ring as true as in the arts and professions. It is less likely greed that moves the movie producer to offer up mind-numbing violence than a social directive that such an offering creates more value than anything else that he might produce. The ostensibly compromised artist might on some occasions be better described as the "market educated" artist, one who has been convinced that her social contribution is well summarized by the quantity of dollars that her creations can fetch. For such a person, an understanding of second-order preferences would likely result in unilateral shifts. No longer would she have to regard her favored productions as obviously of lesser social value. With a little reflection she would see that when artistic license is allowed free reign, those moved to consume her art are seldom moved to act by preferences that they dislike. With a little more reflection, she would see that when bottom lines are allowed to exercise control, her consumers are more frequently acting on unpreferred preferences.

The process of welfare-improving changes becoming a reality that began this section was truly minimalist since the efficiency of such practices was a sufficient condition for their occurrence. The process just considered required a spread of the ideas as a necessary as well as sufficient precondition for change. A third process similarly sees knowledge as necessary but not as sufficient. By this version, change itself is in the nature of a public good and must be collectively achieved.

This third process raises an immediate question, namely, is it incumbent on the theorist to also serve as an architect of change? To the extent that these are very different talents, an attempt by a theorist to also serve as architect can be a serious mistake. For this reason alone I am hesitant to make particular suggestions as to how the modern economy might better serve our second-order preferences. But even if I were more diversified than I appear to think, I would still have to approach the architectural task with great caution. For even when collective action is the only possible solution, particularities of the population being served must be kept critically on the table.

In explaining this position, let me again call on a personal experience. During the summer following my first year of graduate school, I served as a summer intern in the state of New Jersey's Department of Community Affairs. Among the projects assigned during my three-month stint was a cost-benefit analysis to decide whether three small communities would benefit by consolidating their separate sanitation departments into a single system. Our analysis proceeded to estimate how economies of scale would be realized as certain heavy machinery that was currently owned by each would be shared, at little or no inconvenience. There were, to be sure, some cost disadvantages as well, but all things considered, our low and high estimates suggested that some savings were possible if consolidation were to occur.

When the time came to issue a report to a state official, I urged that we stress that the cost-benefit figures should not be allowed to stand by themselves. For despite the caution reflected in the disparity between the high and low estimates, I still came to the conclusion that there were too many details that we simply were not able to take into account because of our unfamiliarity with qualitative details of the communities in question. To this day I do not regard my suggestion as an example of academic caution taken to an extreme. I instead regard it as my first exposure to a necessary humility about the limitations of abstract models. Peculiarities of the communities that were not knowable to researchers as well as peculiarities that were knowable but not quantifiable simply became more significant than I had previously realized. Local knowledge had to come into play before any informed decision could be made.

In the two centuries that have witnessed the spread of free markets, their advocates have been spared most temptations to play dual roles of theorist and architect, since "acting" in response to the critique of interventionist practices did not require the imposition of elaborate new systems to replace the status quo. Instead, all that was required was the *undoing* of old restraints and the giving of a green light for spontaneous market forces to prevail. Yet in recent years, even with this greatly constrained active role, it has been possible for the seemingly simple architectural task of "tearing down" to go too far.

Explanations of why the Russian economy failed so miserably to make a smooth transition from centralized planning to market economy are many and will undoubtedly proliferate in the years ahead. But among the competing explanations is the suggestion that those who advised Russian officials on the implementation of a market economy too often assumed that the free marketers "architectural" role was far simpler than it actually was. According to this bit of hindsight, while "cold turkey" may have been a sound strategy in those nations where a thriving market economy of years past had left institutional traces that were easily reawakened, such a policy was doomed to fail in Russia, where the shift from feudal ways to Stalinism occurred without any intervening era of market capitalism.

I am spared any such temptation to see the implementation of policies designed to account for second-order preferences as an easy one. As noted several times in the preceding chapters, the ways in which societies constrain freedom are numerous. The legal route is often used, but often only as a consequence of the erosion of intermediary institutions. To resolve the issue here would be an instance of going far beyond what I am capable of accomplishing.[1]

Can Pareto Gains Trump Ideological Opposition?

A first principle of welfare economics is that the internalization of externalities is a potential Pareto improvement. The qualifier "potential" is a critical one and has been the cause of considerable controversy at the level of theory.[2] At the level of practical politics, in contrast, the distinction takes on a different sort of importance. It is one thing to inquire if society should be declared better off following some change as long as the winners' gains exceed the losers' losses. It is something else again to ask whether such a change is likely to occur.

The question of whether certain groups stand to lose by the implementation of any regime that takes second-order preferences seriously is an interesting one. Clearly participants in certain industries—be they stockholders or employees—stand to suffer. Participants in the production of that archetype of unpreferred preferences—cigarettes—come most immediately to mind. Less clear is whether certain income groups would stand to gain more than others from the lessening of preference pollution and whether certain groups might actually be made worse off. Might the wealthy find returns to wealth falling to such an extent that the joy of more preferred preferences fails to compensate? Might low-income people for whom the shaping of preferences is a mere "luxury of the haves" find themselves worse off? While these are important questions, nothing that has been presented in the preceding chapters can even begin to point in the direction of answers. Still more questions are raised when the cost-benefit focus is less egoistically centered and takes into account that a person's stand on governmental actions are at least partially based on principle.[3] Are there clearly discernible ideological positions that would emerge if sensitivity to second-order preferences were on the table?

When I began my work on second-order preferences, it seemed transparently clear that the political implications were to the left of center and that it was there that support for my ideas would necessarily be located. Things have not turned out quite that way. While my original criticisms were directed strictly at free markets and thus by association at the conservatives who were most inclined to champion such markets, the plot has thickened considerably, as the chapters in the second part of this book are intended to demonstrate. To be sure, sellers within the market had vested interests in nearly all of the developments that received consideration in those chapters. But just as surely, arguments that are offered in defense of these historical changes are voiced by those having no direct interests in them, and, at least as tellingly, it is on the cultural left that such support can be found. Simply put, liberal opposition to market forces has more to do with the distributions of income, power, and wealth that market forces generate than it does with market forces per se. Indeed, it is hard to imagine any contemporary liberal criticism that could be directed at an imaginary market among equals. In such an Edenic setting, equals would meet to engage freely in voluntary exchanges, and the objectionable phenomenon of productive forces catering to the wealthy while vast segments of the population suffered privation would have been solved. Absent misleading advertisements, persuasive efforts would be beyond reproach.

What is to be made of all this? For the pessimist it might appear that the practical implications of second-order preferences are tolerable to none, at least from an ideological standpoint. The contemporary economic conservative would see more doubts cast upon her beloved vision of the smoothly functioning free market, while the contemporary social liberal would see equally severe doubts thrown in the direction of widening social freedoms. But for the optimist, of course, the glass is half full rather than half empty. As argued in chapter 5, the conventional conservative holds to more than just a love of free markets, and for such a person the rationale for rethinking certain manifestations of choice in the social realm will be appealing indeed. Just as surely, the conventional liberal will find the implications for reining in the epoch of ever fewer market restrictions a healthy antidote. In short, the reactions of different ideologies to second-order preferences would appear to depend on the sphere of life under consideration.

The Broader View: Some Long-Run Implications

The focus throughout this book has been steadfastly microeconomic in scope. In drawing the discussion to a close it will be worth speculating briefly about the implications that sensitivity to second-order preferences holds for the broader economy. As discussed last chapter, the evidence suggests that agents who are unhappy with their preferences to devote time to paid employment are more apt to prefer to prefer less work rather than more, and as a simple corollary, prefer to prefer more leisure rather than less. From a static perspective, the implication seems clear. Unless an increase in work effort per hour worked managed to precisely counter the decrease in work time, output would fall.

Were the discussion to end here, this would of course not be a cause for regret. Ironically, it is among noneconomists that GDP is most indiscriminately used as a proxy for well-being, and thus among noneconomists that doubts about the advisability of preferred preferences would be heard. But among economists it is possible for GDP to be inefficiently *high* as well as inefficiently *low,* and any GDP change that followed the economy-realizing efficiency in preference production would have to be judged favorably irrespective of the direction of the change.

The discussion, however, does not end here. For just as chapter 9 provides reasons for believing that leisure time would rise in an economy engaging in the efficient shaping of tastes, it also provides reasons for believing that savings rates would rise as well. The net effect on the actual amount saved depends on the relative size of these two effects. So, for example, if work time (and earnings) were to fall 25 percent and savings rates were to rise by 5 percent, there would still be a drop in the amount saved, albeit a drop less than 25 percent. But if the drop in work time were just 5 per cent and the rise in savings 25 percent, the absolute amount saved would have risen.

And this in turn raises the possibility that the long-term effect of sensitivity to second-order preferences might be higher rather than lower levels of gross output. For if savings rates correlate closely with rates of real investment, though the short-run consequence of efficiency in the shaping of preferences would likely be lower output, the possibility of increased amounts (and not just rates) of saving would raise growth rates and eventually result in output levels exceeding what they would have been absent any increased sensitivity to second-order preferences.

Two further points merit mention. First, at the risk of some redundancy let me again emphasize that whether or not this last considered scenario is the more accurate has nothing to do with the desirability of seeing preferred preferences prevail. As noted above, from a public relations standpoint those reforms that promise higher growth as a by-product almost always trump those reforms destined to bring lower growth, but from an efficiency standpoint no differentiation can be made. A more efficient economic system may or may not yield higher rates of growth than the present system. Second, while the two scenarios differ as to how their growth rates compare with current growth rates, they do not differ with regard to how their *savings* rates compare with current savings rates. In a world of preferred preferences, average rates of saving would be greater, and thus in a world of preferred preferences the desirability of Keynesian fiscal stimulus would likely increase. A somewhat fortunate by-product of unpreferred preferences to save little has been the ability of the private sector to mop up these modest savings. Greater reliance on expansionary fiscal policy might be a corresponding by-product of liberating unhappy consumers from their profligate ways.

As the philosopher Steven Lukes (1995) so brilliantly managed to convey in his fictional account of a modern-day Pangloss who travels from utopia to utopia, each defined by a particularly rigid adherence to a political vision, applications of abstract principles must be partial and nuanced. I will end by expressing again, as I did at this chapter's beginning, my strong support for such a warning. My intent has been to demonstrate a serious shortcoming of contemporary culture that grows ever more respectful of our preferences for products while growing ever less mindful of our uniquely human capability of having preferences for our preferences. But before reforms can occur, perceptions and understandings must be altered. I hope this work has begun that project.

Notes

1. For a particularly insightful critique of these developments, see Kuttner 1997. The suddenness of the market's rise in popularity has led to the expression of doubts from a variety of quarters. Financier George Soros questions the workability of the increasing reliance on self-interest as a moral principle, noting, "It has allowed the market mechanism to penetrate into aspects of society that were outside its sway until recently" (1998, 82). For similar second thoughts about the wisdom of placing increased reliance on markets, see Amsden, Kochanowicz, and Taylor 1994; Schwartz 1994; Gray 1998; and Luttwak 1999. For a theologian's analysis of the religious nature of the burgeoning faith in markets, see Cox 1999.

2. Since being raised by Michael Harrington (1962) this general position has become part of liberal "conventional wisdom."

3. Since such a position smacks of a socially unacceptable sort of elitism, it is more often encountered in private conversations than in published writings. For a very provocative critique of the effect that mass consumption has had in creating chronic "disappointment" in the American consumer (and a critique not easily pigeonholed as either conservative or liberal), see Scitovsky 1976.

4. See Hirschman 1995 for an analysis of the differences in professional and popular meanings of addiction.

5. This is not to suggest that these more colloquial uses of addiction have never been officially recognized by professionals. As Stearns (1999, 299–304) reports, the American Psychiatric Association recognized compulsive gambling in 1980. But as he also reveals, this was fully fifty years after the popular press began making reference to "gambling addiction."

6. Recent years have witnessed some professional writers extending their definitions of addiction to conform more with popular usage. Psychologist Kimberly S. Young (1998) informs her readers in the first sentence of her book cover that "Internet addiction is real." And as reported by Jesdanun (2000, A11), a recent article in the young journal *Sexual Addiction and Compulsivity* recognized two relatively new addictions at once in describing "cybersex compulsives."

7. According to the sociologist Jackson Toby, the use of *addiction* is inappropriate if the agent has choice of action. In his words, "Whereas the word 'temptation' suggests *choosing* an immoral alternative, the word currently used to describe such behaviors, 'addictions,' suggests that perpetrators are *compelled* to do what they do regardless of their own inclinations" (1998, 64).

163

8. See, in particular, Winston 1980; Becker and Murphy 1988; Leonard 1989; Becker, Grossman, and Murphy 1994; Becker 1996; and Yuengert 2001.

9. Stigler and Becker (1977) argue that an agent's tastes should be treated as unchanging and that otherwise unexplained changes in the agent's choices should be attributed to a changing ability of goods to satisfy these unchanging tastes. For a critique of this argument, see Cowen 1989.

10. Two of Galbraith's early critics, Hayek (1961) and Katona (1964, chap. 7), emphasized the problem of asserting the inherent superiority of preexisting "natural" preferences over socially created preferences. According to Katona, "It makes no sense whatsoever to distinguish between wants, desires, or behavior that we have acquired spontaneously. If the distinction were made, we would find that the ways in which we satisfy our basic needs are the least spontaneous. Habits of eating and drinking, toilet training, and the like, are impressed upon us in early childhood. Sociocultural norms which fashion our behavior and our wants are likewise conditioned in our early childhood, rather than selected spontaneously later" (1964, 55). Taking a different, and more formal, approach, von Weizsacker also suggested that the problem might be a propensity of the market to be too attentive to existing tastes. In his words, "If present preferences are strongly influenced by myopic thinking, by lack of imagination how a different world would look, we should not accept these preferences as the last word" (1971, 371).

11. There is one possible defense of the truthfulness of the three statements that is worth noting. To the extent that consumption decisions are "interpersonal" in nature, then my choice of the McDonald's might be prompted by the fact that others are so behaving. In the best of all possible worlds, I might wish to see the social pressures brought on by others be different than what they are. For development of ideas along these lines, see Hirsch 1976 and Frank 1999. The importance of interdependent utility functions should not be underestimated, but they do not seem of much relevance in the present case, as particularly witnessed by the fact that much food consumption that is regretted goes on in private.

12. There are a number of mainstream economists who would accept the three statements by positing the existence of more than one self within the ostensible self. By this approach what is rational for one of these "persons within the person" to do is not rational for the other. This literature will be reviewed in chapter 2.

13. In previous articles (George 1978, 1984, 1993, 1998) I have alternatively described a preference for a preference as a "metapreference" and, equivalently, as a "second-order preference." Amartya Sen (1974, 1977a) used the former, while philosopher Harry Frankfurt's seminal article (1971) used the latter. Harsanyi (1954) appears to have been the first economist to develop in detail a model that included second-order preferences. Others within economics who have made use of the concept include Gintis 1972, 1974; Hollis 1983; Majumdar 1980; Pattanaik 1980; McPherson 1980, 1982, 1984; van der Veen 1981; Hahn 1982; Hirschman 1982b, chap. 4; 1985; Etzioni 1986; Daniel 1988; McCain 1992; Lutz 1993; Yuengert 1995, 2001; Tomer 1996; Becker 1996, chap. 1; Walsh 1996; and Dowell, Goldfarb, and Griffith 1998.

14. Some have chosen to focus on those instances when an agent's second-order preference is a reflection of the agent's moral beliefs. See, for example, Sen 1974,

1977b and Dowell, Goldfarb, and Griffith 1998. While they are an important subset of second-order preferences, it would be a mistake to treat moral considerations as necessarily present. From a strictly formal perspective, an agent could prefer to act morally while preferring to prefer to act immorally.

Chapter 2

1. "We do not suppose that animals enjoy freedom of the will, although we recognize that an animal may be free to run in whatever direction it wants. Thus, having the freedom to do what one wants to do is not a sufficient condition of having a free will" (Frankfurt 1971, 14).

2. This is not to say that *all* philosophers have elected to remain with *wants* and *desires.* See, for example, Richard Jeffrey 1974.

3. The preference for an element from the set of possibilities should be understood as a preference for the state of the world that is contingent on the choice. This definition of preference as "overall" in scope will be contrasted with a more narrow definition later in the chapter.

4. According to Hausman and McPherson, "Theories of well-being can be classified as either 'formal' or 'substantive.' A substantive theory of well-being says what things are intrinsically good for people. . . . Formal theories of well-being specify how one finds out what things are intrinsically good for people, but they do not say what those things are" (1996, 72). My project would thus be classified as formal rather than substantive.

5. John Harsanyi makes a different distinction. In his words, "[W]e have to . . . distinguish between a person's manifest preferences and his true preferences. His manifest preferences are his actual preferences as manifested by his observed behaviour, including preferences possibly based on erroneous factual beliefs, or on careless logical analysis, or on strong emotions that at the moment greatly hinder rational choice. In contrast, a person's true preferences are the preferences he *would* have if he had all the relevant factual information, always reasoned with the greatest care, and were in a state of mind most conducive to rational choice" (1982, 55). Both the "manifest" and the "true" preference are "overall" in scope, the former being expressed, the latter being what would, ideally, be expressed.

6. There is a variation on the intrinsic-overall distinction that is worth brief mention. According to Kelsey, "[A]n individual with multiple objectives may find it impossible to construct a transitive ordering and hence may have to adopt satisficing behavior" (1986, 77). By this approach, there are conflicting conditional preference rankings (e.g., "If security is my concern, a Volvo is preferred to a BMW but if excitement is my concern, it's the reverse") from which no clear overall ranking emerges.

7. The distinction between preferences over attainable outcomes and preferences over the unattainable has been noted in the philosophy literature. See, for example, Locke 1975, 98–99; and Thalberg 1978, 212–13. For Frankfurt's reply to Locke, see Frankfurt 1975.

8. Interestingly, when second-order preferences have been introduced by economists, it has usually been as a suggested strategy for better fulfilling one's existing preferences. These existing preferences have not, themselves, been suggested to be subject to evaluation by the agent. For examples of this limited use of second-order preferences see Sen 1974, 1977a; Weisbrod 1977; Frank 1987, 1989; and Harrington 1989. This limited use of second-order preferences will be considered in some detail later in this chapter.

9. Gottheil (1996, 108) reports on the findings of Kagel and Battalio (1975) that rats can indeed respond to effective "price" changes and informs the introductory student that "rats behave—and perhaps even think—the way people do." For a fuller account of the economic behavior of animals, see Kagel, Battalio, and Green 1995.

10. See Weisbrod 1977; Sen 1974, 1977a. Herbert Gintis (1972, 1974) also raised significant normative issues. Considerations of his ideas (and the writings that they inspired) will be taken up in the concluding section of chapter 3.

11. Condition (a) is not met either. In an example that will be presented in chapter 4, neither of the two conditions will be fulfilled.

12. Sen 1974, 63. Sen's model has not gone unchallenged. See, in particular, Baier 1977 and Sen's reply (1977b). Sen takes a different position in a later article: "Though a preference may be seen to be 'irrational' even by the person holding it, it does not by any means follow that his preference will actually change—immediately or ever—and cease to have that quality. In such a situation it would not be unreasonable for a person to decide that he must be guided not by his actual preferences only, but also by his 'metarankings' reflecting what he would like his preferences to be" (1983, 25).

13. Bronfenbrenner 1980, 320. His remarks were in defense of an earlier article (Bronfenbrenner 1977).

14. For a relatively early example of a "multiple-utility" argument, see Harsanyi 1955. The major contributors to the "multiple selves" tradition include Elster 1979, 1982, 1985, 1986, 1989a, 1989b; Schelling 1978, 1980, 1984; Thaler and Shefrin 1980, 1981; Becker and Murphy 1988; Cowen 1991, 1993; Chaloupka 1991; and Ainslie 1992. See Brennan 1989, 1993 for a critical review of "multiple utility" frameworks and a defense of the orthodox "single utility" assumption. For a critique of Brennan's argument, see Lutz 1993. For a philosopher's account of "self-deception and self-control," see Mele 1987.

15. See, in particular, Strotz 1955–56; Herrnstein 1988, 1990; Loewenstein and Thaler 1989; Herrnstein and Prelec 1992; Prelec and Herrnstein 1991; Hoch and Loewenstein 1991; Laibson 1997; and Laibson, Repetto, and Tobacman 1998.

16. Hausman and McPherson 1996, 77.

17. Laibson 1997, 465. Laibson formalizes a tradition begun less formally by Schelling (1978, 1980, 1984). Also see Baigent 1981; Maital 1986; Levy 1988; Archibald 1994; and Sunstein and Ullmann-Margalit 1999.

18. Boland 1981, 1034. Robert Nelson imparts a quasi-religious quality to rationality with the observation, "If earlier eras spoke of a person acting justly or being good, in the message of economic theology much the same meaning is conveyed when it is today said that someone is acting or being 'rational'" (1991, 7).

19. This is not to suggest that having a preference that one prefers not to have is the *only* cause of internal discontent. As I have argued elsewhere (George 1993), there are at least two other sorts of regret. First, an agent may simply regret the fact that there is a positive opportunity cost associated with his or her choice. Second, an agent may "dislike" all the available options, including the one he or she prefers to the others. In neither of these situations is discord between the first and second order suggested. Brennan (1993, 157) is correct in noting that regret over having to bear an opportunity cost is not clear evidence of a tension between the orders of preference, but is mistaken in offering this opportunity-cost explanation of regret (or "inner tension") as the only explanation.

20. More accurately, the preferred preference might have been in the choice set but been judged too "expensive" to bring into being. Hence, a discontented obese person might forgo enrolling in a program guaranteed to reshape his tastes because of the price of such a program.

21. Sen's earlier considered use of second-order preferences had moral implications (leaving one's opponent better off by forgoing the dominant strategy) but was presented as mainly motivated by prudential concerns. In other words, the payoff realized by an agent was not taken to depend on how the other player fared. Kuran specifically casts the second-order preference as morally motivated: "Values . . . are judgments about preference orderings or about the choices that preferences have generated; they are standards of rightness in either character or conduct" (1997, 232).

22. Timothy Brennan has made a similar point: "[T]he notion that choice can be divorced from preference . . . would weaken the empirical foundations and normative power of efficiency analysis" (1990, 121).

23. Cowen 1991. Cowen is not the only one to have raised the issue. Jon Elster observes, "Weakness of the will is defined in formal terms, and has no substantive implications about the kinds of motives and wants that are involved" (1985, 250) and goes on to note that in addition to the short-term "spontaneous self" being the source of an agent's problems of will, the long-term planner-self might also on occasion be the source of the problem. Criticisms of a similar sort have been directed at Laibson's work by Robert E. Hall, who notes that it "deals with people who consume too much, in the sense that they would consume less if they had a good commitment mechanism. I wonder, though, if there are not other people with the opposite problem: they are inconsistent in weighting current consumption below any future consumption" (Laibson, Repetto, and Tobacman 1998, 176).

Chapter 3

1. Dau-Schmidt (1990) suggests that a fundamental purpose of criminal law (unlike civil law) is to shape tastes. For another attempt by a legal theorist to trace the implications of the economic theory of will to torts and criminal law, see Cooter 1991. Also see Sunstein 1997, chap. 10.

2. Bowles 1998, 105. Kuran (1995, 23) explicitly defines higher-order preferences in this way.

3. Two of my articles (George 1984, 1993) are exceptions to this generalization.

4. Hirschman 1982b, 69. For similar suggestions that the act of preferring one preference ranking to another implies the imminent occurrence of the preferred ranking, see Lutz and Lux 1988, 113; Daniel 1988, 247; and Garvey 1997, 14. An earlier quote from Hirschman bears repeating since it may go part of the way in explaining why interest in those first-order preferences that change to correspond with second-order preferences has been the rule. "If . . . the two kinds of preferences are permanently at odds so that the agent always acts against his better judgment . . . this [second-order preference] cannot only be dismissed as wholly ineffective, but doubts will arise whether it is really there at all" (1985, 9).

5. There have been recent instances of individuals suing tobacco companies for causing them to prefer cigarettes. It is difficult to imagine anyone attempting a similar tactic with respect to a product that was not so widely reviled. As will be considered in a later chapter, a necessary condition of such lawsuits appears to be that the individual has been, or may be, subject to objectively observable harm as a result of consuming the product.

6. It is true that the costs of changing preferences will be partially passed on to consumers in the form of a more expensive product, but that is not equivalent to saying that the spillover benefit has been internalized.

7. See Rhoads 1990 for an extended discussion of consumer attitudes toward certain sorts of preference change.

8. It is for simplicity that figure 4.3 shows the demand curve intersecting the vertical axis at a price below zero. In such a case the imposition of the preference change harms all recipients—all would voluntarily permit such a change only if a subsidy accompanied the change. A more complicated case would be one that had some actors valuing a preference change and would thus pay a positive price, while most disvalued the same change. In such a case the demand curve would intersect the horizontal axis. As long as the "supply curve" intersects the horizontal axis to the right of this "demand curve," there would be an excessive amount of the preference change occurring, but not all of those experiencing the change would be harmed. Some would be experiencing a spillover benefit.

9. For simplicity of presentation, since the amount being spent on product X remains unchanged, there is no shift in the demand curve for product Y. The price elasticity of each product is equal to one, and consumption has moved to 12X and 8Y for each agent.

10. The strength of the market's hold on contemporary economic thought, and the inhibiting effect this has had on new "visions," is particularly well treated by Heilbroner and Milberg (1995).

11. The situation being described is a variation on Jon Elster's description of "sour grapes" (1983). Implicit in the "sour grapes" scenario is an agent's moving from a state of having something be available to a state of having it no longer available, and in so doing changing from preferring the good to not preferring it. In the present case, in contrast, the failure to prefer the hot dog is not a defensive reaction to its being taken from my choice set. It's an initial reality that the availability of hot dogs suddenly alters.

12. According to one unsuccessful argument the growing economy was doomed to suffer from overproduction in the absence of advertising that would successfully tempt consumers with never before considered sources of utility. Only by creating wants for their products could sellers remain profitable, unlike an earlier age when demand was alleged to be guaranteed. Thus Goodwin refers to the "consumerist mentality that assures that the things produced will be purchased" (Goodwin, Ackerman, and Kiron 1997, xxx). Micromotives are offered as a cure for a recurrent macroeconomic problem, insufficient demand, and as Keynes sought to demonstrate, micromotives would not be able to address such a problem.

Chapter 4

1. If it were impossible to change the second-order preference, a move from 1 to 3 would represent a clear welfare gain within the logic of the model thus far developed. It hence becomes problematic to understand the general rejection of such a move by most gays. As one possible explanation, remaining at 1 might be a long-term strategy for changing the second-order preference in a way the agent would wish to see it change. If this were true, moving to 3 would provide short-term benefit (having one's preferred preference and acting on it) but would not be in the agent's long-term interest since remaining at 1 (having one's unpreferred preference and acting on it) might raise the probability of shifting the second-order preference in a desirable direction. It might be argued that the apparent tension represented by state of affairs 1 would be eliminated once this strategy is adopted as long as preferences are defined in an "overall" sense. Such an agent would now have an *overall* second-order preference for men while still experiencing an *intrinsic* second-order preference for women.

2. Frankfurt 1971, 16. For a critique of Frankfurt's position, see Watson 1989, 118–20.

3. For richer attempts to link Aristotle with contemporary economic thought, see Levy 1982 and Worland 1984.

4. There is one difference. The "harmonic" agent has the *same* second-order preference and *different* first-order preference and choice than does the "conflicted" agent. In contrast, the self-indulgent agent has a *different* second-order preference but the *same* first-order preference and choice as does the incontinent. This distinction has no particular significance to the main point that is being raised.

5. This is not to suggest that Aristotle was the only ancient philosopher to hold such a belief nor that mainstream economists were the only ones to counter it. The philosopher Gary Watson attributes such positions to Plato and David Hume, respectively. In his words, "On Hume's account, Reason is not a source of motivation, but a faculty of determining what is true and what is false, a faculty concerned solely with 'matters of fact' and 'relations among ideas.' . . . For Plato, however, the rational part of the soul is not some kind of inference mechanism. It is itself a

source of motivation. In general form, the desires of Reason are desires for 'the Good'" (1989, 111).

6. While Frankfurt chose to emphasize that discord between second order and third order is a rarity, it has been a point of contention, as will be discussed later in this chapter.

7. For expository convenience an element in the second-order preference ranking is expressed in terms of only the first element. To illustrate, "preference for L" appears rather than " L pref A pref H." While "preference for L" describes two rankings ("L pref A pref H" and "L pref H pref A"), this finer distinction is not important for what is here under discussion.

8. The point was first raised by Hayek 1961.

9. There are exceptions to this generalization. The Austrian economists as well as Chicago economists, particularly those who align themselves with libertarian social philosophy, have been known to occasionally emphasize the virtues of freedom as an "end in itself," irrespective of what effects such freedom might have on the well-being of agents. For an excellent satire on the distinctions between a political regime strictly following a classical utilitarian regimen and one following a strictly libertarian, see Lukes 1995.

10. Dworkin 1989, 55. For an excellent collection of philosophical writings on autonomy, see Christman 1989. For a treatment of the subject by economists, see Heap et al. 1992.

11. See Young 1989, 79, for a good defense of this position.

12. One might wish to argue that to be a sane, well-informed individual would entail having a second-order preference ranking such that the most preferred ranking was indeed attainable. This possibility arose in the discussion of the conflicted gay person at the beginning of this chapter. As will be discussed in the section to follow, while it is possible that one would prefer to have a first-order preference such that the most preferred element was attainable, it is not necessary that this be so. One who is fated to always prefer to smoke may seek to prefer this preference or may prefer retaining the preference to not prefer smoking.

13. The preference relationship is being treated as a strong one. There is a weaker relationship where any item in a ranking is "at least as good" as any item to its right. In such a case, an item is indeed "weakly preferred" to itself. This does not affect the basic claim being made here.

14. A qualification is necessary. While the second-order preference literature has not chosen to repackage the discussion with the help of "complex elements," the idea has been broached elsewhere. The literature on "extended preferences" in a somewhat roundabout way arrived at the ranking of what might be called "very complex elements," each of which consisted of not only an element and a preference ranking of elements, but other features as well. This literature developed in the context of addressing the question of whether ordinalism would permit something generally thought to be the exclusive preserve of cardinalism, namely, interpersonal comparisons of well-being. Such extended preferences, according to Kenneth Arrow (1977) and John Harsanyi (1977) would make possible such comparisons, a conclusion contested by John Broome (1998), but which will not be pursued here. Separate from this literature, Roger McCain (1992, 185) does con-

struct complex elements, albeit only in a footnote. His work will be taken up later in this section.

15. John Harsanyi (1954) presented a structure along the lines of what appears in figures 4.2a and 4.2b in the context of evaluating preference change. Though he did not explicitly speak of second-order preferences, he appears to be the first to offer an analytical context for these structures. There is some irony in this. For the argument made in his perhaps better-known article of a year later (1955) was more in the nature of the "multiple selves" tradition. Kenneth Boulding also predated Frankfurt in mentioning higher-order preferences. As he observed, "When we distinguish ethical from 'unethical' behavior or 'higher' from 'lower' standards of behavior we are in effect *evaluating the value orderings* themselves" (1957, 449).

16. It is possible to show this while remaining strictly within the ordinal approach, but since a cardinal utility approach is the easier, that is what will be used here.

17. McCain 1992, 185. McCain was attempting to draw some conclusions from an earlier article of mine (George 1984), but nowhere in that earlier article did I construct the complex elements here under discussion.

18. While Mill could engage in a ranking of 2 and 3 as a mental exercise, it was Harry Frankfurt's main argument (1971) that a pig could not. According to Frankfurt, as earlier discussed, the defining feature of humans is the ability to have preferences over preferences.

19. For the only other pair having no shared elements, 1 is preferred to 3 by assumption for all three rankings.

20. This claim could be interpreted as requiring noncomparability, but a more likely interpretation is that the agent is required to be indifferent between the two states. It is the latter that will be assumed for the remainder of this discussion.

21. Surprisingly, Richard Jeffrey (1974, 385) argues that one might not choose one's preferred preference even if in a position to do so and even if the same elements are available both before and after the preference change. His argument rests on the assumption that it is possible to have a ranking in which some of the elements are "activities" and some "preferences" (1974, 390). So, for example, his argument allows for the possibility of [(N pref S) pref (S) pref (N) pref (S pref N)]. Since any ranking implicitly invokes the ceteris paribus assumption, a ranking such as this is impossible. A look at just the first two elements in the Jeffrey ranking will show why this is so. If the "background" associated with (N pref S) is other than S (i.e., is N), then the ceteris paribus assumption is violated since for the second element N *cannot* be true (since S is true). If the background associated with the second element, S, is other than (N pref S), that is, is (S pref N), the ceteris paribus assumption is likewise violated since for the first element (S pref N) cannot be true, since (N pref S) is true.

It follows that the only complete statement of the first two elements shown that is consistent with the ceteris paribus assumption is [(N pref S) and S] preferred to [(N pref S) and S]. This is, of course, an impossibility. Thus, the elements with the ranking that Jeffrey builds his argument around would appear to be insufficient, and the argument is unsustainable if each element is permitted to include both a preference and an activity. In this section, it is precisely such complex elements that are being considered.

22. Clearly, it could be otherwise. As many professors like to remind students, a sizable portion of education can be usefully regarded noninstrumentally. But the existence of students who think otherwise makes this example a reasonable one.

23. As far as I am aware, only Frankfurt (1971, 9) has considered something along these lines (an intrinsic preference). However, since he builds his argument around the notion of desire rather than preference, his claim is not equivalent to what I am suggesting here. As earlier noted, Frankfurt offers as an example a physician who desires to have a desire for an illicit drug, not so that he may act upon it, but simply as a means of better understanding an addict's experience.

24. The same distinction between "intrinsic" and "overall" would apply at the second-order level as well. This is of no immediate consequence and will not be taken up here.

25. But just as clearly, there are instances where the reverse occurs, identified as "the grass is greener" phenomenon by Elster (1983, 109ff.). Self-restraint, if intended to change the preferences for the better, would fail in cases such as these.

Chapter 5

1. McChesney 1999, 137. Wachtel made a similar point a decade earlier (1989, 195).

2. This point was pursued in more detail in an earlier article (George 1989). Also see Altman 1999. Economists who have studied social conventions from the "new institutionalist" perspective in recent years (e.g., Choi 1993) have tended to approach their subject from a social evolutionary perspective. While this perspective does not rule out the possibility that efficient practices will erode, it tends to draw attention away from such events. Curiously, Thorstein Veblen, who introduced an evolutionary perspective to economics a century ago, was not at all inclined to draw any necessary connection between survivability and efficiency (Veblen 1967).

3. This assumes that *any* preference shifts that sellers induce must be undesirable. As stressed earlier, this need not be the case and is only being assumed in this example for simplification. The analysis could go forward with the assumption that some agents create worse tastes (and do so too often) and some superior tastes (but too seldom). The same conclusions would be reached but with unnecessary complexity for what is here being demonstrated.

4. As Marwell and Ames (1981) discovered, economics majors were more inclined than other students to fall into the prisoner's dilemma. For an extension of this finding see Frank, Gilovich, and Regan 1993. For contrary findings, see Yezer, Goldfarb, and Poppen 1996.

5. Gwartney, Stroup, and Sobel 2000, inside cover. Figures are from *Economic Report* 1999; *Survey of Current Business,* March 1999.

6. The title of the book by Ottosen and Thompson (1996)—*Reducing Unem-*

ployment: A Case for Government Deregulation—makes clear their view of one thing deregulation might accomplish.

7. See Yergin and Stanislaw 1998 for an extended treatment of the contribution of increasing globalization to the erosion of the economic power of governments.

8. For an insightful consideration of the different sorts of motivations, some self-interested and some not, behind the actions of government figures, see Kelman 1990.

9. An unusually strong claim regarding the adequacy of nongovernmental mechanisms is made by Powelson, reflecting on the "moral economy" that might prevail in some "future world." In his words, "Despite its emphasis on freedom, the moral economy is one of social control. However, controls are not imposed by governments that determine how society ought to be run and pass laws to make it run that way. Rather, they are negotiated by citizen groups who determine the law, the monetary system, the manner of contracts, and labor practices, and who implement environmental practices that assure clean air and water, preserve the forests and soil, and prevent global warming and destruction of the ozone layer" (Powelson 1998, 8). Gold (1992, 19) notes certain changes in conservative attitudes toward government in the United States over the last twenty years. While traditional conservatives were inclined to regard government as the cause of, but not the solution for, social breakdown, the religious Right that gained strength in the late 1970s often sought solutions through the legislative process.

10. "Traditional Catholics" are the only group whose primary self-definition is nonpolitical.

11. Cuneo 1997, 19. For another analysis of conservative Catholicism, American style, see Weaver and Appleby 1995.

12. According to Donald Lambro, "Many voters like the libertarian message of smaller government, but . . . do not want to throw their vote away if Libertarian candidates have no chance of winning" (1998, 43). He goes on to note that "there is no question . . . that Americans are becoming increasingly interested in libertarian ideas such as privatizing or contracting out government functions, allowing workers to put Social Security contributions into their own personal retirement accounts and dismantling the IRS" (1998, 43).

13. Lasch 1991, 515. Others have made similar arguments. Sociologist Alan Wolfe argues that "the right won the economic war, [and] the left won the cultural war." Another commentator similarly notes, "[Young people] see no contradiction in holding down day jobs in the unfettered global marketplace—the Reaganite dream, and left nightmare—and spending weekends immersed in a moral and cultural universe shaped by the 60's." (Both quotes appear in Bronner 1999, sec. 4, p. 5.) Also see Butt 1972, 265. As argued by Kuran (1995), to the extent that private beliefs are masked by public pronouncements, the stability of the "conservative" coalition may be precarious. If enough libertarian conservatives become unhappy to be allied with Christian conservatives, and enough believe that other libertarian conservatives think the same way, a dramatic "cascade" effect is likely to occur, and opposition to the coalition suddenly acceptable.

14. Some have attempted to draw connections between postmodernism and the

neoclassical vision of human choice. See, for example, Davis 1994 and MacNeill 1996.

15. Market critic Paul L. Wachtel traces the increased defense of spontaneous choice back to Freud. By this account, some aspects of Freud's thought "seemed to lend support to the idea of the naturalness of consumer desires. In his focus on the single individual and the vicissitudes of his desires, Freud implicitly minimized the role of others in shaping spontaneous upwellings from within" (Wachtel 1989, 126).

16. As was discussed earlier in this chapter, as the distance between time of choice and time of actual consumption varies, so too does the choice itself vary. This point will be encountered again in each of the remaining chapters.

Chapter 6

1. Lewis 1996, 24. In just the last year the *Philadelphia Inquirer* has begun showing not just the opinion of the critics in its listing of movies, but box office success as well.

2. McChesney 1999, 33. Cowen (1998) argues that commercial culture has permitted the arts to flourish. Communications theorist Neil Postman (1985) offers a far less optimistic thesis that light entertainment has become the culture's common currency and has undermined the arts as a result.

3. This is not to say that in every capacity in contemporary society the trend is to be nonjudgmental about the desires of others. It might be argued that religious and secular organizations that have as their purpose the altering of tastes are flourishing in contemporary America. This would not be inconsistent with the spread of the "brokering style" within the marketplace and might actually be interpreted as a consequence of this spread. Just as the rise of businesses that counter the effects created by pollution might be a reaction to the creation of "too much" pollution, so the spread of preference shaping institutions outside the market might indicate an abdication of this function by sellers.

4. As Garrison Keillor points out, though a negative sort of "elitism" is usually associated with those who are "critic-sensitive" rather than "market-sensitive" in their creations, the categorization might more properly be reversed. In commenting on a shift in the policy of the *New Yorker* magazine toward a more "reader friendly" format, he states, "Some people considered the magazine elitist because it published a few writers who wrote better than anybody else in the world, but great writing is truly democratic, open to all. What's really snooty is to put out commercial garbage for an audience that you yourself feel superior to" (Keillor 1996, 34).

5. According to Michael Schudson (1984), advertising has little effect on sales and persists largely as a ceremonial declaration that one has "arrived." If this is correct, there may be some companies who would indeed like to drop out of the process but haven't the nerve. This, in turn, could be construed as a conflict between the orders of preferences.

6. The spread of cable television over the past two decades has altered this means of payment only slightly. By most any imaginable criterion for evaluating time, the cable viewers still spend far more time watching commercials than sending checks to their cable companies.

7. So widespread and well known is this particular sort of "other-directed" second-order preference that a farce aimed at fairly young children has been written in which the protagonist disappoints parents and teachers alike by revealing a preference for books rather than for television (Heide 1982). The author apparently reasoned that even young children could recognize the absurdity of adults preferring that their children develop preferences to read less and watch television more. For a critical analysis of television's effect on the young, see Minow and LaMay 1995.

8. For some examples of this sort, see Washburn and Thornton 1996.

9. This was reported in an account of a conference at which Gerbner was a participant (Boldt 1996).

10. McChesney, for example, argues, "With tremendous pressure to attract audiences but to keep costs down and not take chances, the standard route of the media giants is to turn to the tried and true formulas of sex and violence. . . . To the extent that the system factors in audience desires, it does so in a quite limited and commercially exploitable manner. . . . Programming that features lurid and infantile discussions of sexual behavior, like talk shows hosted by Howard Stern or Jerry Springer, costs virtually nothing to produce and does not need to 'develop' an audience" (McChesney 1999, 34).

11. Recent evidence is hard to find. But in an article written in the 1970s, Scitovsky reports, "According to one [questionnaire] of the people watching television, 24 percent 'occasionally feel like doing something else,' another 12.5 percent 'often' felt that way, and a further 6.5 percent 'almost always' have that feeling. Yet, all of them continue watching!" (Scitovsky 1986, 77). Curiously, though a survey conducted by United Media Enterprises (1983) (and included in the report's appendix) asked participants whether they watched too much, too little, or the right amount of television, nowhere in the 130-page report were the results noted.

12. This charge was frequently made during the 1995 House Appropriations subcommittee hearing on whether to continue the federal subsidy of public broadcasting. As noted in the *New York Times,* "The Corporation for Public Broadcasting . . . has long been a favorite target for conservatives who have accused its operators of elitism with a liberal bias" (Gray 1995, A22). Charges of "cultural elitism" have come from other quarters as well. One commentator noted that frequently heard charges that commercial television is destructive of childhood innocence are likely to "raise objections from more liberal camps" and "seem certain to encourage cries of cultural elitism" (Mason 1998, B4).

13. Fernandez 1998, A20. The figures cited in the article are from Department of Labor, USDA Food Cost Review.

14. It is interesting to consider that the role of the professor may be somewhat similar. Beyond the high school level, it has long seemed that self-education is possible. It is also extremely rare, partly because no official accreditation is attained, but formal education allows precommitment strategies to emerge.

15. For a particularly insightful look at how the manner of presentation influences perceptions of economic fairness, see Kahneman, Knetsch, and Thaler 1986.

16. Legal considerations might also help to shed some light on this policy. As David Laibson states, contracts that entail no explicit loss to the aggrieved party if broken "are generally unenforceable in the United States" (Laibson 1997, 448). He goes on to note, "U. S. Contract law is based around the 'fundamental principle that the law's goal on breach of contract is not to deter breach by compelling the promisor to perform, but rather to redress breach by compensating the promisee' (Farnsworth 1990, p. 935). Hence, courts allow contracts to specify 'liquidated damages' which reflect losses likely to be experienced by the promisee, but courts do not allow 'penalties' which do not reflect such losses" (Laibson 1997, 448 n. 5).

Chapter 7

1. Leach (1993) provides a particularly interesting account of shifts that were occurring early in the twentieth century.

2. This comes through most clearly in the following passage: "One New York man expressed his . . . despair by explaining that when he was fifteen, he wanted to have sex with every woman in the world. When he was eighteen, he wanted to have sex with every woman in New York. When he was twenty, he wanted every woman on Manhattan's Upper West Side. Then, he decided he would settle for every woman on his block. Now, in his mid-twenties, he just wants to no longer be a virgin" (Michael et al. 1994, 49). Clearly not a conflict over preferences, but rather over the limitations that he faces.

3. See Gatens 1991 for a philosopher's perspective on this issue and Rosenberg 1982 for an historical account of how positions have shifted over the years.

4. The working assumption has been that seduction is more acceptable, that is, that one is more free to impose a preference for sex. Within marriage, it might be argued, there are certainly instances in which one historically has felt "pressures" to create a preference within the other. If the concern with second-order preferences is indeed weakening, we would expect to see social pressures to remain "sexually attractive" to one's spouse weakening.

5. Gallagher 1996, 227. A very similar position is voiced by British conservative political thinker turned market critic John Gray. As he states, "By privileging individual choice over any common good [the market] tends to make relationships revocable and provisional. In a culture in which choice is the only undisputed value and wants are held to be insatiable, what is the difference between initiating a divorce and trading in a used car?" (1998, 37).

6. Hewlett and West 1998, 241–43. A political trend in this direction appears to be occurring: "Covenant marriage, a legal experiment that began two years ago in Louisiana in response to high divorce rates, has spawned a national movement that would make it harder to enter and exit marriages" (Lowy 1999, 13A).

7. As the Attorney General's Commission on Pornography reported in 1986, "In both clinical and experimental settings, exposure to sexually violent materials

has indicated an increase in the likelihood of aggression" (qtd. in Baird and Rosenbaum 1991, 41). For a wide range of empirical studies, see Malamuth and Donnerstein 1984.

8. Mishan 1972, 159. For similar concern from a psychologist about the direction that sexology was taking, see Farber 1972.

9. Reference to these groups appears in Giddens 1992, 85.

Chapter 8

1. See, in particular, Fabian 1990 for a vivid account of this dominant view of the problems with gambling that prevailed in the nineteenth century.

2. This, however, is a very shaky reed on which to build an argument for restricting any of these activities. For as the textbooks are fond of reminding the student, that an act has associated with it physical harm (or increased risks of physical harm) is not a sufficient reason for declaring it not to be in the consumer's best interest. While it is true that cigarettes lessen life expectancy, it is equally true that driving does the same.

3. As Fabian, for example, says, "Those who managed savings institutions saw gambling games as direct competitors for the small surplus of the laboring poor, and . . . they argued that such surpluses could serve the interests of society either by augmenting the pool of capital available for investment or by purchasing necessities" (1990, 61).

4. Marcum and Rowen view horse-track betting as more "isolated" than the more recent sorts of gambling offerings. In their words, "[S]ince tracks are usually not easily accessible, the time and expense of going to them requires premeditation, which tends to discourage impulsive betting" (1974, 28).

5. At least two other factors have been at work, one contributing to lower density, the other to higher density. Falling transportation costs have raised the demand for privacy, while the rise in population has put upward pressure on the relatively fixed resource, land. Apparently this third factor has not been enough to offset the first two since by all accounts square footage of housing and lot size continue to rise.

6. For a development of this theme, see Lesieur 1977, 1ff.

7. As defined on the opening page of the introductory chapter, "preference falsification" is "the act of misrepresenting one's genuine wants under perceived social pressures" (Kuran 1995, 3).

8. But there are exceptions. An alcoholic in denial might announce to himself that he does not have a drinking problem while finding that co-members of Alcoholics Anonymous lead him to prefer to announce the opposite.

Chapter 9

1. See Combee and Norton 1991, 18–19 for passages from the Old Testament that warn against usury. Also in this selection of readings is a more developed

antiusury argument offered by Thomas Aquinas in *Summa Theologica* (Combee and Norton 1991, 43–44).

2. These remarks were made by Evans Clark and appear in Leach 1993, 300.

3. Medoff and Harless 1996, 9. Both of the quoted figures are expressed in 1969 dollars.

4. As reported in the *Business Week* of March 6, 1995, "The number of U.S. cards has soared: Visa and MasterCards increased from 208.3 million in 1990 to 266.5 million at the end of 1993" (Holland and Melcher 1995, 92).

5. Laibson 1997, 461. As Laibson notes elsewhere, competitive pressures have weakened the precommitment capabilities of 401(k) plans, which were originally instituted as a means of encouraging retirement savings. As he observes, "Almost all (90 percent) of the plans surveyed . . . have begun to allow participants to use their 401(k) balance as collateral for a loan" (Laibson, Repetto, and Tobacman 1998, 145).

6. This is the point raised by Cameron, who notes that "debt behaviour is part of the dynamic of capitalism. Problem debtors may be created to satisfy the temporary requirements of some sectors of an inherently unstable macroeconomic system" (1994, 217).

7. "In the generation after World War I . . . people from every rank and persuasion believed that industrial productivity, symbolised by Ford's assembly lines and the munitions factories of World War I, was about to realise an historic dream—the satiation of human physical needs. This, in turn, would necessarily lead to greater time free from work and create new opportunities for organised public leisure" (Cross 1993, 3).

8. While Schor built her argument around the assumption that the average worker's labor supply curve was backward bending, her interpretation is consistent with a positively sloped curve. I discuss this at more length in an earlier article (George 1997, 39–40.)

9. Roberts and Rupert 1995. For a less sanguine analysis of the substitution of market-produced goods for self-produced goods, see Offe and Heinze 1996.

10. The first of these estimated figures was derived from U.S. Bureau of the Census 1993, table 700, p. 448; the second is from the same publication, table 696, p. 445.

11. In a more recent work Schor (1998) develops the consumption side of her argument further. The inefficiency that is implicit in her choice of titles *(The Overspent American)* is Veblenian in nature rather than a reaction to preferences that the agents would rather be without. Also see Frank 1999. One news reporter views unionization as the best way of combating overwork, writing, "Only when there's a labor movement that's strong enough to limit weekly hours to 40, or to make normal the idea of taking off the whole month of August, can those in the salaried class bring some sanity to their lives as well. I often wonder whether busy professionals will be able to endure until a strong union movement returns" (Geoghegan 1999, A17).

12. William Safire (2000, 10) credits Wayne E. Oates with coining *workaholic* in a 1968 article—"On Being a 'Workaholic'"—that appeared in a pastoral magazine.

Chapter 10

1. For a careful consideration of settings in which legal solutions are required and those in which social norms will suffice, see legal theorist Richard Epstein 1998, chap. 2.

2. See Kaldor 1939 and Hicks 1939 for the original statements of necessary compensation criteria. See Scitovsky 1941 for a specification of an additional criterion and Little 1957, chap. 6, for a summary of the theoretical controversy that followed.

3. Kelman (1991) argues that a much too narrow view of self-interest currently dominates within political science today.

References

Ainslie, George. 1992. *Picoeconomics: The Strategic Interaction of Successive Motivational States within the Person.* Cambridge: Cambridge University Press.

Altman, Morris. 1999. "The Methodology of Economics and the Survival Principle Revisited and Revised: Some Welfare and Public Policy Implications of Modeling the Economic Agent." *Review of Social Economy* 57, no. 4: 427–49.

Amsden, Alice H., Jacek Kochanowicz, and Lance Taylor. 1994. *The Market Meets Its Match: Restructuring the Economies of Eastern Europe.* Cambridge: Harvard University Press.

Anderson, Elizabeth. 1993. *Value in Ethics and Economics.* Cambridge: Harvard University Press.

Archibald, R. B. 1994. "How Many Paychecks? An Example of a Self-Imposed Constraint." *Economic Inquiry* 32, no. 4: 696–702.

Aristotle. 1973. *Aristotle's Ethics.* Trans. J. L. Ackrill. New York: Humanities Press.

Arrow, Kenneth. 1977. "Extended Sympathy and the Possibility of Social Choice." *American Economic Review Papers and Proceedings* 67:219–25.

Assiter, Alison. 1989. *Pornography, Feminism, and the Individual.* London: Pluto Press.

Baier, Kurt. 1977. "Rationality and Morality." *Erkenntnis* 11:197–223.

Baigent, Nick. 1981. "Rational Choice and the Taxation of Sin: Comment." *Journal of Public Economics* 16:253–59.

Baird, Robert M., and Stuart E. Rosenbaum, eds. 1991. *Pornography: Private Right or Public Menace?* Buffalo, N.Y.: Prometheus Books.

Baumohl, Bernard, Valerie Marchant, Joshua Cooper Ramo, and Bill Saporito. 1997. "When Boomers Become Busted." *Time,* March 31, 64.

Becker, Gary S. 1996. *Accounting for Tastes.* Cambridge: Harvard University Press.

Becker, Gary S., Michael Grossman, and Kevin M. Murphy. 1994. "An Empirical Analysis of Cigarette Addiction." *American Economic Review.* 84, no. 3: 396–418.

Becker, Gary S., and Kevin Murphy. 1988. "A Theory of Rational Addiction." *Journal of Political Economy* 96, no. 4: 675–700.

Bell, Daniel. 1976. *The Cultural Contradictions of Capitalism.* New York: Basic Books.

———. 1980. *The Winding Passage: Essays and Sociological Journeys, 1960–1980.* Cambridge, Mass.: Abt Books.

Black, Hillel. 1961. *Buy Now, Pay Later*. New York: William Morrow.

Board of Governors of the Federal Reserve System. 1994. "Statement Submitted to the Subcommittee on Consumer Credit and Insurance of the Committee on Banking, Finance and Urban Affairs, U.S. House of Representatives, February 9, 1994." *Federal Reserve Bulletin,* April, 296–301.

Boland, Lawrence A. 1981. "On the Futility of Criticizing the Neoclassical Maximization Hypothesis." *American Economic Review* 71:1031–36.

Boldt, David. 1996. "TV Violence Gets Left-Right Punch." *Philadelphia Inquirer,* June 25, B1.

Booth, Wayne. 1974. *Modern Dogma and the Rhetoric of Assent*. Chicago: University of Chicago Press.

Boulding, Kenneth E. 1957. "Some Contributions of Economics to Theology and Religion." *Religious Education* 5:446–50.

Bowles, Samuel. 1998. "Endogenous Preferences: The Cultural Consequences of Markets and Other Economic Institutions." *Journal of Economic Literature* 36, no. 1: 75–111.

Brennan, Timothy J. 1989. "A Methodological Assessment of Multiple Utility Frameworks." *Economics and Philosophy* 5:189–208.

———. 1990. "Voluntary Exchange and Economic Claims." *Research in the History of Economic Thought and Methodology* 7:105–24.

———. 1993. "The Futility of Multiple Utility." *Economics and Philosophy* 9:155–64.

Bronfenbrenner, Martin. 1977. "Poetry, Pushpin, and Utility." *Economic Inquiry* 15:95–110.

———. 1980. "Liberty and the Higher Pleasures: Reply." *Economic Inquiry* 18:319–20.

Bronner, Ethan. 1999. "Left and Right Are Crossing Paths." *New York Times,* July 11, sec. 4, pp. 1, 5.

Broome, John. 1998. "Extended Preferences." In *Preferences,* ed. C. Fehige and U. Wessels, 271–87. New York: W. de Gruyter.

Butt, Ronald. 1972. "The Mistakes Liberals Make." In *The Case against Pornography,* ed. D. Holbrook, 264–67. London: Tom Stacey.

Cameron, Samuel. 1994. "Household Debt Problems: Towards a Micro-Macro Linkage." *Review of Political Economy* 6, no. 2: 205–20.

Chaloupka, Frank. 1991. "Rational Addictive Behavior and Cigarette Smoking." *Journal of Political Economy* 99, no. 4: 722–42.

Choi, Young Back. 1993. *Paradigms and Conventions: Uncertainty, Decision Making, and Entrepreneurship*. Ann Arbor: University of Michigan Press.

Christman, John, ed. 1989. *The Inner Citadel: Essays on Individual Autonomy*. Oxford: Oxford University Press.

Clark, John Maurice. 1936. *Preface to Social Economics*. New York: Farrar and Rinehart.

Clotfelter, Charles T., and Philip J. Cook. 1989. *Selling Hope: State Lotteries in America*. Cambridge: Harvard University Press.

———. 1990. "On the Economics of State Lotteries." *Journal of Economic Perspectives* 4, no. 4: 105–19.

Collins, Jim. 1989. *Uncommon Cultures: Popular Culture and Post-Modernism.* New York: Routledge.

Combee, Jerry, and Edgar Norton. 1991. *Economic Justice in Perspective: A Book of Readings.* Englewood Cliffs, N.J.: Prentice-Hall.

Cooper, Carol Marie. 1998. "Fruit to Walls to Floor, Ads Are on the March." *New York Times,* February 26, A1, C8.

Cooter, R. D. 1991. "Lapses, Conflict, and Akrasia in Torts and Crimes: Towards an Economic Theory of the Will." *International Review of Law and Economics* 11, no. 1: 149–64.

Cowen, Tyler. 1989. "Are All Tastes Constant and Identical? A Critique of Stigler and Becker." *Journal of Economic Behavior and Organization* 11:127–35.

———. 1991. "Self-Constraint versus Self-Liberation." *Ethics* 101:360–73.

———. 1993. "The Scope and Limits of Preference Sovereignty." *Economics and Philosophy* 9:253–69.

———. 1998. *In Praise of Commercial Culture.* Cambridge: Harvard University Press.

Cox, Harvey. 1999. "Notes and Comments: The Market as God." *Atlantic Monthly,* March, 18–23.

Cross, Gary. 1993. *Time and Money: The Making of Consumer Culture.* New York: Routledge.

Cuneo, Michael W. 1997. *The Smoke of Satan: Conservative and Traditionalist Dissent in Contemporary American Catholicism.* New York: Oxford University Press.

Daniel, Coldwell, III. 1988. "A Critique of the Controversy about the Stability of Consumers' Tastes." *Journal of Economic Education* 19:245–53.

D'Antonio, William V. 1999. "The American Catholic Laity in 1999." *National Catholic Reporter,* October 29, 12.

Dau-Schmidt, Kenneth G. 1990. "An Economic Analysis of the Criminal Law as a Preference-Shaping Policy." *Duke Law Journal* 1990, no. 1: 1–38.

Davis, John B. 1994. "Personal Identity and Multiple Selves Analysis." Typescript.

Dean, Carolyn J. 1996. *Sexuality and Modern Western Culture.* New York: Twayne.

Dixit, Avinash, and Victor Norman. 1978. "Advertising and Welfare." *Bell Journal of Economics* 9:1–18.

Dowell, Richard S., Robert S. Goldfarb, and William B. Griffith. 1998. "Economic Man as Moral Individual: Modeling Moral Preferences in Utility Functions and Related Budget Constraints." *Economic Inquiry* 36, no. 4: 645–53.

Duesenberry, James. 1952. *Income, Saving, and the Theory of Consumer Behavior.* Cambridge: Harvard University Press.

Dworkin, Gerald. 1989. "The Concept of Autonomy." In *The Inner Citadel: Essays on Individual Autonomy,* ed. J. Christman, 54–62. Oxford: Oxford University Press.

Eagleton, Terry. 1996. *The Illusions of Postmodernism.* Oxford: Blackwell.

Economic Report of the President. 1987 (January). Washington, D.C.: Government Printing Office.

Economic Report of the President. 1998 (February). Washington, D.C.: Government Printing Office.

Ellis, Havelock. 1931. *More Essays of Love and Virtue.* Garden City, N.Y.: Doubleday, Doran.

Elster, Jon. 1979. *Ulysses and the Sirens: Studies in Rationality and Irrationality.* Cambridge: Cambridge University Press.

———. 1982. "Sour Grapes-Utilitarianism and the Genesis of Wants." In *Utilitarianism and Beyond,* ed. A. K. Sen and B. Williams, 219–38. Cambridge: Cambridge University Press.

———. 1983. *Sour Grapes: Studies in the Subversion of Rationality.* Cambridge: Cambridge University Press.

———. 1985. "Weakness of Will and the Free-Rider Problem." *Economics and Philosophy* 1:231–65.

———. 1989a. *The Cement of Society.* Cambridge: Cambridge University Press.

———. 1989b. *Nuts and Bolts for the Social Sciences.* Cambridge: Cambridge University Press.

———, ed. 1986. *The Multiple Self.* Cambridge: Cambridge University Press.

Epstein, Richard A. 1995. *Simple Rules for a Complex World.* Cambridge: Harvard University Press.

Etzioni, Amitai. 1986. "The Case for a Multiple-Utility Conception." *Economics and Philosophy* 2:159–83.

Fabian, Ann. 1990. *Card Sharps, Dream Books, and Bucket Shops.* Ithaca, N.Y.: Cornell University Press.

Farber, Leslie H. 1972. "Sex in Bondage to the Modern Will: 'I'm Sorry Dear.'" In *The Case against Pornography,* ed. D. Holbrook, 83–102. London: Tom Stacey.

Farnsworth, E. Allan. 1990. *Contracts.* Boston: Little, Brown.

Fernandez, Bob. 1998. "Restaurants Are Fattening Region's Economy." *Philadelphia Inquirer,* July 26, A1, A20.

Frank, Robert H. 1987. "If *Homo Economicus* Could Choose His Own Utility Function, Would He Want One with a Conscience?" *American Economic Review* 77:593–604.

———. 1989. "If *Homo Economicus* Could Choose His Own Utility Function, Would He Want One with a Conscience? Reply." *American Economic Review* 79:595–96.

———. 1999. *Luxury Fever: Why Money Fails to Satisfy in an Era of Excess.* New York: Free Press.

Frank, Robert H., T. Gilovich, and D. Regan. 1993. "Does Studying Economics Inhibit Cooperation?" *Journal of Economic Perspectives* 7:159–71.

Frankfurt, Harry G. 1971. "Freedom of the Will and the Concept of a Person." *Journal of Philosophy* 68:5–20.

———. 1975. "Three Concepts of Free Action: II." *Proceedings of the Aristotelian Society* 49:113–25.

Galbraith, John Kenneth. 1958. *The Affluent Society.* New York: New American Library.

Gallagher, Maggie. 1996. *The Abolition of Marriage: How We Destroy Lasting Love.* Washington, D.C.: Regnery.

Garvey, John H. 1997. "The Real Reason for Religious Freedom." *First Things,* March, 3–19.

Gatens, Moira. 1991. *Feminism and Philosophy: Perspectives on Difference and Equality.* Bloomington: Indiana University Press.

Geoghegan, Thomas. 1999. "Unions Can Save the Workaholic." *New York Times,* September 17, A17.

George, David. 1978. "The Market System and Second-Order Wants." *Forum for Social Economics* (spring): 42–44.

———. 1984. "Metapreferences: Reconsidering Contemporary Notions of Free Choice." *International Journal of Social Economics* 11, nos. 3–4: 92–107.

———. 1989. "Social Evolution and the Role of Knowledge." *Review of Social Economy* 47:55–73.

———. 1993. "Does the Market Create Preferred Preferences?" *Review of Social Economy* 51:323–46.

———. 1997. "Working Longer Hours: Pressure from the Boss or Pressure from the Marketers?" *Review of Social Economy* 55:33–65.

———. 1998. "Coping Rationally with Unpreferred Preferences." *Eastern Economic Journal* 24, no. 2: 181–94.

———. 2000. "Driven to Spend: Longer Work Hours as a Byproduct of Market Forces." In *Working Time: International Trends, Theory, and Policy Perspectives,* ed. L. Golden and D. M. Figart, 127–42. London and New York: Routledge.

Gergen, Kenneth J. 1991. *The Saturated Self: Dilemmas of Identity in Contemporary Life.* Basic Books.

Giddens, Anthony. 1992. *The Transformation of Intimacy: Sexuality, Love, and Eroticism in Modern Societies.* Stanford: Stanford University Press.

Gintis, Herbert. 1972. "A Radical Analysis of Welfare Economics and Individual Development." *Quarterly Journal of Economics* 86:572–99.

———. 1974. "Welfare Criteria with Endogenous Preferences: The Economics of Education." *International Economic Review* 15:415–29.

Gitlin, Todd. 1997. "The Anti-Political Populism of Cultural Studies." *Dissent* (spring): 77–82.

Gold, Howard J. 1992. *Hollow Mandates: American Public Opinion and the Conservative Shift.* Boulder, Colo.: Westview Press.

Goodman, Robert. 1995. *The Luck Business: The Devastating Consequences and Broken Promises of America's Gambling Explosion.* New York: Free Press.

Goodwin, Neva R., Frank Ackerman, and David Kiron, eds. 1997. *The Consumer Society.* Washington, D.C.: Island Press.

Gottheil, Fred M. 1996. *Principles of Microeconomics.* Cincinnati: South-Western College Publishing.

Gray, Jerry. 1995. "House Committee Discusses Public Broadcasting Budget." *New York Times,* Current Events Edition, January 20, A22.

Gray, John. 1998. *The Delusions of Global Capitalism.* New York: New Press.

Gwartney, James K., Richard L. Stroup, and Russel S. Sobel. 2000. *Macroeconomics: Private and Public Choice.* 9th ed. Fort Worth, Tex.: Dryden Press.

Hahn, Frank. 1982. "On Some Difficulties of the Utilitarian Economist." In *Utilitarianism and Beyond,* ed. A. K. Sen and B. Williams, 187–98. Cambridge: Cambridge University Press.

Hahnel, Robin, and Michael Albert. 1990. *Quiet Revolution in Welfare Economics.* Princeton: Princeton University Press.

Harrington, Joseph E., Jr. 1989. "If *Homo Economicus* Could Choose His Own Utility Function, Would He Want One with a Conscience? Comment." *American Economic Review* 79:588–93.

Harrington, Michael. 1962. *The Other America: Poverty in the United States.* New York: Macmillan.

Harsanyi, John C. 1954. "Welfare Economics of Variable Tastes." *Review of Economic Studies* 21:204–13.

———. 1955. "Cardinal Welfare, Individualistic Ethics, and Interpersonal Comparisons of Utility." *Journal of Political Economy* 63:309–21.

———. 1977. *Rational Behavior and Bargaining Equilibrium in Games and Social Situations.* Cambridge: Cambridge University Press.

———. 1982. "Morality and the Theory of Rational Behaviour." In *Utilitarianism and Beyond,* ed. A. K. Sen and B. Williams, 39–62. Cambridge. Cambridge University Press.

Hausman, Daniel M., and Michael S. McPherson. 1996. *Economic Analysis and Moral Philosophy.* Cambridge: Cambridge University Press.

Hayek, Friedrich. 1961. "The Non-Sequiter of the 'Dependence' Effect." *Southern Economic Journal* 27:346–48.

Heap, Shaun Hargreaves, Martin Hollis, Bruce Lyons, Robert Sugden, and Albert Weale. 1992. *The Theory of Choice: A Critical Guide.* Cambridge: Blackwell.

Heide, Florence Parry. 1982. *The Problem with Pulcifer.* New York: Mulberry Books.

Heilbroner, Robert, and William Milberg. 1995. *The Crisis of Vision in Modern Economic Thought.* Cambridge: Cambridge University Press.

Herrnstein, Richard J. 1988. "Lost and Found: One Self." *Ethics* 98:566–78.

———. 1990. "Behavior, Reinforcement, and Utility." *Psychological Science* 1, no. 4: 217–23.

Herrnstein, Richard J., and Drazen Prelec. 1992. "Melioration." In *Choice over Time,* ed. G. Loewenstein and J. Elster, 235–63. New York: Russell Sage Foundation.

Hewlett, Sylvia Ann, and Cornel West. 1998. *The War against Parents: What We Can Do for America's Beleaguered Moms and Dads.* New York: Houghton Mifflin.

Hicks, John R. 1939. "The Foundations of Welfare Economics." *Economic Journal* 49:696–712.

Hirsch, Fred. 1976. *Social Limits to Growth.* Cambridge: Harvard University Press.

Hirschman, Albert O. 1982a. "Rival Interpretations of Market Society: Civilizing, Destructive, or Feeble." *Journal of Economic Literature* 20:1463–84.

————. 1982b. *Shifting Involvements: Private Interest and Public Action.* Princeton: Princeton University Press.

————. 1985. "Against Parsimony: Three Easy Ways of Complicating Some Categories of Economic Discourse." *Economics and Philosophy* 1:7–21.

————. 1991. *The Rhetoric of Reaction: Perversity, Futility, and Jeopardy.* Cambridge: Belknap Press of Harvard University Press.

Hirschman, Elizabeth C. 1995. "Professional, Personal, and Popular Culture Perspectives on Addiction." *American Behavioral Scientist* 38, no. 4: 537–52.

Hoch, Stephen J., and George Loewenstein. 1991. "Time-Inconsistent Preferences and Consumer Self-Control." *Journal of Consumer Research* 17:492–507.

Hogan, John. 1998. "Parents—the New Proletariat?" *Greater Philadelphia Democratic Left,* June–July, 7.

Holland, Kelly, and Richard A. Melcher. 1995. "Plastic: Are Banks over Their Limit?" *Business Week,* March 6, 92.

Hollis, Martin. 1983. "Rational Preferences." *Philosophical Forum* 14:246–62.

Jeffrey, Richard C. 1974. "Preferences among Preferences." *Journal of Philosophy* 71:377–91.

Jesdanun, Anick. 2000. "Taking Count of 'Cybersex Compulsives.'" *Philadelphia Inquirer,* March 1, A11.

Joyce, Kathleen M. 1979. "Public Opinion and the Politics of Gambling." *Journal of Social Issues* 35, no. 3: 144–65.

Juster, F. T., and F. P. Stafford. 1990. "The Allocation of Time: Empirical Findings, Behavioral Models, and Problems of Measurement." *Journal of Economic Literature* 29, no. 2: 471–522.

Kagel, John H., and Raymond C. Battalio. 1975. "Experimental Studies of Consumer Demand Behavior Using Laboratory Animals." *Economic Inquiry* 13, no. 1: 22–38.

Kagel, John H., Raymond C. Battalio, and Leonard Green. 1995. *An Experimental Analysis of Animal Behavior.* Cambridge: Cambridge University Press.

Kahneman, Daniel, Jack L. Knetsch, and Richard Thaler. 1986. "Fairness as a Constraint on Profit Seeking: Entitlements in the Market." *American Economic Review* 76, no. 4: 728–41.

Kaldor, N. 1939. "Welfare Propositions in Economics and Interpersonal Comparisons of Utility." *Economic Journal* 49:549–52.

Katona, George. 1964. *The Mass Consumption Society.* New York: McGraw-Hill.

Keillor, Garrison. 1996. "*New Yorker* Magazine Goes to Dogs." In *Dumbing Down: Essays on the Strip-Mining of American Culture,* ed. K. Washburn and J. Thornton. New York: W. W. Norton.

Kelman, Steven. 1990. "Congress and Public Spirit: A Commentary." In *Beyond Self-Interest,* ed. J. J. Mansbridge, 200–206. Chicago: University of Chicago Press.

Kelsey, D. 1986. "Utility and the Individual: An Analysis of Internal Conflicts." *Social Choice and Welfare* 3:77–87.

Kuran, Timur. 1995. *Private Truths, Public Lies: The Social Consequences of Preference Falsification.* Cambridge: Harvard University Press.

————. 1997. "Moral Overload and Its Alleviation." In *Economics, Values, and*

Organization, ed. A. Ben-Ner and L. Putterman, 231–66. New York: Cambridge University Press.

Kuttner, Robert. 1997. *Everything for Sale: The Virtues and Limits of Markets.* New York: Alfred A. Knopf.

Laibson, David. 1997. "Golden Eggs and Hyperbolic Discounting." *Quarterly Journal of Economics* 112:443–77.

Laibson, David I., Andrea Repetto, and Jeremy Tobacman. 1998. "Self-Control and Saving for Retirement." *Brookings Papers on Economic Activity* 1:91–196.

Lambro, Donald. 1998. "Small but Stalwart Party Claims Large Influence." *Insight,* August 17, 43.

Lane, Robert E. 1991. *The Market Experience.* Cambridge: Cambridge University Press.

Lasch, Christopher. 1991. *The True and Only Heaven: Progress and Its Critics.* New York: W. W. Norton.

Leach, William. 1993. *Land of Desire: Merchants, Power, and the Rise of a New American Culture.* New York: Vintage.

Leete, L., and J. B. Schor. 1994. "Assessing the Time-Squeeze Hypothesis: Hours Worked in the United States, 1969–89." *Industrial Relations* 33:25–43.

Leonard, Daniel. 1989. "Market Behavior of Rational Addicts." *Journal of Economic Psychology* 10:117–44.

Lesieur, Henry R. 1977. *The Chase: Career of the Compulsive Gambler.* Garden City, N.Y.: Anchor Press/Doubleday.

Levy, David. 1982. "Rational Choice and Morality: Economic and Classical Philosophy." *History of Political Economy* 14:1–36.

———. 1988. "Utility-Enhancing Consumption Constraints." *Economics and Philosophy* 4, no. 1: 69–88.

Lewis, Michael. 1996. "All Grossed Out." *New York Times Magazine,* May 19, 24.

Little, I. M. D. 1957. *A Critique of Welfare Economics.* 2d ed. London: Oxford University Press.

Locke, Don. 1975. "Three Concepts of Free Action: I." *Proceedings of the Aristotelian Society* 49:95–112.

Loewenstein, George, and Richard H. Thaler. 1989. "Intertemporal Choice." *Journal of Economic Perspectives* 3, no. 4: 181–93.

Lowy, Joan. 1999. "'Covenant Marriage' Movement Gains in U.S." *Detroit News,* June 6, 13A.

Lukes, Steven. 1995. *The Curious Enlightenment of Professor Caritat.* London: Verso.

Luttwak, Edward. 1999. *Turbo Capitalism: Winners and Losers in the Global Economy.* New York: HarperCollins.

Lutz, Mark A. 1993. "The Utility of Multiple Utility: A Comment on Brennan." *Economics and Philosophy* 9:145–54.

Lutz, Mark A., and Kenneth Lux. 1988. *Humanistic Economics: The New Challenge.* New York: Bootstrap Press.

MacNeill, Allan. 1996. "Modernism and the Economics of Consumption." Typescript.

Maital, Shlomo. 1986. "Prometheus Rebound: On Welfare-Improving Constraints." *Eastern Economic Journal* 12, no. 3: 337–44.

Majumdar, Tapas. 1980. "The Rationality of Changing Choice." *Analyse & Kritik* 2:172–78.

Malamuth, Neil M., and Edward Donnerstein, eds. 1984. *Pornography and Sexual Aggression.* Orlando, Fla.: Academic Press.

Marcum, Jess, and Henry Rowen. 1974. "How Many Games in Town—the Pros and Cons of Legalized Gambling." *Public Interest* 36: 25–52.

Marwell, G., and R. Ames. 1981. "Economists Free Ride, Does Anyone Else? Experiments on the Provision of Public Goods." *Journal of Public Economics* 15:295–310.

Mason, M. S. 1998. "Throwing the Book at Children's Television." *Christian Science Monitor,* October 1, B4.

May, Rollo. 1972. "Paradoxes of Sex and Love in Modern Society." In *The Case against Pornography,* ed. D. Holbrook, 13–35. London: Tom Stacey.

McCain, Roger A. 1992. *A Framework for Cognitive Economics.* Westport, Conn.: Praeger.

McChesney, Robert W. 1999. *Rich Media, Poor Democracy: Communication Politics in Dubious Times.* Urbana: University of Illinois Press.

McCloskey, Donald. 1985. *The Rhetoric of Economics.* Madison: University of Wisconsin Press.

McGee, Michael Calvin. 1985. *"On Feminized Power": The Van Zelst Lecture in Communication.* Evanston, Ill.: Northwestern University School of Speech.

McGinn, Daniel. 1997. "Deadbeat Nation: Why Are So Many People in Bankruptcy Court?" *Newsweek,* April 14, 50.

McPherson, Michael S. 1980. "Liberty and the Higher Pleasures: In Defense of Mill." *Economic Inquiry* 18:314–18.

———. 1982. "Mill's Moral Theory and the Problem of Preference Change." *Ethics* 92:252–73.

———. 1984. "On Schelling, Hirschman, and Sen: Revising the Concept of the Self." *Partisan Review* 51:236–47.

Medoff, James, and Andrew Harless. 1996. *The Indebted Society: Anatomy of an Ongoing Disaster.* Boston: Little, Brown.

Mele, Alfred R. 1987. *Irrationality: An Essay on Akrasia, Self-Deception, and Self-Control.* New York: Oxford University Press.

Michael, Robert T., John H. Gagnon, Edward O. Laumann, and Gina Kolata. 1994. *Sex in America: A Definitive Survey.* Boston: Little, Brown.

Mill, John Stuart. 1962. *On Liberty.* Ed. M. Warnock. London: Fontana.

Miller, Peter M., and Michel Hersen. 1975. "Research on Addictive Behaviors: Current Needs." Editorial. *Addictive Behaviors* 1:1–2.

Minow, Newton N., and Craig L. LaMay. 1995. *Abandoned in the Wasteland: Children, Television, and the First Amendment.* New York: Hill and Wang.

Mishan, E. J. 1972. "The Economic Steam behind Pornography." In *The Case against Pornography,* ed. D. Holbrook, 157–60. London: Tom Stacey.

Molinaeus, Carolus. 1991. "A Treatise on Contracts and Usury." In *Economic Jus-*

tice in Perspective: A Book of Readings, ed. J. Combee and E. Norton, 48–54. Englewood Cliffs, N.J.: Prentice-Hall.

Nelson, Robert H. 1991. *Reaching for Heaven on Earth: The Theological Meaning of Economics.* Savage, Md.: Rowman and Littlefield.

Offe, Claus, and Rolf G. Heinze. 1996. "Beyond the Labor Market: Reflections on a New Definition of 'Domestic' Welfare Production." In *Modernity and the State,* ed. Claus Offe, 121–46. Cambridge: MIT Press.

Office of Management and Budget. 1999. *Historical Tables: Budget of the United States Government.* Washington, D.C.: Government Printing Office.

O'Neill, John. 1998. *The Market: Ethics, Knowledge, and Politics.* New York: Routledge.

Ottosen, Garry K., and Douglas N. Thompson. 1996. *Reducing Unemployment: A Case for Government Deregulation.* Westport, Conn.: Praeger.

Pattanaik, Prasanta K. 1980. "A Note on the 'Rationality of Becoming' and Revealed Preference." *Analyse & Kritik* 2:179–82.

Penelhum, Terence. 1979. "Human and External Desires." *Monist* 62:304–19.

Pollak, R. A. 1978. "Endogenous Tastes in Demand and Welfare Analysis." *American Economic Review: Papers and Proceedings* 68, no. 2: 374–79.

Postman, Neil. 1985. *Amusing Ourselves to Death: Public Discourse in the Age of Show Business.* New York: Viking Penguin.

Powelson, John P. 1998. *The Moral Economy.* Ann Arbor: University of Michigan Press.

Prelec, Draxen, and R. J. Herrnstein. 1991. "Preferences or Principles: Alternative Guidelines for Choice." In *Strategy and Choice,* ed. R. J. Zeckhauser, 319–40. Cambridge: MIT Press.

Price, Charlene C. 1996. "Sales of Food Away from Home Expanding." *Food Review,* May, 30–32.

Purdy, Jedidiah S. 1998. "The God of the Digerati." *American Prospect* 37 (March–April): 86–90.

Quinn, Kevin, and Tina R. Green. 1998. "Hermeneutics and Libertarianism: An Odd Couple." *Critical Review* 12, no. 3:207–24.

Radin, Margaret Jane. 1996. *Contested Commodities.* Cambridge: Harvard University Press.

Rhoads, Steven E. 1990. "Economists on Tastes and Preferences." In *From Political Economy to Economics and Back?* ed. J. H. Nichols Jr. and C. Wright, 79–103. San Francisco: Institute for Contemporary Studies Press.

Robbins, Lionel. 1952. *An Essay on the Nature and Significance of Economic Science.* 2d ed. London: Macmillan.

Roberts, K., and P. Rupert. 1995. "The Myth of the Overworked American." *Economic Commentary* (Federal Reserve Bank of Cleveland), January 15.

Rosenberg, Howard. 1997. "Opponents of TV Violence May Not Constitute a Majority of Viewers." *Philadelphia Inquirer,* May 26, C8.

Rosenberg, Rosalind. 1982. *Beyond Separate Spheres: Intellectual Roots of Feminism.* New Haven: Yale University Press.

Safire, William. 2000. "Wordplayers: Coiners Come and Go, but Coinages Live On." *New York Times Magazine,* January 2, 10–12.

Samuelson, Paul A. 1967. *Economics.* 7th ed. New York: McGraw-Hill.

Schelling, Thomas C. 1978. "Egonomics, or the Art of Self-Management." *American Economic Review: Papers and Proceedings* 68, no. 2: 290–94.

———. 1980. "The Intimate Contest for Self-Command." *Public Interest* 60:94–118.

———. 1984. "Self-Command in Practice, in Policy, and in a Theory of Rational Choice." *American Economic Review: Papers and Proceedings* 74, no. 2: 1–11.

Schor, Juliet B. 1991. *The Overworked American: The Unexpected Decline of Leisure.* Basic Books.

———. 1998. *The Overspent American: Upscaling, Downsizing, and the New Consumer.* New York: Basic Books.

Schrag, Calvin O. 1997. *The Self after Postmodernity.* New Haven: Yale University Press.

Schudson, Michael. 1984. *Advertising, the Uneasy Persuasion: Its Dubious Impact on American Society.* New York: Basic Books.

Schwartz, Barry. 1994. *The Costs of Living: How Market Freedom Erodes the Best Things in Life.* New York: W. W. Norton.

Schwartz, Hugh. 1998. *Rationality Gone Awry? Decision Making Inconsistent with Economic and Financial Theory.* Westport, Conn.: Praeger.

Scitovsky, Tibor. 1941. "A Note on Welfare Propositions in Economics." *Review of Economics and Statistics* 23:77–78.

———. 1976. *The Joyless Economy.* New York: Oxford University Press.

———. 1986. *Human Desire and Economic Satisfaction: Essays on the Frontiers of Economics.* New York: New York University Press.

Sen, Amartya K. 1974. "Choice, Orderings, and Morality." In *Practical Reason,* ed. S. Korner, 54–67. Oxford: Blackwell.

———. 1977a. "Rational Fools: A Critique of the Behavioural Foundations of Economic Theory." *Philosophy and Public Affairs* 6:317–44.

———. 1977b. "Rationality and Morality: A Reply to Kurt Baier." *Erkenntnis* 11:225–32.

———. 1983. "Liberty and Social Choice." *Journal of Philosophy* 80:5–28.

Seplow, Stephen. 1996. "Less Violence No Hit with Viewers." *Philadelphia Inquirer,* June 2, A1, A12.

Soros, George. 1998. *The Crisis of Global Capitalism: Open Society Endangered.* New York: Public Affairs.

Stearns, Peter N. 1999. *Battleground of Desire: The Struggle for Self-Control in Modern America.* New York: New York University Press.

Stigler, George J., and Gary S. Becker. 1977. "De Gustibus Non Est Disputandem." *American Economic Review* 67:76–90.

Strossen, Nadine. 1995. *Defending Pornography: Free Speech, Sex, and the Fight for Women's Rights.* New York: Scribner.

Strotz, R. H. 1955–56. "Myopia and Inconsistency in Dynamic Utility Maximization." *Review of Economic Studies* 23:165–80.

Sunstein, Cass R. 1997. *Free Markets and Social Justice.* New York: Oxford University Press.

Sunstein, Cass R., and Edna Ullmann-Margalit. 1999. "Second-Order Decisions." *Ethics* 110:5–31.

Thalberg, Irving. 1978. "Hierarchical Analyses of Unfree Action." *Canadian Journal of Philosophy* 8, no. 2: 211–25.

Thaler, Richard H. 1991. *Quasi Rational Economics.* New York: Russell Sage Foundation.

Thaler, Richard H., and N. M. Shefrin. 1980. "Rules and Discretion in a Two-Self Model of Inter-Temporal Choice." Working paper, Cornell University.

———. 1981. "An Economic Theory of Self-Control." *Journal of Political Economy* 89:392–406.

Titmuss, Richard M. 1972. *The Gift Relationship: From Human Blood to Social Policy.* New York: Vintage.

Toby, Jackson. 1998. "Medicalizing Temptation." *Public Interest* 130: 64–78.

Tomer, John F. 1996. "Good Habits and Bad Habits: A New Age Socio-Economic Model of Preference Formation." *Journal of Socio-Economics* 25, no. 6: 619–38.

Twitchell, James B. 1999. *Lead Us into Temptation: The Triumph of American Materialism.* New York: Columbia University Press.

United Media Enterprises. 1983. *Where Does the Time Go? Report on Leisure in America.* New York: Newspaper Enterprise Association.

U.S. Bureau of the Census. 1993. *Statistical Abstract, 1993.* Washington, D.C.: Government Printing Office.

U.S. Department of Labor Statistics. 1989. *Handbook of Labor Statistics: Bulletin 2340.* (August). Washington D.C.: Government Printing Office.

van der Veen, Robert J. 1981. "Meta-Rankings and Collective Optimality." *Social Science Information* 20:345–74.

Veblen, Thorstein. 1967. *The Theory of the Leisure Class.* New York: Penguin.

von Weizsacker, C. C. 1971. "Notes on Endogenous Change of Tastes." *Journal of Economic Theory* 3:345–72.

Wachtel, Paul L. 1989. *The Poverty of Affluence: A Psychological Portrait of the American Way of Life.* Philadelphia: New Society Publishers.

Walsh, Vivian. 1996. *Rationality, Allocation, and Reproduction.* Oxford: Clarendon Press.

Washburn, Katharine, and John Thornton, eds. 1996. *Dumbing Down: Essays on the Strip-Mining of American Culture.* New York: W. W. Norton.

Watson, Gary. 1989. "Free Agency." In *The Inner Citadel: Essays on Individual Autonomy,* ed. J. Christman, 109–22. Oxford: Oxford University Press.

Weaver, Mary Jo, and R. Scott Appleby, eds. 1995. *Being Right: Conservative Catholics in America.* Bloomington: Indiana University Press.

Weber, Max. 1930. *The Protestant Ethic and the Spirit of Capitalism.* Trans. Talcott Parsons. London: George Allen and Unwin.

Wechsler, Pat. 1997. "This Lesson Is Brought to You By." *Business Week,* June 30, 68–69.

Weisbrod, Burton A. 1977. "Comparing Utility Functions in Efficiency Terms; or, What Kind of Utility Functions Do We Want?" *American Economic Review* 67:991–95.

Winerip, Michael. 1998. "Looking for an Eleven O'Clock Fix." *New York Times Magazine,* January 11, 30–63.

Winston, G. C. 1980. "Addiction and Backsliding: A Theory of Compulsive Consumption." *Journal of Economic Behavior and Organization* 1:295–324.

Wolf, Susan. 1989. "Sanity and the Metaphysics of Responsibility." In *The Inner Citadel: Essays on Individual Autonomy,* ed. J. Christman, 137–51. Oxford University Press.

Wolfson, Adam. 1997. "Are We All Liberals Now?" *Commentary* 103, no. 6: 48–50.

Worland, Stephen T. 1984. "Aristotle and the Neoclassical Tradition: The Shifting Ground of Complementarity." *History of Political Economy* 16, no. 1: 107–34.

Worsnop, Richard L. 1996. "Consumer Debt." *CQ Researcher,* November 15, 1011.

Yellen, Janet L. 1996. "Statement before the Subcommittee on Financial Institutions and Regulatory Relief, Committee on Banking, Housing, and Urban Affairs, U.S. Senate, July 24, 1996." *Federal Reserve Bulletin,* September, 815–19.

Yergin, Daniel, and Joseph Stanislaw. 1998. *The Commanding Heights: The Battle between Government and the Marketplace That Is Remaking the Modern World.* New York: Simon and Schuster.

Yezer, Anthony M., Robert S. Goldfarb, and Paul J. Poppen. 1996. "Does Studying Economics Discourage Cooperation? Watch What We Do, Not What We Say or How We Play." *Journal of Economic Perspectives* 10, no. 1: 177–86.

Young, Kimberly S. 1998. *Caught in the Net: How to Recognize the Signs of Internet Addiction—and a Winning Strategy for Recovery.* New York: John Wiley and Sons.

Young, Robert M. 1989. "Autonomy and the 'Inner Self.'" In *The Inner Citadel: Essays on Individual Autonomy,* ed. J. Christman, 77–90. New York: Oxford University Press.

Yuengert, Andrew. 1995. "Free Markets and Character." Typescript.

———. 2001. "Rational Choice with Passion: Virtue in a Model of Rational Addiction." *Review of Social Economy* 59: 1–21.

Index